# FASHION MARKETING

D1536107

## Dotty Boen Oelkers

SOUTH-WESTERN
CENGAGE Learning

Australia • Brazil • Japan • Korea • Mexico • Singapore • Spain • United Kingdom • United States

**SOUTH-WESTERN**
CENGAGE Learning

**Fashion Marketing**
by Dotty Boen Oelkers

**Editor-in-Chief**
Jack Calhoun

**Vice President/Executive Publisher**
Dave Shaut

**Senior Publisher**
Karen Schmohe

**Executive Editor**
Eve Lewis

**Project Manager**
Penny Shank

**Production Manager**
Patricia Matthews Boies

**Production Editor**
Colleen A. Farmer

**Director of Marketing**
Carol Volz

**Senior Marketing Manager**
Nancy A. Long

**Marketing Coordinator**
Yvonne Patton-Beard

**Manufacturing Coordinator**
Kevin L. Kluck

**Cover and Internal Designer**
Tippy McIntosh

**Editorial Assistant**
Linda Keith

**Production Assistant**
Nancy Stamper

**Compositor**
GGS Information Services

**Printer**
C&C Offset Printing Co., Ltd.

**About the Author**
**Dotty Boen Oelkers** is an author and educator. She has been recognized as Administrator of the Year while working as a Director of Career and Technology Education in Texas. Dotty was previously a marketing education teacher and a fashion merchandise manager. She currently owns her own business, Developing Educational Solutions, which provides consulting and staff development to school districts.

# REVIEWERS

**Priscilla R. McCalla**
Professional and Program
  Development Director
DECA
Reston, VA

**Janet Butler**
Omaha, NE

**Monica Caillouet**
Gonzales, LA

**Shelly Devos**
Auburn, IL

**Teresa Fary**
Virginia Beach, VA

**Sissy Long**
Pensacola, FL

**Ronda Matthews**
Gonzales, LA

**Pam Naylor**
Birmington, AL

**Jo Winstanley**
Grosse Pointe Woods, MI

# Expect More From South-Western...
## ...And Get It!

## Marketing Yourself
Knowing how to sell yourself is critical to business success today. *Marketing Yourself*, a brand new title, utilizes a marketing framework to develop a self-marketing plan and portfolio. The self-marketing plan is based on the analysis of student marketable skills and abilities. Every student text includes a Portfolio CD.

Text/Portfolio CD Package      .38-43640-9

## Hospitality Marketing
Discover new ways to cover the marketing curriculum using the hospitality industry as the learning vehicle. Hospitality Marketing covers topics such as hotel image and location, use of technology in the industry, information and risk management, and marketing strategies for product and service planning.

Text      0-538-43208-X
Module (includes **Exam**_View®_ CD, Instructor's Resource CD,
     Video, and Annotated Instructor's Edition)      0-538-43209-8

## Sports and Entertainment Marketing
Explore the intriguing world of sports and entertainment from the perspective of marketing. Sports and Entertainment Marketing covers topics such as college and amateur sports, professional sports, public images, marketing entertainment, marketing plans, and legal issues.

Text      0-538-69477-7
Module (includes **Exam**_View®_ CD, Instructor's Resource CD,
     Video, and Annotated Instructor's Edition)      0-538-69478-5

## Mean Jeans Manufacturing Co. 3E
*Mean Jeans* is a unique simulation based on the operations of an imaginary, small business community. Students learn by doing as they become responsible for the daily operations and success of 15 businesses and agencies that interact with *Mean Jeans*, a maker of denim products. Great capstone simulation!

Student Reference Book (one per student)      0-538-43204-7
Operations Manual (see catalog for info)      0-538-43205-5
Supplies and Resources CD (one per class)      0-538-43206-3

## Business 2000
This innovative series of 12 titles provides you with the tools needed to customize your marketing courses. Using a modular format, you can create your own course by combining several topics or use the books separately to enhance an existing course. The Multimedia Module available with each title includes an Annotated Instructor's Edition, Instructor's Resource CD, **Exam**_View®_ CD, and Video. The *B2000* web site contains additional activities for every lesson in every book. Here are a few of the titles in the B2000 Series—see our catalog for ordering information:

| | | |
|---|---|---|
| *Selling* | *Marketing* | *E-Commerce* |
| *Entrepreneurship* | *Advertising* | *Retail* |
| *Customer Service* | *Business Management* | |

## Entrepreneurship: Ideas in Action 2E
Take students step-by-step through the entire process of owning and managing a business. Focus their attention on the real skills required of entrepreneurs—start with meeting a market need and work through planning, financing, incorporating technology, hiring, managing, and avoiding legal problems. Students learn by doing using the innovative, activity-based Business Plan Project built into every chapter.

Text      0-538-43600-X
Student Workbook      0-538-43602-6

*Instructor Support and Other Materials Available*

**SOUTH-WESTERN**
CENGAGE Learning™

## Join us on the Internet at school.cengage.com

# FASHION MARKETING
## CONTENTS

## CHAPTER 1
### The Fashion Industry 2
Lesson 1.1 Fashion Marketing Basics **4**
Lesson 1.2 The Next Hot Item **9**
Lesson 1.3 Capitalizing on Style **13**
Lesson 1.4 Beating the Competition **17**
*Chapter Review* **22**

## CHAPTER 2
### The Basics of Fashion 26
Lesson 2.1 Fashion Origins **28**
Lesson 2.2 Fashion Components **33**
Lesson 2.3 Design and Color **38**
Lesson 2.4 Textiles and Construction **42**
*Chapter Review* **48**

## CHAPTER 3
### Marketing Fashions 52
Lesson 3.1 Information, Please **54**
Lesson 3.2 The Right Product, The Right Place **58**
Lesson 3.3 The Right Price **62**
Lesson 3.4 The Right Promotion = Sales **67**
*Chapter Review* **72**

## CHAPTER 4
### Fashion Economics 76
Lesson 4.1 Supply and Demand **78**
Lesson 4.2 The Competition **82**
Lesson 4.3 Financial Records **87**
Lesson 4.4 Sources of Money **92**
*Chapter Review* **98**

## CHAPTER 5
### The Centers and the Designers 102
Lesson 5.1 America's Fashion Centers **104**
Lesson 5.2 European Fashion **110**
Lesson 5.3 Asian and Other Emerging Centers **115**
*Chapter Review* **122**

## CHAPTER 6
### Promoting a Fashion Image 126
Lesson 6.1 Advertising Fashion **128**
Lesson 6.2 Promoting Through Events **133**
Lesson 6.3 Selling Fashion **139**
*Chapter Review* **144**

## CHAPTER 7
## Using Technology in Fashion Marketing 148
Lesson 7.1 Production Processes 150
Lesson 7.2 Research and Technology 155
Lesson 7.3 Distribution Technology 160
*Chapter Review* 166

## CHAPTER 8
## Merchandising and Buying 170
Lesson 8.1 Surrounding Style 172
Lesson 8.2 Displaying Style 177
Lesson 8.3 Buying Style 184
*Chapter Review* 190

## CHAPTER 9
## Data-Driven Decisions 194
Lesson 9.1 Collecting Information 196
Lesson 9.2 Analyzing and Reporting 202
Lesson 9.3 Using Data 207
*Chapter Review* 212

## CHAPTER 10
## Creating a Fashion Business 216
Lesson 10.1 A Business Plan 218
Lesson 10.2 Risk Management 224
Lesson 10.3 Leadership 228
*Chapter Review* 234

## CHAPTER 11
## Laws, Labor, and Ethics 238
Lesson 11.1 The Law 240
Lesson 11.2 Labor 245
Lesson 11.3 Piracy and Ethics 250
*Chapter Review* 256

## CHAPTER 12
## Fashion Marketing Careers 260
Lesson 12.1 Fashion Businesses 262
Lesson 12.2 Fashion Careers 268
Lesson 12.3 Finding and Keeping a Fashion Career 273
*Chapter Review* 280

GLOSSARY 284
INDEX 000
PHOTO CREDITS 298

# TO THE STUDENT

Welcome to *Fashion Marketing.* You are entering a world of beauty, style, and promotion. Marketing is the tool that has allowed the United States' economy to be one of the most successful in the world. The fashion industry is an important part of our modern economy. Consumers spend millions of dollars each year on clothing and related accessories.

You will learn the basic functions of marketing and how these functions are applied to fashion. Whenever a marketing function is presented in a lesson, it is marked with an icon indicating which marketing function is being used.

 **MARKETING-INFORMATION MANAGEMENT**   **FINANCING**   **PRICING**   **PROMOTION**   **PRODUCT/SERVICE MANAGEMENT**   **DISTRIBUTION**   **SELLING**

To help you on your journey through the world of *Fashion Marketing,* this text has a number of special features to highlight interesting or unusual aspects of fashion.

**The Latest Style** begins each lesson and encourages you to explore the material in the upcoming lesson. The Latest Style also gives you opportunities to work with other students.

**Try It On** provides you with an opportunity to assess your comprehension of material. Ongoing review and assessment will help you to better understand the material.

**Final Fit** provides exercises at the end of each lesson to reinforce understanding and to provide critical thinking.

Each chapter ends with a review of vocabulary and basic concepts. The **Chapter Review** includes Think Critically exercises, which provide opportunities to apply concepts, and Make Connections exercises, which provide connections to other disciplines.

**DECA Prep** provides preparation for DECA competitive events in every chapter.

**PROJECT: The COLLECTION POINT**

**The Collection Point** provides an individual or group project for students to apply the marketing concepts in the chapter.

# WINNING STRATEGIES

**Winning Strategies** presents successful strategies used in real-life fashion businesses.

**Cyber Marketing** investigates Internet marketing and how the Internet is a major tool for today's fashion marketers.

**Trend Setters** acquaints you with people who have succeeded in fashion marketing careers.

**Fashion Flashback** provides a historical perspective of the fashion industry and its related marketing issues.

**Fashion Do's and Don'ts** examines legal and ethical issues that exist in the fashion industry.

**Time Out** introduces you to interesting facts and statistics about fashion marketing.

Dedicated web site **fashion.swlearning.com** that provides activities and links for each chapter.

*Fashion Marketing* will provide you with an interesting journey through the world of marketing. Grab your coat and let's go shopping!

# CHAPTER 1

# THE FASHION INDUSTRY

## LESSONS

**1.1 FASHION MARKETING BASICS**

**1.2 THE NEXT HOT ITEM**

**1.3 CAPITALIZING ON STYLE**

**1.4 BEATING THE COMPETITION**

# WINNING STRATEGIES

## POLO RALPH LAUREN

The timeless image projected by Polo Ralph Lauren Corporation has always dominated its distinctive line of apparel, fragrance, accessories, and home products. Polo Ralph Lauren markets a line of fresh, aristocratic clothing evoking a look of old wealth living on country estates. The company has an uncommon approach to marketing that promotes a consistent image as well as fashions.

The unique marketing technique has propelled Polo Ralph Lauren into a major corporation in the fashion industry. Founded in 1968 by Ralph Lauren, the company designs, markets, and distributes fashions internationally. International licensing partners operate Polo stores in more than 60 countries. Polo's long-term growth strategies include

- continuing to expand globally, especially in Japan and Europe
- adding brands that address new customer groups
- opening more of its own specialty stores
- improving the margin of profit.

Ralph Lauren has been the driving force in developing a company that casually dresses people who work or want to work in corporate businesses, rather than the world's elite. Born in Bronx, New York, as Ralph Lifshitz, he changed his name and started the company with a small loan. The Polo look has always been preppy and casual and has appealed to those on the way up the corporate ladder.

### THINK CRITICALLY
1. Discuss why Polo Ralph Lauren has been popular for more than 30 years.
2. Why would Polo Ralph Lauren market an image as well as fashions?

# CHAPTER 1
## Lesson 1.1

# FASHION MARKETING BASICS

## GOALS

**Describe** the basic concepts of fashion marketing.

**Define** the seven key marketing functions.

## The Latest Style

Fashion retailers make decisions about what image they will project to consumers. The combination of clothing and accessories, the price lines and brands, and the way garments are displayed, advertised, and delivered to consumers are all a mix of marketing elements that contribute to the identity of a store. The mix of the marketing elements may be focused on a specific customer group.

Nordstrom is a chain of 75 department stores known for catering to its customer with tuxedoed pianists entertaining shoppers. When sales began to sag, Nordstrom tried changing its image and launched a $40 million "Reinvent Yourself" promotional campaign. Additionally, the store changed about one-third of its women's clothing lines to brands that appealed to young, hip consumers and began playing hip-hop music. The changes made long-time customers unhappy and did not quickly attract the hoped-for new customers.

Work with a group. Choose two department stores with which you are familiar. Make a list of characteristics that are different about the two stores. Then make a list of characteristics that are similar. Discuss differences in their targeted customer groups.

## MARKETING CONCEPTS

Fashion marketing has glamour and mystique about it that may trick some people into thinking it has its own set of rules. In reality, fashion marketing follows the same rules as marketing for any other product.

### WHAT IS FASHION MARKETING?

Fashion marketing is an important business function of the fashion industry that includes planning, pricing, promoting, and selling fashion products. The American Marketing Association defines **marketing** as "planning and executing the conception, pricing, promotion, and distribution of ideas, goods, and services to create exchanges that satisfy individual and organizational objectives."

Fashions provide more than just the basic human need of clothing and home furnishings. Fashions fulfill a need to reflect an image of one's self to the world. By combining the basic marketing elements, fashion marketing helps people clarify their own image and makes a profit for those engaged in the business. The **marketing mix** is how the basic elements—product, price, promotion, and distribution—are combined to meet customer needs and wants.

**Product** is what a business offers customers to satisfy needs. Fashion products include suits, shirts, jeans, shoes, belts, purses, and home furnishings such as rugs and chairs.

**Price** is the amount that customers pay for products. The price of fashion products is dependent on the cost of producing the item, the markup (a percentage added to the cost to generate a profit), and the customer demand.

**Promotion** includes all of the ways a customer is encouraged to buy the product. Promotion includes advertising, publicity, personal selling, and public relations.

**Distribution** involves getting the product to the customer. It includes all of the steps from getting the raw material for fabric to the textile manufacturer to making a garment available to a customer.

# TRY IT ON

**What is marketing? What are the elements of the marketing mix?**

_____

_____

_____

# KEY MARKETING FUNCTIONS

One or more of seven key marketing functions takes place whenever a product is marketed. The seven key functions are marketing-information management, financing, product/service management, pricing, promotion, distribution, and selling.

## USING THE KEY MARKETING FUNCTIONS

**Marketing-Information Management** involves gathering and using information about what consumers want. This information is critical to deciding how to make a product that will sell. Fashion changes from season to season and from year to year. Determining what will sell requires fashion marketers to keep in touch with their customers. They must decide far in advance on the design of a garment, acquire the fabric and other materials, produce the garment, sell it to retailers, and deliver it for customer viewing when the customer wants it and is ready to buy it.

**Financing** involves planning ways to cover the costs of successfully operating the business. This planning includes how to cover operating expenses while waiting for income from the first sales. A textile manufacturer may require payment for fabric when it is delivered to a fashion designer, which is long before the customer pays for the garment. The designer may need to borrow money and pay finance fees, which adds costs to the price of the final product. It takes careful budget planning to assure that the product is priced to cover all costs plus a profit and is what a customer is willing to pay.

**FUNCTIONS OF MARKETING**

MARKETING-INFORMATION MANAGEMENT

SELLING

FINANCING

DISTRIBUTION

PRICING

PRODUCT/ SERVICE MANAGEMENT

PROMOTION

© 2000, Marketing Education Resource Center, Columbus, Ohio

**Pricing** is the process of setting the value or cost at the right level. The price of a fashion product is dependent on the cost of production plus a profit. Customer demand can also adjust the price up or down. The price must cover all of the elements of the key marketing functions.

- The costs of gathering information about what customers want
- The costs of financing the business
- The costs of design, fabric, and construction to produce the product
- The costs of advertising and promotion
- The costs of moving the product to the consumer
- The costs of selling the product to the final consumer
- Some profit for all of the people involved in each of these steps

**Promotion** is communicating with customers about the product to achieve the desired result—customer demand for and purchase of the product. Promotion includes advertising, personal selling, publicity, and public relations. Fashion marketers create an image of who wears a brand of clothing through promotion. Using entertainers to advertise a brand leads consumers to believe they can be like the entertainer if they wear that brand.

**Product/Service Management** is designing, producing, maintaining, improving, and/or acquiring products or services to meet customer needs. With information about what customers want and financing to make it happen, fashion marketers can start to work on the product. Designer R. Scott French used high-priced lingerie as the inspiration for his line of moderate-priced lingerie. He used quality construction and fabrics to create a line of trendy lingerie, serving customers seeking a novel item at a more affordable price. He turned an idea into a product line that succeeded.

**Distribution** involves moving the product each step from the design idea to the consumer. The number of businesses involved in the actual

Chico's FAS is a trendy women's sportswear chain. When Chico's did 11.7 percent better one month compared to the same month a year before, the gain in sales was directly attributed to promotions not used in the prior year. An additional catalog was mailed and TV commercials were used.

planning and movement of the product is a major factor in the final price. The channels of distribution can include *intermediaries* who help a designer or manufacturer get the product into retail stores. Distribution also includes the actual transportation of the product—for example, by truck or by air.

**Selling** assists the customer in identifying and satisfying a want or a need. Selling helps the customer understand the benefits of quality. For example, if customers buy only the lowest-priced garment, they may find that the garment does not last. They may spend time and money purchasing again, sooner than expected. If they are aware that another, more expensive garment will retain its shape or color through repeated wearing and cleaning, it might be the most cost-effective purchase.

## USING THE BASICS

The seven key functions—marketing-information management, financing, product/service management, pricing, promotion, distribution, and selling—are basic to all marketing. When applied to fashion marketing, they provide a foundation on which to develop a fashion business. Developing a strong knowledge of how to interconnect all seven functions is an expectation for all successful fashion marketing careers. A designer who does not understand the key functions will need to learn them or partner with someone who does. Business managers must understand and use the key functions in a way to please customers and make a profit, or the business will struggle to exist.

## CYBER MARKETING

In February 2001, **www.JCPenney.com** introduced an online feature called "Just for Me." The program allowed customers to "try on" clothing by entering their measurements into the site. According to JCPenney, the virtual model technology was tested to determine if it was something customers would use to help with their swimsuit purchasing decisions. By March 2002, the feature was gone.

### THINK CRITICALLY

**1.** Why would JCPenney remove such a forward-thinking feature from its web site?

**2.** Visit **www.JCPenney. com**. What alternatives have been provided to help women find the right swimsuit?

## TRY IT ON

**Name three of the key marketing functions. Give a fashion marketing example of each.**

## UNDERSTAND MARKETING CONCEPTS
Circle the best answer for each of the following questions.

**1.** Marketing, as a business function, is
   **a.** encouraging customers to purchase products.
   **b.** another term for grocery shopping.
   **c.** creating and maintaining satisfying exchange relationships.
   **d.** none of the above.

**2.** The elements of the marketing mix are
   **a.** purchasing, distribution, financing, and price.
   **b.** product, price, promotion, and distribution.
   **c.** purchasing, planning, advertising, and distribution.
   **d.** planning, distribution, price, and advertising.

## THINK CRITICALLY
Answer the following questions as completely as possible. If necessary, use a separate sheet of paper.

**3. Communication** Think of a recent fashion purchase you made. Imagine how the seven key marketing functions were involved in getting the item to you, and write a narrative describing their role.

_____

_____

_____

_____

_____

**4.** You have been hired to help a designer market formal wear for teens. Use all of the marketing mix elements to briefly describe what you would do.

_____

_____

_____

_____

_____

_____

_____

# THE NEXT HOT ITEM

## The Latest Style

**R**arely are fashion items totally new. Most fashions are a version of garments from the past. The *silhouette* or the *outline* of an outfit has characteristics taken from a previous time period. During the twentieth century, silhouettes were repeated about every 25 to 30 years. For example, hemlines on women's skirts and dresses were at or above knee length in the 1930s, the 1960s, and again in the 1990s.

This cycle seems to be shortening and blurring in the 2000s. Many silhouettes are seen as "in fashion" all at once. The cycle has hit a new phase of confusion. The trend of casual work clothing that swept through the 1990s added to the confusion about what was "in." As people again began to wear more serious attire to work in the 2000s, styles have started to refocus.

Work with a partner. Discuss other reasons why fashions might lack a focus in the early years of the twenty-first century.

**Describe** the stages of the fashion cycle.

**Analyze** the relationship between today's fashions and the history of fashion.

## THE FASHION CYCLE

**F**ashion reflects the economy and attitude of consumers and, at the same time, intrigues and appeals to consumers. If you are observant, you might notice people at a concert or an airport and realize that there is similarity in the clothing of many people—especially people of the same age or status. You may see similarity in the shape of their shoes or the length or cut of their pants. You are observing a phase of the **fashion cycle**—the time from when a style is introduced until it is no longer purchased.

### THE PHASES

Fashions have a life cycle that most simply can be described as having three phases: introductory, peak, and decline.

PROMOTION

The *introductory phase* is early in the life of the product. Many fashion retailers will herald the new season of clothing as fresh and innovative, something that the consumer would be foolish to miss. The sellers wish to create excitement through promotion of the fashions. Journalists and celebrities are invited to special shows to introduce the next season's collection. Trend setters are usually already wearing the garments.

SELLING

The *peak phase* describes the time during which sales of the items to the consumer are at the highest level. The target market is generally wearing the item. A **target market** refers to a specific audience of people—for example, all of the people in the United States ages 13 to 18 years. This does not mean that every single person in this group is wearing the item, but it does mean that you will frequently observe members of the target group wearing the item. Trend setters have generally moved on to newer items.

PRICING

The *decline phase* of a fashion item occurs when the masses have tired of the item and are no longer buying it. People may continue to wear the item, but the retail stores begin to lower the price to a level that will squeeze out the last possible sales. Remaining garments are finally sold in bulk to stores that sell closeout fashions. Eventually the item is no longer available.

## STYLE MATTERS

The length of time an item stays in one of the three phases is dependent on the style. **Fads** are those items that quickly move through the three phases and disappear from the fashion scene. Fads generally are outlandish in style or color and do not appeal to the real trend setters.

**Classic styles** last many decades. A classic style is timeless, meaning it is flattering to the wearer and is not easily dated as to when it was purchased. Classics are not outlandish in style or color, but are subtle and refined. Classics have a style that is appreciated over many years.

# TRY IT ON

**What is the difference between a fad and a classic item of clothing?**

_____

_____

_____

# RETRO FASHIONS

**W**hen the President of Afghanistan, Hamid Karzai, made his first world tour during the U.S. war against terrorism, he wore an ankle-length overgarment called a *chapan* with a skin hat called a *karakul*. Both are traditional northern Afghan apparel. Under the chapan, he wore a single-breasted black suit jacket over a traditional southern Afghan knee-length shirt with a banded collar and loose-fitting trousers. His outfit reflected tradition, history, and the presence of a leader. Karzai made a striking appearance and succeeded in making an excellent first impression on a watchful world.

**TIME OUT**

Ferrari activewear is being marketed to teens who are interested in Formula One auto racing. The sport, which has been popular in Europe for many years, is catching on in the United States. The fashion items are similar to ones worn by the Ferrari Formula One racing team.

## STYLE

Hamid Karzai has style. He successfully mixed Middle Eastern, Western contemporary, and historical styles. About 30 years ago, John Fairchild, publisher of *Women's Wear Daily*, was quoted in the *Dallas Times Herald* as stating that "style is an expression of individualism mixed with charisma. Fashion is something that comes after style." The prevailing style may define what is fashionable at a specific time and place, with some styles lasting as classics.

## REFLECTIONS

**PRODUCT/ SERVICE MANAGEMENT**

Historically, what people wear has reflected the general economic health and attitudes of the United States and other Western civilizations. When the economy is good and people feel secure, people wear brighter, more casual clothes. When the economy is weak or there is world tension, people tend to wear more serious clothing. After the terrorist attacks on September 11, 2001, Calvin Klein showed a totally black collection that was criticized for being too somber. Other designers such as R. Scott French were successful at the same time with a much lighter look that said, "Let's move on."

Designers whose Spring 2002 collections were presented prior to September 11, 2001, became symbols of self-centered excess that permeated the industry. After the tragic events, the luxurious designer fashions seemed too excessive for the times. For the next six months, consumers were confused and not buying what was offered. As time passed and the economy improved, so did high fashion sales.

## FASHION INFLUENCE

The influence of designers as the authorities of fashion has passed into history. Today, what customers will buy is influenced by what they have read and seen other people wear or not wear.

**Fashion Flashback**

In October 2001, Marshall Field's celebrated the return of the "28 Shop" within its flagship department store in Chicago. Marshall Field's originally introduced the "28 Shop" in the 1940s. The exclusive, special-occasion shop was accessed through the 28 East Washington Street entrance via an elevator lined with velvet benches. Wealthy customers were shown evening gowns while seated in one of 28 individual, elegant dressing rooms designed by a movie set designer. A butler and hostess catered to customers' every need.

**THINK CRITICALLY**
1. What image does the 28 Shop project of shopping in the 1940s?
2. Do you think this shop had mass appeal? Why or why not?

## TRY IT ON

**What events or attitudes might influence the direction of fashion?**

_____

_____

_____

_____

## Final Fit

### UNDERSTAND MARKETING CONCEPTS

Circle the best answer for each of the following questions.

**1.** The three phases of a fashion cycle include
  **a.** design, construction, and distribution.
  **b.** price, product, and promotion.
  **c.** introductory, peak, and decline.
  **d.** none of the above.

**2.** Generally, the colors and styles worn by people in the United States reflect
  **a.** economic conditions and attitudes.
  **b.** what is on sale.
  **c.** their age and income.
  **d.** what they think looks good on them.

### THINK CRITICALLY

Answer the following questions as completely as possible. If necessary, use a separate sheet of paper.

**3.** Why does the clothing worn by leaders influence public opinion regarding their ability to serve?

_____

_____

_____

**4. Communication** Write a short paragraph about why a classic style has a long life cycle and continually returns to popularity.

_____

_____

_____

_____

_____

_____

# CAPITALIZING ON STYLE

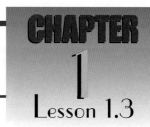

## The Latest Style

**W**hen U.S. retailers hit a difficult selling season, they are often not able to find hot, fast-selling items that will set them apart. In this situation, many retailers will turn to a tried-and-true item, such as the turtleneck. With so many similar turtlenecks from which to choose, customers may decide not to buy at full price. Retailers are then forced to mark down the items to sell them.

Turtlenecks are seen as a commodity, not as trendy item that creates excitement. If customers do not see anything new or exciting that gives them a reason to shop at a specific store, they don't buy. When price, not style, is the only attraction, sales will decline.

Work with a group. Discuss how retailers could combine turtlenecks with other, more exciting items to create the right product mix for increased sales.

**Define** fashion product mix.

**Discuss** product/ service management as it relates to a defined customer.

## MAKING THE RIGHT SELECTION

**E**ach season, there are thousands of fabrics made into thousands of apparel items from which to choose. Selecting the right items from the right supplier at the right price requires knowing what customers want and adjusting to those wants. By making these selections, a retail store defines the repeat customer it wants to attract.

### CATEGORIZING THE GOODS

PRODUCT/ SERVICE MANAGEMENT

**Product mix** refers to all the products an organization sells. In fashion marketing, the product mix is the combination of styles, product classifications, and price lines created by a designer or carried by a retail store.

Retail stores can be categorized by the items they carry and customers they target. There are five predominant types of fashion retailers in the United States: department stores, discount stores, off-price stores, chain stores, and boutiques.

*Department stores*, such as Dillard's, Nordstrom, and Macy's, offer a variety of merchandise besides fashion items. The four largest department stores in the United States are Sears, JCPenney, Federated Department Stores, and May Department Stores. Each of these chains has an image that is projected by its product mix of items predominantly sold at the store.

*Discount stores*, such as Target® and Kmart, offer clothing that is low priced. Discount stores are one of the fastest-growing areas of retailing.

*Off-price stores*, such as T.J. Maxx® and Marshall, offer irregular or closeout fashions at 20 to 80 percent off first-quality prices. The off-price industry accounts for hundreds of millions of dollars a year in retail sales.

*Chain stores*, like Talbots and The Limited, can be found in most malls throughout the United States. They offer a consistent line of products to a target customer.

*Boutiques,* such as Tootsie's, a fine women's specialty store located in major cities such as Houston and Atlanta, are smaller stores with a specific customer in mind.

# TRY IT ON

**What are the elements of a product mix?**

_____

_____

_____

## THE STYLE

Specialty stores are generally very focused and must select a style to emphasize. Some of the most commonly used descriptions to characterize style are classic, trendy, young designer, designer, and couture.

- *Classic* is traditional, with a long product life cycle. The classic is appealing to many people in a wide age group and various sizes.
- *Trendy* refers to forward-looking fashion or an updated version of a classic. Trendy is the most current style, in the opinion of the beholder.
- *Young designer* describes garments created by designers who are just starting out. It is usually a very creative style and use of fabric.
- *Designer* garments are high-quality, high-fashion items that are sold under one of the well-known designer labels.
- *Couture* refers to original, one-of-a-kind garments made with the highest standards of the highest quality fabrics.

## CLASSIFYING A COLLECTION

**PRODUCT/ SERVICE MANAGEMENT**

In addition to style, the function or the occasion for which garments are intended to be worn can be used to categorize them. Examples of such classifications are sportswear, activewear, and careerwear as well as eveningwear and wedding apparel.

*Sportswear* can include items worn for work or play. For men, it can include sportcoats or jeans, but it is generally considered a casual version of the garment. This uniquely American classification can be confusing since it generally does not refer to garments worn while participating in sports.

*Activewear* refers to apparel worn while taking an active part in a sport. Activewear includes clothing such as soccer uniforms or workout shorts and shirts.

*Careerwear* or *business attire* is generally traditional in design since it focuses on the workplace. In the 1990s, what was considered careerwear swung to a very casual interpretation, but began drifting back to a more traditional interpretation in the 2000s. Careerwear has a fashion cycle of its own, characterized as longer with more subtle, gradual changes.

*Eveningwear* has evolved to mean special occasion or formal wear, including cocktail, prom, or other formal-event apparel. The fabric and style of eveningwear are considered more elegant and formal than other classifications. *Wedding apparel* is related to eveningwear but includes wedding gowns, mother-of-the-bride dresses, and bridesmaid dresses, which are rarely worn more than once and are not appropriate for other events.

Other classifications include social apparel, lingerie, and accessories. Some garments defy classification because they can have multiple uses.

## PRICING IT RIGHT

Deciding on styles and classifications of clothing to design or offer for sale is heavily influenced by the final sale price. A garment may be perfect, but if it costs too much for the target customer, it will not sell.

Some of the factors included in the final price of a garment are the fabric, construction, distribution, promotion, and profit for those involved. Bringing together the right combination of product mix—style, classification, and price—makes for a successful collection and brings in customers to shop and buy.

The strong desire to own trendy fashions can cause some people to act unethically. During Spring 2001, bowling shoes by Prada, Kenneth Cole, and Camper were selling for $100 or more a pair, but many people in the under-age-30 crowd were not paying for the shoes. They were renting them at bowling alleys and never returning them. *The Wall Street Journal* quoted Melissa Scales, a staff assistant at the National Merit Scholarship Corporation in Evanston, Illinois, as saying " I don't feel bad because I went to high school in that same town [where she took the shoes], and I probably gave them hundreds of my hard earned dollars. I felt like I deserved a pair of shoes." Nationwide, bowling alleys were losing hundreds of pairs of shoes each year, and the costs were being passed on to bowlers with higher prices per game.

**THINK CRITICALLY**
**1.** Is failing to return rented bowling shoes stealing? Why or why not?
**2.** Do you think honest bowlers should have to pay for shoes stolen by others? Who should pay for the shoes? Discuss your opinion.

## TRY IT ON

**What must be considered in determining the final price of a garment?**

_____

_____

_____

_____

## UNDERSTAND MARKETING CONCEPTS

Circle the best answer for each of the following questions.

**1.** Product mix refers to
  **a.** encouraging customers to purchase products.
  **b.** the selection of styles, product classifications, and price lines.
  **c.** creating and maintaining designer collections.
  **d.** buying only designer apparel.

**2.** Some of the ways to classify garments by function include
  **a.** sportswear, activewear, eveningwear, and careerwear.
  **b.** retail, wholesale, designer, and fad.
  **c.** shoes, hats, coats, and gloves.
  **d.** denim, silk, cotton, and nylon.

## THINK CRITICALLY

Answer the following questions as completely as possible. If necessary, use a separate sheet of paper.

**3. Research**  Ask five other students to classify the clothing carried by three small chain stores in your area into one or more of the following: sportswear, activewear, careerwear, or eveningwear and wedding apparel. Is some stores' merchandise more easily classified than others? Do some stores clearly target one or two classifications of apparel?

_____

_____

_____

_____

_____

**4.** Why is it important for designers and retailers to understand who their customers are before deciding on a product mix?

_____

_____

_____

_____

_____

_____

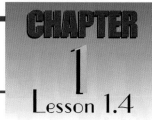

# BEATING THE COMPETITION

## The Latest Style

**P**roviding what the customer wants means gathering and using information in a way that improves product offerings. Abercrombie & Fitch opened a new chain of stores called Hollister Co., which focused on 14- to 18-year-olds. Younger teens want fashions that are different from the college-age group targeted by the namesake stores. The new stores are in the same malls as the Abercrombie & Fitch stores, but they offer lower prices and have merchandise that the younger crowd wants.

A third store called abercrombie caters to 7- to 14-year-olds. Separating the merchandise by tighter age groups and price lines is intended to more precisely focus on trends in the product mix. The clothing is casual in all three stores, but the atmosphere and price lines are different.

Work with a group. Discuss the potential for damaging Abercrombie & Fitch's business by siphoning customers to the lower-priced goods at Hollister Co. and abercrombie. How can Abercrombie & Fitch gather information about the likes and dislikes of 14- to 18-year-olds?

**Discuss** trends in fashion marketing.

**Describe** the use of emerging technology to reach target markets.

## DISCOVERING TRENDS

**MARKETING-INFORMATION MANAGEMENT**

**W**hen a fashion collection hits the mark and is setting a trend, everyone knows it. A **trend** is when fashion takes a particular direction and the style is acknowledged as being right for the time. According to Linda Griffin, a fashion journalist, when a designer is showing a collection that is right, the audience is already wearing similar styles. This phenomenon happens when good designers know their customers. Staying ahead of the flow of trend development is a never-ending job for designers and retailers, and it requires constant marketing-information management.

Charismatic sales people are given credit for the phenomenal sales of the Tokyo fashion chain, Egoist. Egoist is known as one of the most successful retailers of trendy fashions because the salespeople are setting the trends. Customers come in to see what the sales people are wearing, talk with them, and then buy, buy, buy.

## TARGETING THE TREND

Trends start in many different places. Fashion insiders seem to just know what is going to be "in," and they spread the word among themselves and those who track fashion trends. Trends can be very segmented and may only pertain to a specific market *niche*, such as an age group. Lerner New York is one of The Limited stores. Lerner targets a 33-year-old, working mother of two as its customer. The Lerner customer wants fashions very different from those of a high school student. Trying to sell both of these customers on the same trend could be a sales disaster.

## RESEARCHING TRENDS

**MARKETING-INFORMATION MANAGEMENT**

The fashion industry and those who monitor it spend much time and money trying to determine the next direction of the flow of trends. Information about what consumers want can be gathered in multiple ways, including interviews, visual surveys, and sales data collection. People who need to know about consumers spend time observing them where they work and play. Noting the colors, fabrics, and styles the trend setters are wearing hints at what people will want next. What celebrities wear is frequently seen as a gauge of what is to come. In the late 1990s and early 2000, celebrities were wearing outrageous costumes with maximum skin exposure. By early 2002, the trend had swung to more traditional styles.

## TRY IT ON

**What is a trend? Where do trends start?**

_____

_____

_____

# TECHNO FASHIONS

Every aspect of fashion, from a designer's idea to the final purchase made by a consumer, has been impacted by technology. Technology has increased the speed at which ideas can be turned into sales.

## INSTANT GRATIFICATION

**SELLING**

Customers see a garment in a movie or on TV and almost instantly search the Internet to find out where they can buy it. Web sites for entertainment venues are linked with those of major retailers handling the fashion products used in the entertainment. The downside is that the trend setters quickly tire of items once they are available to everyone.

For example, the web site Shop the Soaps at **www.abcshowstore.com** offers merchandise connected to ABC soap operas. The merchandise is directly related to what is happening on a show. The merchandise is not trend setting, but it offers the merchant a new sales opportunity and information about its customer/viewer.

## THE VALUE OF INFORMATION

**MARKETING-INFORMATION MANAGEMENT**

The Internet allows companies whose business is researching and predicting trends to monitor and transmit information instantly to their customers. Worth Global Style Network (WGSN) is a subscription service that offers designers, manufacturers, buyers, and retailers information about the fashion business. Obtaining and managing information in a timely manner can be critical to success. Having access to intelligence about fashion trends through an online service reduces the time it would take using other media. Technology shortens the distance between trend setters and wide availability in retail stores.

## CHANGING THE FASHION LANDSCAPE

Technology has changed not only the way information is transmitted to users but also the way designers and manufacturers create garments. Prior to the use of technology, designers created hand sketches of garments that were then turned into patterns for cutting fabric. Each step was completed by hand. Tasks that took weeks now take days. Now designers who have an idea in their head, but whose sketching talents are limited, can use software to create the design and pattern.

Technology allows consumers access to fashion information and photos direct from the designer and manufacturer. Retailers who once feared online shopping have found ways to use it to their advantage to increase sales. Technology is making fashion marketing more efficient.

Very busy people find that online shopping for high-end fashion fits their crazy schedules. Web sites such as **www.eLuxury.com** offer name-brand, designer fashions that are trendy yet classic. eLuxury caters to customers by offering the assistance of a real personal shopper, either by e-mail or a toll-free call. Available gift selections can be sorted by recipient, occasion, brand, and price range. The selections offered are designed for people who are buying gifts for women. People who need a gift that is elegant, wrapped, and delivered in a hurry can find what they need.

**THINK CRITICALLY**
Describe the people who might be the target market for eLuxury.

# TRY IT ON

**What impact has the Internet had on marketing-information management?**

_____

_____

_____

## TrendSetters

### SELVEN O'KEEF JARMON

A grass roots marketing plan has worked well for Selven O'Keef Jarmon, a young, successful designer. Meeting people, putting together projects that serve as ad campaigns, and getting tons of press has led to sales of his upscale clothing line. "You must believe in what you do, learn how to do fashion, put out a collection, and show it over and over as if it is a work of art," Jarmon said, describing what it takes to be a successful designer. "People who know people who know people want to help me get where I need to be because they love my work. The individual has to do the work, and there is an immense amount of work involved in creating a collection," says Jarmon.

Jarmon acquired his interest in fashion from his aunts who made hats and accessories for the ladies of their church. Jarmon worked as a design assistant for a Los Angeles sports and swimwear manufacturer, then returned to his home in Houston to begin his own line of women's wear. A fortuitous meeting on an airline with the owner of Tootsie's led to Jarmon designing a private label for the upscale women's boutique. His signature collections range from high-end blouses starting at $145 to evening gowns for $3,000. "I have created an audience and have enough income to take it to the next level," states Jarmon about his plans for opening a New York address. "It is so important to be in a city where everything is there in terms of fabric, pattern makers, and the wholesale market."

### THINK CRITICALLY

**1.** Why do you think Selven O'Keef Jarmon says that it is important to know people in the fashion business?

**2.** How might a young designer meet people in the fashion business?

## UNDERSTAND MARKETING CONCEPTS

Circle the best answer for each of the following questions.

**1.** When a garment is part of a trend, it means
   **a.** it would make a great gift.
   **b.** it is classified as couture fashion.
   **c.** the item reflects the direction of fashion.
   **d.** it is a luxury item.

**2.** Obtaining information about trends via the Internet means
   **a.** you will need to check the source of the information.
   **b.** information can be received instantly.
   **c.** you need to target your customer.
   **d.** planning, distribution, price, and advertising.

## THINK CRITICALLY

Answer the following questions as completely as possible. If necessary, use a separate sheet of paper.

**3.** Think of a recent fashion purchase you made. Describe it by style, function, and price level. What was the most determining factor in your decision to buy?

_____

_____

_____

**4.** Describe the merchandise and décor of a retail store that caters to you and your friends. Classify the product mix offered by style and functional classification.

_____

_____

_____

_____

_____

_____

_____

**CHAPTER 1**

# REVIEW

## REVIEW MARKETING CONCEPTS
**Write the letter of the term that matches each definition. Some terms will not be used.**

_____ **1.** Planning and executing the conception, pricing, promotion, and distribution of ideas, goods, and services

_____ **2.** A specific audience of people to whom a business hopes to sell

_____ **3.** How the elements–product, price, promotion, and distribution–are combined to meet customer needs and wants

_____ **4.** What a business offers customers to satisfy needs

_____ **5.** The combination of styles, product classifications, and price lines created by a designer or carried by a retail store

_____ **6.** All of the ways a customer is encouraged to buy the product

**a.** classic style
**b.** distribution
**c.** fad
**d.** fashion cycle
**e.** marketing
**f.** marketing mix
**g.** price
**h.** product
**i.** product mix
**j.** promotion
**k.** target market
**l.** trend

**Circle the best answer.**

**7.** Assisting in the design and development of new products is
   **a.** financing.
   **b.** marketing-information management.
   **c.** product/service management.
   **d.** none of these.

**8.** Advertising a garment in a magazine is an example of
   **a.** promotion.
   **b.** product/service management.
   **c.** purchasing.
   **d.** none of these.

**9.** The phase when sales of a fashion item are at the highest level is
   **a.** the fast track.
   **b.** the peak phase.
   **c.** the classic.
   **d.** a fad.

**10.** Some of the most common styles are
   **a.** trendy.
   **b.** designer.
   **c.** classic.
   **d.** all of these.

# THINK CRITICALLY

**11.** In pairs, discuss why fashion trend researchers spend time observing people at work and play. Write down what they might do with the information they gather through observation.

POINT YOUR
BROWSER

fashion.swlearning.com

_____

_____

_____

_____

_____

**12.** You are the manufacturer of a new men's clothing line. Who is your target market? What stores do you want to sell your clothing line?

_____

_____

_____

_____

_____

**13.** Why do political leaders spend time and money carefully choosing the clothing to wear at public events and during media appearances? Why does it matter?

_____

_____

_____

_____

_____

**14.** Describe the kinds of information a business needs to know about teenage customers' likes and dislikes before designing and manufacturing a new line of clothing. How can they get this information?

_____

_____

_____

_____

_____

## MAKE CONNECTIONS

**15. Marketing Math**   Using a $3 bottle of fabric paint, you created an original design and printed it on a T-shirt that cost you $10. It looks great, and a small store in your neighborhood wants to buy 30 of your shirts. There may be more stores that you can sell to later. You can buy blank T-shirts online for $5 each, plus a total of $4 shipping and handling. A bottle of fabric paint costs $3 and will do five shirts. You want to make at least $100 profit. How much will you charge the store for each shirt?

_____

_____

_____

_____

_____

_____

**16. Ecology**   When people shop online for clothing, are they helping to improve air quality and reduce pollution? Why or why not?

_____

_____

_____

_____

_____

**17. Technology**   In groups, discuss how a fashion manufacturer might use the Internet to save time and money. Make a list of five ways.

_____

_____

_____

_____

_____

_____

## SPECIALTY STORE PROMOTIONS PLANNING

www.deca.org
/publications/HS_
Guide/guidetoc.html

You are the special events director for an upscale designer clothing store located in a fashion mall. The mall is located where two major highways interconnect several miles outside of a large city. Other large cities are within an hour's drive. A sluggish economy, stiff competition from major department stores, and successful designer outlet stores have resulted in decreased sales for your specialty store. You must devise a series of special events during October, November, and December (the busiest months for your store) to increase business. You must consider promotions that will increase customer traffic and special sales strategies that may be used without losing money. Also, the store needs to develop stronger, personalized customer relations and loyalty.

Outline and describe a special promotions weekend for your clothing store. Then design a newspaper advertisement that describes the weekend promotions and sets your store apart from competitors. Describe other forms of advertisement you would use to make the public aware of the promotions and draw them off the highways and from the major cities. Once customers are in the store, describe actions that will be taken to encourage customer loyalty and repeat business.

# PROJECT: The COLLECTION POINT

You are working with a small retailer who wants to target career-oriented young people, ages 23 to 30, as the customers for her apparel store. The retailer wants help in deciding what product mix to select. She plans to hold prices at a moderate level—above what discount stores offer but below upscale prices.

**Work with a group and complete the following activities.**

**1.** Determine what additional information you need to know about the target customer.

**2.** Create a spreadsheet with style options and functional classification options as column headings.

**3.** Search the Internet for information about the following brand names: Polo, Tommy Hilfiger, Marc Jacobs, Nine West, and Jones New York. You may include additional brands of your choice.

**4.** In rows on your spreadsheet, list the brand names and place a checkmark under the style and classification options that apply to each brand.

**5.** Write a one-page report that explains your chart and makes a recommendation of the brands that should be carried in the store and why they would appeal to the target customer.

# CHAPTER 2

# THE BASICS OF FASHION

## LESSONS

### 2.1 FASHION ORIGINS

### 2.2 FASHION COMPONENTS

### 2.3 DESIGN AND COLOR

### 2.4 TEXTILES AND CONSTRUCTION

# WINNING STRATEGIES

## THAI SILK COMPANY

At the end of World War II, U.S. intelligence agent Jim Thompson moved to Thailand because he was fascinated with the country and its beautiful handwoven silk textiles. In 1946, hand-weaving silk was a dying home-based industry. The demand for silk fabric was very low throughout the world, having been replaced by less expensive, machine-made fabrics. Thompson thought handwoven silk was so striking that he took samples to New York to find buyers for this luxurious fabric and, as a result, founded the Thai Silk Company Limited. He is credited with saving the silk industry in Thailand, which now employs more than 20,000 people.

Known worldwide for woven silks, Thai Silk Company has fabric showrooms in New York, Atlanta, and London. There are also 35 Jim Thompson specialty stores that sell silk neckties and scarves. The company has expanded its brand to home furnishings and women's sportswear in the Jim Thompson stores of Tokyo and Paris.

The marketing of the expanded brand focused on the mystique of Jim Thompson, emphasizing his secretive former job and mysterious disappearance. Thompson first went to Thailand during World War II as an agent of the U.S. Office of Strategic Services, which is now the Central Intelligence Agency. In 1967, Thompson went on vacation in Malaysia and mysteriously disappeared in the jungle. No clues related to his disappearance have ever been found.

### THINK CRITICALLY

1. How would the popularity of Asian styles impact the type of promotion used by the Jim Thompson stores?

2. How could the Jim Thompson brand capitalize on its fine reputation for silk fabric to help promote its new lines of women's clothing and home furnishings?

# CHAPTER 2
## Lesson 2.1

# FASHION ORIGINS

## GOALS

**Explain** the relationship of fashion history to today's fashions.

**Identify** the impact of cultural diversity on fashion.

## The Latest Style

In 1868, French fashion designers formed a trade association to organize the showing of each season's new collections in Paris and to promote the French fashion industry. The organization is called the Chambre Syndicale de la Couture Parisienne. Additionally, the organization negotiates with labor, promotes education for future fashion careers, and enforces copyright laws.

To belong to the exclusive organization, all designs must be created in the member firm. A design firm must have at least one *atelier* (a workroom), at least 15 technical staff employees, and at least 60 garments showing in a collection twice a year.

In 1973, two branches were added to the association. One branch is for fashion firms that design women's prêt-à-porter (pret-a-por-tay), and the other is for fashion firms that design men's prêt-à-porter. *Prêt-à-porter* means ready-to-wear garments as opposed to original, made-to-measure garments. The two newest branches are currently the most financially successful of the organization.

Work with a group. Discuss why it would be beneficial for a fashion design firm to join with other firms in a trade organization. Make a list of possible benefits.

## WHERE IT BEGAN

France was considered the center of fashion for almost 400 years, from the 1600s into the 1900s. Especially in Paris, a number of factors came together to focus the world on French fashions. Local and

international patrons, artists, skilled workers, a tremendous fabric and notions industry, and the right economic conditions fused to make Paris the preeminent fashion center.

## FRENCH FLAVOR

In the 1600s, French royalty and wealthy landowners employed their own dressmakers and tailors. Wealth was concentrated within a small group who had an endless desire for lavish fashions. The garments were shown off at balls, galas, receptions, and other social events, creating a climate where fashion was a major cultural element.

At the time, there was no middle class. People were either among the wealthy, or they were poor peasants. The peasants wore homemade and cast-off garments. If a peasant family owned a good set of clothes, it was handed down from generation to generation and became the folk dress of the peasant culture.

The excesses of the courts and the wealthy partially led to the French Revolution that began in 1789. After the Revolution, the importance and influence of royalty diminished, class distinctions blurred, and *haute couture* (hoat koo-tour) design firms grew. **Haute couture** means high-fashion, individually designed, original, handmade garments. A **couturier** (koo-tour-i-er) is the main creator and designer for a haute couture firm. The individual designers began creating designs for sale to the general public, rather than working for only one family.

## COUTURIERS

During the growth of Paris as the fashion center, the designers benefited from close proximity to other artists and their patrons. The couture houses soon gained prominence and could demand new, exciting fabrics for each season's collection of fashions, thus keeping the textile industry healthy.

The idea of the couturier as the master of fashion first led to the dominance and then to the decline of the haute couture fashion firms. In 1868, when the couturiers joined together to form the Chambre Syndicale de la Couture Parisienne, recognition of Paris as the fashion center was increasing. The Chambre Syndicale empowered the designer, rather than the customer, to decide what was fashion. This eventually worked against the haute couture fashion firms since good business practice requires that the customer be pleased.

## SUPPORTING ROLES

For a couture house to exist, a vast pool of skilled labor was required to back up the couturier. Assistant designers, production managers, pattern makers, tailors, and fitters were also needed to produce a collection. To provide the training needed for all of the positions, schools were established to train young people and prepare them to step into the fashion business.

**Fashion Flashback**

During the late 1700s, the first clothing designed specifically for boys was called the *skeleton suit*. The outfit had long, high-waisted trousers, generally buttoned onto a very short jacket. Charles Dickens said the suits "gave a boy's legs the appearance of being hooked on just under his armpits." The skeleton suit is significant because it was designed for a child and was not a copy of an adult garment. It remained popular for half a century.

**THINK CRITICALLY**
What special characteristics would allow a garment to remain in style for 50 years?

## GLOBALIZATION

**PRODUCT/ SERVICE MANAGEMENT**

Industrialization, technology, globalization, and the spread of democracy broadened the demand for fashion. Consequently, the fashion industry grew to meet the demand. Many social, political, and industrial factors helped spread the fashion center from Paris to multiple centers throughout the world. Democratization of fashion, making it available to the masses, quickly spread as technology improved production processes, communication, and transportation. Well-made, fashionable garments quickly became available in many parts of the world.

The growth of a middle class with income to purchase fashions, not just basic clothing, fueled the growth of the fashion industry. As the customer base broadened, the fashion center spread because the control shifted from the designer to the customer. Paris now shares the fashion spotlight with other cities, such as Milan and New York.

## MASS PRODUCTION

Haute couture designer gowns seen on celebrities at the Academy Awards on Sunday evening are copied and advertised by Wednesday. The copies, called **knockoffs**, are available for purchase at reasonable prices within two weeks. Haute couture houses fight back by copying their own garments in less expensive versions and selling them to retailers.

The high cost of creating original garments limits the pool of customers. Expensive, custom, made-to-measure originals have given way to mass-produced, reasonably priced, ready-to-wear garments that have broadened fashion from an art to a major business industry. The haute couture fashion design houses have turned to mass-produced, ready-to-wear garments in order to survive.

## TRY IT ON

**Why was Paris the center of fashion?**

# THE ELEMENTS OF CULTURE

There is an evolution of fashion trends that flows among Europe, Asia, and the United States. The three cultures admire each other's fashions and cyclically adopt them. The elements of a culture that influence fashions include the language, religion, art, customs, values, and symbols, as well as what other people in the culture are wearing. *Americanization* takes place when the characteristics of a cultural element attributed to the United States are transferred to other countries. The elements of other cultures are also very visible in the United States.

## RESTRICTING INFLUENCES

Even today, many cultures have self-imposed rules that regulate how men and women can dress. Modest dress is associated with many religions and certainly impacts fashions of cultures where the majority of people are associated with a particular religion. While the fashion magazine *Bibi* shows South Asian women dressed with bare midriffs, some South Asian women cover themselves from head to toe, including their faces. Muslim women follow dress codes that can be very restrictive and include complete coverage in public with a head-to-toe garment called a *burka*. Social stigma keeps many Muslim women from wearing swimsuits in public, while others dress with few restrictions.

## THE MULTICULTURAL CONSUMER

The American population as a whole grew about 13 percent from 1990 to 2000, according to the U.S. Census, but the minority population grew about 34 percent. Minority shoppers are fashion buyers and are growing in importance to retailers. Retail sales data shows that minority shoppers pay full price for items 37 percent of the time, while Caucasian shoppers do so only 25 percent of the time.

Smart fashion marketers will take the time needed to understand and serve all customers. Understanding diverse cultures can help the fashion marketer spot trends that will lead to sales.

Experiencing the diversity of cultures is an exciting adventure. Gaining an understanding of cultures beyond your own can open doors in fashion marketing, from providing insight to what may be the next trend to understanding diverse customers and providing for them.

*Bibi* is a fashion magazine for South Asians. South Asia is made up of India, Bangladesh, Pakistan, Sri Lanka, Nepal, Maldives, Bhutan, and other nearby countries. *Bibi* shows traditional South Asian clothing combined with Western apparel. Traditional South Asian shirts called *cholis* are snug and leave midriffs bare. Cholis look great with Western-style jeans.

# TRY IT ON

**What elements of a culture influence its fashion?**

## UNDERSTAND MARKETING CONCEPTS
Circle the best answer for each of the following questions.

1. Paris was the center of fashion because
   a. French royalty was very interested in fashion.
   b. a wealthy class of people wanted fashions.
   c. fabric and talented people were available.
   d. of all of the above.

2. Some of the elements of culture are
   a. couture, burkas, and skeleton suits.
   b. fashion, religion, and language.
   c. peasants, royalty, and upper class.
   d. textiles, seamstresses, and tailors.

## THINK CRITICALLY
Answer the following questions as completely as possible. If necessary, use a separate sheet of paper.

3. **Research**  Look up the origin of pants. When did men start wearing pants? Why are they called pants? Write a paragraph about the history and evolution of pants.

_____

_____

_____

_____

_____

_____

4. **Economics**  Why do people in fashion marketing need to understand cultural diversity? What impact might the cultural diversity of customers have on a business?

_____

_____

_____

_____

_____

# FASHION COMPONENTS

## The Latest Style

**W**hen teens complained to department stores that prom dresses were too provocative, the stores listened. When stores offered only plunging necklines, thigh-high-slit skirts, and bikini-style tops with low-riding skirts, the teens made it clear they wanted more glamorous gowns with a classy style. Wanting to look trendy but not revealing, the teens complained and found plenty of support from other teens. Designers and retailers reacted by providing a wider selection of young, chic dresses that covered the wearer.

When fashion trends swing too far one way, this generally indicates it is time for the pendulum to swing back. Retailers and designers must stay in touch with their customers to anticipate fashion trends.

Work with a group. Discuss how stores can stay ahead of teen trends. Suggest ways that a store can obtain feedback from teens.

**GOALS**

**Identify** the major environmental influences on fashion demand.

**Define** softlines, and describe the three segments.

## THE SUM OF THE PARTS

**F**ashion is at once a big business, an art form, and the prevailing style. Fashion combines all of the components—design, color, fabric, construction, function, and history—into a style. **Style** is a particular look in fashion that sets it apart. Environmental factors heavily influence the demand for what is considered style at any given time. Social, technological, economic, regulatory, and competitive forces are external environmental factors that influence the demand for a style. **Demand** refers to the quantity of a particular fashion item that the public is willing and able to buy.

### DEMAND FACTORS

People will buy styles worn by those they admire, and fashion marketers are

in competition to dress celebrities. Celebrities, including athletes, actresses, and political figures, project an image that influences what the public wears.

When First Lady Laura Bush selected clothing for the presidential inauguration, the fashion world gave little notice. Mrs. Bush's style has been described as rock-solid and middle of the road. She is considered modest and not a trend setter.

Contrast Mrs. Bush with former First Lady Jacqueline Kennedy. During the 1960s, she portrayed an image that is still used today as an example of elegance in personal style. Mrs. Kennedy had an impeccable sense of style for any occasion and perfectly planned her appearance with grace and dignity. The "Jackie look" is legend.

In addition to trend setters who work with competing designers, the demand for a style is heavily influenced by technology. People around the world see styles on TV or in movies and can buy them over the Internet.

The influence of economic conditions can also heat or chill the demand for a style. If people are barely able to meet their basic needs of food and shelter, style becomes less of a factor in making clothing selections. The price of a particular style always affects its demand. Owning an original garment from a haute couture firm may be something people would really enjoy, but the astronomical price keeps the demand low.

Social factors, including culture, values, and beliefs, also influence the styles a person wears. In the 1920s, women in Western countries started shortening their skirts and created a huge demand for the new, shorter style, while women in conservative cultures and religions continued covering their legs with long garments.

The gender and age of wearers also determine which fashions they are likely to buy. Men's, women's, and children's fashions are impacted by each other or cause reverse reactions as one age group wants to be different from the other.

**FASHION DO'S & DON'TS**

Dress code wars among teens, parents, and schools occur in a cyclical nature. As fashions change, the battles come and go. Issues such as skirt length, bare midriffs, exposed underwear, head coverings, and low-riding pants tend to be the focus issues.

School rules and fashion trends frequently conflict. Parents also join in the battle when they feel teens are being too racy for the occasion. JCPenney pulled a back-to-school TV ad after parents complained. The ad depicted a mother helping her daughter pull down her jeans to show more midriff.

THINK CRITICALLY
1. Do you think schools need dress codes? Why or why not?
2. Who should set the rules for appropriate school attire?

# TRY IT ON

**What is meant by style?**

_____

_____

_____

_____

# TYPE CASTING

**C**lothing, shoes, and accessories are referred to as *soft-lines* or *soft goods*. **Softlines** are those items generally made of fabrics or leather and include women's wear, men's wear, and children's wear. These three segments sometimes merge when garments are appropriate for all three categories. For example, women, men, or children could wear a T-shirt, with size being the only distinction.

## WOMEN'S WEAR

Women's wear is considered the leading edge of fashion and is the most financially competitive of the three softline segments. Women's wear has the most dramatic swings in styles, colors, and fabrics, making it an even more challenging business. The fashion industry loves to make women look good and is in a constant buzz to stay ahead of what its customer wants. The demand for fashionable clothing is perpetuated by the extensive availability of garments and widespread information about who is wearing what.

What women wear has always reflected their social and political status. Women who live in socially or politically restrictive environments dress accordingly in restrictive clothing, either by choice or by force. Women who have the means generally like to change with fashion cycles. Even in very restricted situations, women manage to maintain some sense of fashion.

In addition to the functional categories such as sportswear and eveningwear, women's wear is broken down into size ranges. *Misses* is a regular woman's size in even numbers, from 2 to 14. *Petite* is sized for women who are less than 5'4" tall. *Junior* sizes are odd numbers from 1 to 13 for a younger figure, and *women's* sizes are the plus sizes for larger women.

## MEN'S WEAR

Prior to the 1800s, men's fashions were as elaborate and decorative as women's fashions. Since the early 1800s, men's wear has not had the dramatic swings in styles and color associated with women's wear. The economic rise of the middle class in Western countries during the 1800s was due to the growth of democracies and the Industrial Revolution. The economic change led men to establish a middle-class look that has been slow to change. Men's wear becomes more casual in response to a good economy and more formal when the economy and job market

According to *Women's Wear Daily*, African-American females spent about $4 billion on apparel and another $3.6 billion on accessories in 2000. Since African-American women are represented in all income levels, marketing to their culture is one way to target them as customers.

become more demanding. Although it does reflect the changes in the economy, men's wear remains slower to change in style.

Men's clothing in Western countries has all of the functional categories of women's wear, including sportswear, activewear, and evening-wear. Accessories for men's wear, including belts, shoes, and ties, are a high-volume fashion business that can enhance sales for the manufacturer and retailer and appropriately finish a well-groomed look.

Men's wear in the United States is sized by chest, waist, and inseam measurements, with jacket length designated as regular, long, or short. Dress shirts are sized by collar and sleeve measurements. Sportswear shirts come in small, medium, and large.

Trend setters in men's wear include celebrities and many of the U.S. presidents. President John Kennedy is often credited with killing the men's hat industry by not wearing a hat at his 1961 inauguration. In the 2000s, George W. Bush gave a boost to activewear by frequently wearing comfortable outdoor clothing. Many male actors, musicians, and professional athletes have their own line of clothing.

## CHILDREN'S WEAR

The children's wear market is heavily influenced by what adults are wearing and offers trendy, durable, and comfortable garments. Children's wear has two customers, the child and the parent. Both customers must be pleased for the line to be a success.

At times during the history of children's fashions, children were seen as mini-adults and were subjected to confining, pretentious clothing that was designed to reflect the social status of the parents. When adult clothing is simple and casual, children's clothing repeats the theme and becomes more relaxed.

# TRY IT ON

**Why does current men's wear change more slowly than women's wear?**

_____

_____

_____

**UNDERSTAND MARKETING CONCEPTS**

Circle the best answer for each of the following questions.

1. What is considered softlines in fashion?
   a. garments for plus sizes
   b. software for fashion designers
   c. clothing, shoes, and accessories
   d. layers of clothing

2. Women's wear is made in
   a. only two sizes.
   b. all sizes.
   c. junior, misses, petite, and women's sizes.
   d. little and big sizes.

**THINK CRITICALLY**

Answer the following questions as completely as possible. If necessary, use a separate sheet of paper.

3. Describe major influences that affect the demand for fashions.

   _____

   _____

   _____

   _____

   _____

4. **Communication** Write a paragraph about the economic and historical changes that influenced the current style of men's clothing. Discuss your ideas with a small group of students and compare your thoughts.

   _____

   _____

   _____

   _____

   _____

# CHAPTER 2
## Lesson 2.3

# DESIGN AND COLOR

## GOALS

**Explain** the principles and elements of design.

**Explain** the importance of color in fashion.

## The Latest Style

Inspiration for fashion comes from many sources, including trend setters, environmental influences, and everyday items and events. Using an automobile that is a retro-design of a vintage car as an inspiration for fashion can attract media attention for both the designer and the automobile company.

Ford Motor Company hired eight American designers to use the Ford Thunderbird as a design inspiration for women's and men's wear. Designer William Reid used denim with metallic details reflecting the car's trim for a dressy design. Accessory designers Richard Lambertson and John Truex created a handbag from the convertible's soft-top fabric. Gene Meyer honored the Thunderbird with a bold leather jacket embossed with the car's emblem on the chest. John Bartlett reflected the car's pin-pricked leather seats in a red mesh T-shirt. Larry Leight of Oliver Peoples Eyewear designed sunglasses with a sloping frame modeled after the Thunderbird's windshield.

Work with a group. Discuss where ideas for new fashion products begin. Why would an auto manufacturer hire fashion designers to use a car for inspiration?

## BY DESIGN

PRODUCT/
SERVICE
MANAGEMENT

**S**uccessful and legendary classic styles are not theatrical, but memorable. The principles and elements of design are used to create both eye-pleasing and financially successful styles.

### THE PRINCIPLES

The **principles of design** are the fundamental rules that guide good design, whether for a garment, a home furnishing, or a print media advertisement. These design principles include balance, contrast, rhythm, unity, and proportion.

*Balance* can be achieved by placing equal weights at equal distance from the center to create *formal balance*. *Informal balance* can be achieved by moving a heavier weight toward the center and moving a lighter weight to the outer edge.

*Contrast* or *emphasis* is what attracts your attention at first glance. Opposites in size or color stand out because of contrast. A dark area in the midst of light, such as black pockets on a white shirt, creates contrast and catches your eye.

*Rhythm* creates eye movement and occurs when an element is repeated. The eye can be directed by repeating color, such as a white collar and white cuffs on a dark dress.

*Unity* links the visual elements, making them appear to belong together. Wearing a tie that contains small amounts of the color of the jacket helps unite the outfit.

*Proportion* relates the size and shape of all the elements used in a design. In fashion, proportion is created with lines and shapes. A short jacket with a long skirt can be in proportion.

## THE ELEMENTS

The **elements of design** include lines, shapes, texture, and color. The principles are applied to the elements, which come together to define the design.

*Lines* can be curved or straight and flowing or pointed. Lines give direction and divide the design with seams, waist lines, or even sleeves.

*Shapes* or *silhouettes* are formed when lines enclose a space. The basic fashion silhouettes include hourglass, rectangle, and triangle.

*Texture* is the feel of the design and can be created using different weaves of a fabric or visually with lines.

The use of *color* in the design can affect moods, feelings, and emotions.

When the principles of design are applied to the elements, a work of art is created. All designs contain the elements, but application of the principles determines how pleasing the design will be to the viewer.

**CYBER MARKETING**

At **www.apparelsearch .com/glossary.htm** is a dictionary of textile and apparel industry terms. This list includes terms that describe fabrics, garments, styles, and accessories. Definitions include some historical information on the origins of many of the words.

Students wanting to learn the jargon of the industry can use the short, factual bits of information as an electronic encyclopedia of fashion. The historical references in many of the definitions add interest to the items.

**THINK CRITICALLY**
Why might a fashion company be interested in providing free access to fashion vocabulary and historical information on its web site?

# TRY IT ON

**Give an example of how shapes can be balanced.**

_____

_____

_____

_____

# COLOR

**C**olor is so important to fashion that whole associations exist just to predict the trends in color. Two of the associations are the Color Marketing Group and the Color Association of the United States (CAUS).

## FORECASTS

**MARKETING-INFORMATION MANAGEMENT**

CAUS, founded in 1915, is the oldest of the associations. It was established when World War I made it difficult to get *color forecasts* from Europe, where color trends were being forecast at the time. The U.S. textile industry needed the color information for upcoming production runs. A committee of U.S. textile professionals was formed to choose the colors. The colors were made available to the textile industry as an American "color card" and were issued twice a year to provide directions in color trends. The information included formulas for mixing the colors, so the colors were standardized across the industry. The color forecasts are now divided into segments of the industry, such as women's fashions, men's fashions, and home/interior fashions. The forecasts are sent to approximately 1,000 members.

## COLOR TRADITIONS

Culturally, colors can take on significant meanings that can be fashionably applied to garments. In many Asian cultures, red means happiness and is worn for celebrations. Jewish tradition uses red as a sign of love and blue for glory. In the United States, patriotism is represented with

red, white, and blue. The colors of the U.S. flag were standardized by CAUS and are called "Old Glory red" and "Old Glory blue."

Colors affect people's senses and attract or repel buyers. A designer generally depends on the color forecasts to develop a plan for the current collection of garments so that the garments will fit with what is trendy. Colors that appeal to consumers can make a good design a great-selling garment.

# TRY IT ON

**What events or attitudes might influence the direction of fashion?**

## UNDERSTAND MARKETING CONCEPTS

Circle the best answer for each of the following questions.

1. The elements of design include
   a. lines, shapes, texture, and color.
   b. documents, marketing, pricing, and dimension.
   c. management, distribution, and production.
   d. balance, repetition, contrast, proportion, and emphasis.

2. The principles of design include
   a. men's wear, women's wear, and children's wear.
   b. lines, shapes, texture, and color.
   c. balance, contrast, rhythm, unity, and proportion.
   d. designers, retailers, and manufacturers.

## THINK CRITICALLY

Answer the following questions as completely as possible. If necessary, use a separate sheet of paper.

3. Why is color so important in fashion?

_____

_____

_____

_____

_____

4. **Communication**  Choose a garment and write a paragraph describing it. Explain how the principles of design were applied to the elements.

_____

_____

_____

_____

_____

# CHAPTER

# 2

## Lesson 2.4

# TEXTILES AND CONSTRUCTION

# GOALS

**Explain** the origins of common natural and man-made fibers.

**List** the aspects of quality garment construction.

## The Latest Style

In 1909, Anna and Laura Tirocchi immigrated to the United States from Italy, and within two years had established a dress-making shop in a mansion in Providence, Rhode Island. The shop was called A. & L. Tirocchi Gowns, and it served famous and wealthy people from 1915 until 1947. The sisters acquired fabric and ideas from Paris for the fashions that they created.

During the 1920s, business turned from custom garments to high-fashion, ready-to-wear and pre-designed, ready-to-cut clothing. After closing in 1947, the virtually intact shop was re-discovered in 1989, complete with garments and textiles as well as business records. The contents of the shop chronicled the history of women's fashions and the increasing freedom of women during that time. The historically significant shop contents were donated to the Rhode Island School of Design, and some can be seen at http://tirocchi.stg.brown.edu/.

Work with a group. Discuss what might be learned from examining garments and fabrics used over the 30-plus years of this business.

# THE FOUNDATION

**PRODUCT/ SERVICE MANAGEMENT**

**G**arments are made of textiles. Although the textile industry is not seen as a glamorous segment of fashion marketing, it is the foundation of the industry. Textiles serve fashion marketing as the trend barometer, the scientific research arm, the political seismograph, and the reflector of current art. Fashion designers create using textiles. Designers look to the textile industry to forecast what's coming for next season and to offer a new medium for the designer to shape. The textile industry is a global industry and the "fabric" of fashion marketing, both literally and figuratively.

## NATURE'S FABRICS

In the early 1900s, the majority of fabrics were made from three natural fibers—silk, wool, and cotton. **Fibers** are the thin threads that are spun into yarn. Yarn is woven into fabric. Fibers are called natural when they come from living plants or animals. Each of the three natural fibers has a mystique and history of its own.

*Silk* was used to richly dress royalty and aristocrats. Silk is lightweight and can keep the skin warm or cool. Silk is made from the cocoon of the silkworm, which eats only mulberry leaves. Unraveling the continuous

fiber spun by the worm produces a filament. A **filament** is a long, continuous fiber, and a silk filament may be as much as 1,100 yards long. Because silk fiber has triangular shapes in its makeup, it reflects light and appears shiny.

*Wool* fibers are produced from animal hair called fleece. Most wool is from sheep. Other animal fleece, such as from angora goats or llamas, is also called wool. Australia produces more wool than any other country.

*Cotton* fibers are produced from the seed pods of the cotton plant. Cotton blossoms wither and fall, leaving a green pod called a boll. The cotton bolls ripen and pop open, exposing the fluffy cotton fibers. Cotton comprises more than 40 percent of the fiber production in the world, with India and the United States being major producers.

One of the major uses of cotton fabric is the production of denim. The fabric originated in Nimes, France, and was originally called *serge de Nimes*. The name was later shortened to denim. Denim was used by Levi Strauss to produce a long-lasting pant worn by California miners. Today, denim's popularity barely fades before its cycle starts over.

## MAN-MADE FIBERS

Fibers may be produced using a combination of cellulose and chemicals or may be produced with chemicals alone. **Cellulose fibers** are produced

Cotton Incorporated publishes a weekly series of articles based on research about American consumer attitudes and behaviors. Cotton Incorporated is a company dedicated to increasing the demand for cotton through research and promotion.

using plants combined with chemical processes. Fibers produced with only chemicals are called **synthetics**. Both cellulose and synthetic fibers are referred to as *man-made fibers*.

Cellulose fabrics include rayon, acetate, and triacetate. Since silk worms only eat mulberry leaves, Hillaire de Chardonnet, a Frenchman, first produced cellulose fibers in the late 1880s by using the leaves and chemically reproducing the process used by the worms. The fibers he produced are now known as rayon.

Synthetic fibers include polyester, nylon, spandex, and acrylic. Major international chemical companies use petroleum-based chemicals to produce synthetic fibers.

From cottage industries hundreds of years ago to technology-based mass production today, the textile industry is a global force that influences every garment made in the world. The mass production of fabric made possible the movement of fashion from royalty to the masses.

The textile industry has always led and supported the fashion industry. Before a designer can begin to create an idea, the designer must have material with which to work. Consumers must like all of the elements—color, texture, line, shape, and mass—of the textiles used before they will choose to buy the garments created.

## TRY IT ON

**Why are some fibers called natural fibers?**

# UNDER CONSTRUCTION

**PRODUCT/ SERVICE MANAGEMENT**

To turn fabric into an apparel line requires knowledge of garment construction, including patternmaking, fabric marking, garment assembly, and selection of findings. **Findings** are all of the notions, besides the main fabric, that are needed to complete the garments and include zippers, buttons, thread, lining materials, and trims.

## PUTTING IT TOGETHER

Recognizing the characteristics of quality garment construction takes time and knowledge. Comparing the construction of high-quality and low-quality garments can help a novice understand the characteristics of quality. The cost of a garment is directly related to the techniques used in construction of the garment. Garments can be very inexpensively constructed, but may soon start to deteriorate and be returned by the consumer to the retailer. A retailer who receives multiple returns with the same construction problem will expect the manufacturer to correct or pay for the problem, costing the manufacturer its profit.

**Stitching** The interlocking or interlooping of thread used to join two pieces of fabric is called **stitching**. The joint at which the two pieces of fabric meet is called a **seam**. Stitching is second only to the fabric in importance to the quality of a garment. If you have ever had a hem fall out or a seam pop open, then the type of stitching used was the problem. For example, a simple chainstitch that is interlooped uses only one thread, unravels easily, and is very inexpensive. A garment constructed with quality

has more expensive stitches that use more thread and require more production time. For example, an interlocked stitch is strong but costs more.

**Quality** Turning a garment inside out can help you learn about construction and quality. Look for no raw edges, no loose thread, and no broken stitches. On the outside, look for buttonholes that are sized right for the button and have an adequate amount of thread to withstand use. If the zipper comes apart when stress is applied to the two sides, it is called *ratcheting* and indicates a cheap zipper that will not last.

Loro Milan ties are sold online. The web site at **www.loromilan.com** provides a simple yet elegant way to buy Italian silk ties at inexpensive prices. The site also provides information about the history of silk, the history of ties, the manufacturing of ties, and the various ways to tie a tie.

**THINK CRITICALLY**
Why would Loro Milan provide historical information about ties and silk on its web site? Who might want the information about how to tie a tie?

Companies that develop high-quality garments perform three types of inspections, with the first while the garment is still under construction. A second inspection is done when the product is finished, and a third and final inspection is done on all, or at least on random samplings of, the garments produced.

# TRY IT ON

**Why does quality cost more?**

_____

_____

_____

## MARGARET WALCH

**M**argaret Walch has a career that impacts the colors of much of the clothing purchased in the United States. As director of the Color Association of the United States (CAUS), she assists with forecasting the colors used by the American textile, fashion, and interior design industries.

After earning a bachelor's degree in history and fine art and a master's degree in social history, Margaret Walch began her career as a journalist. She worked in the United States and London for a textile magazine, *American Fabrics*. Back in the United States, she wrote the *Color Source Book* and began working for CAUS, eventually moving up to the position of director. She helps educate fashion marketers about the importance of color to successful marketing and frequently lectures on color to business organizations, such as May Department Stores, Nike, and the American Society of Interior Designers.

Ms. Walch also edits *CAUS News*, the association's newsletter, and has written two other books on color including *Living Colors: The Definitive Guide to Color Palettes through the Ages*. The history of colors used in fashion and decoration is used in predicting the essence of future colors. Ms. Walch is considered an international expert on color and its impact on people. She has focused her career around color.

**THINK CRITICALLY**
**1.** Why do you think color is so important to fashion marketing?
**2.** Discuss with a partner how color impacts you and the clothing choices you make. Write a paragraph about the colors you like and how they make you feel.

## UNDERSTAND MARKETING CONCEPTS
Circle the best answer for each of the following questions.

1. What is meant by natural fibers?
   a. light-colored fibers
   b. fibers favored by naturalists
   c. high fibers
   d. fibers originating from plants or animals

2. Two types of stitches are
   a. terms and textiles.
   b. seams and stress.
   c. needles and handles.
   d. interlocking and interlooping.

## THINK CRITICALLY
Answer the following questions as completely as possible. If necessary, use a separate sheet of paper.

3. **Social Studies**   Select a natural fiber and research the specific geographic regions in which that natural fiber is developed and why. Present a short report to the class about your findings.

_____

_____

_____

_____

_____

4. **Communication**   Write a paragraph about why denim has been a popular fabric for more than 100 years. Include some information about what styles are currently popular in denim.

_____

_____

_____

_____

_____

_____

# CHAPTER 2 REVIEW

## REVIEW MARKETING CONCEPTS

Write the letter of the term that matches each definition. Some terms will not be used.

_____ **1.** A long, continuous fiber

_____ **2.** Thin threads that are spun into yarn

_____ **3.** The interlocking or interlooping of thread to join two pieces of fabric

_____ **4.** Fibers produced using plants and chemical processes

_____ **5.** Man-made fibers that are produced totally from chemicals

_____ **6.** Clothing items of fabrics or leather

_____ **7.** Joint where two pieces of fabric meet

_____ **8.** Include zippers, buttons, and thread

_____ **9.** A less expensive copy of a haute couture designer garment

**a.** cellulose fibers
**b.** couturier
**c.** demand
**d.** elements of design
**e.** fibers
**f.** filament
**g.** findings
**h.** haute couture
**i.** knockoff
**j.** principles of design
**k.** seam
**l.** softlines
**m.** stitching
**n.** style
**o.** synthetics

**Circle the best answer.**

**10.** Three segments of fashions are
  **a.** small, medium, and large.
  **b.** men's, women's, and children's.
  **c.** style, design, and color.
  **d.** none of these.

**11.** Fashion is no longer centered only in France because of
  **a.** economics.
  **b.** global communications.
  **c.** technology.
  **d.** all of these.

**12.** What are the three major natural fibers?
  **a.** nylon, rayon, and acetate
  **b.** polyester, cotton, and linen
  **c.** silk, cotton, and wool
  **d.** rayon, spandex, and wool

**13.** Environmental factors affecting demand include
  **a.** fibers and filaments.
  **b.** acetate and rayon.
  **c.** style and design.
  **d.** social, technological, and economic.

# THINK CRITICALLY

**14.** Spend five minutes discussing with another student why cultures influence fashions. Make a list of reasons a fashion marketer needs to know about multiple cultures.

POINT YOUR BROWSER

fashion.swlearning.com

_____

_____

_____

_____

_____

**15.** How has the development of textiles influenced the fashion industry? Describe the importance of fabric to the fashion industry.

_____

_____

_____

_____

**16.** Why was France originally the center of fashion? Why are there multiple centers of fashion now? How did the spread of democracies and technology move the center of fashion from France?

_____

_____

_____

_____

**17.** Describe the origins of denim. How did the fabric get its name? Of what fiber is it made?

_____

_____

_____

_____

CHAPTER 2 REVIEW

## MAKE CONNECTIONS

**18. Marketing Math**   You want to produce 100 garments that you can sell for $75.00 each. It takes 5 yards of fabric that costs $7.50 per yard to make each garment. The findings you want for each garment cost $15.00, and it will take a garment manufacturer 1/2 hour to produce each garment at $14.00 per hour. How many garments will you have to sell to pay for the fabric, findings, and construction costs?

_____

_____

_____

_____

_____

**19. Ecology**   Why are some fabrics considered man-made and others considered natural? Which ones are made of totally renewable resources?

_____

_____

_____

_____

_____

**20. Technology**   How has technology changed the production of textiles? How has this changed fashion? Why does global communication over the Internet and TV affect fashion?

_____

_____

_____

_____

_____

_____

_____

## FASHION RETAIL MANAGEMENT

You are the manager of an upscale clothing store that pays sales associates commission on sales. Competition among the sales associates at your store is fierce. Frequently, more than one sales associate approaches the same customer for a possible sale. This has led to arguments among sales associates and has lost business.

Sales associates at your store are expected to be fashion experts who know how clothes should look with the proper fit. You have noticed that sometimes sales associates are so anxious to complete a sale that they are not totally honest with customers. Customers are sold clothing that does not fit correctly.

The policy at your clothing store is "free alterations for the life of the garment." Most sales associates are not eager to help customers who bring in older clothing for alterations. Sales associates feel that the time taken to size older clothes reduces their sales of new clothing. Your store owner believes that the free lifetime alterations policy results in loyal customers.

As manager of the store, you must present a strategy to the owner to improve customer service and the image of sales associates. You must devise the best strategy for paying sales associates, altering clothing, and establishing long-lasting customer relations. The bottom line is to achieve maximum sales with the best service. You have ten minutes to devise your strategy, and you will be given ten minutes for the role play to present your strategy to the store owner.

## PROJECT: The COLLECTION POINT

You are working with a fashion manufacturer to predict trends in fashion based on what has happened in the past. You want to see if you can increase the speed at which styles in men's wear make dramatic changes similar to women's fashion trends.

**Work with a group and complete the following activities.**

1. Research men's wear fashion history on the Internet or at the library. Go to **www.google.com** and search for men's fashion history, or use information and books from your school library.

2. Write a description of a period of time when men's and women's clothing in Europe were similar in decoration and colors. Include information about the environmental characteristics of the time that impacted men's fashions.

3. Discuss your ideas with the group, and prepare a two-minute presentation on the topic. Use computer presentation software to create your presentation. Insert pictures of clothing from the time period, if possible.

# CHAPTER 3

# MARKETING FASHIONS

## LESSONS

3.1 INFORMATION, PLEASE

3.2 THE RIGHT PRODUCT, THE RIGHT PLACE

3.3 THE RIGHT PRICE

3.4 THE RIGHT PROMOTION = SALES

# WINNING STRATEGIES

## ZARA

What started as a mom-and-pop-type business in the 1960s is now an international fashion company. Zara is a chain of almost 1,000 stores in 31 countries, including approximately 40 stores in the United States, that handles fashion marketing from design to retail sales. A team of more than 200 designers creates the moderately priced apparel. Trendy ideas are gleaned from high-end fashions and from customers to create more than 12,000 different garments each year.

Among Zara's marketing techniques is the fast, in-house manufacturing by parent company Inditex. With some of the world's largest design and production facilities, fashions can move from an idea to the stores in as little as two weeks. Zara depends on word of mouth and repeat customers for promotion and does no advertising.

A unique approach of Zara is the use of its salespeople to collect marketing information. The salespeople are equipped with wireless organizers that transmit trends, customer requests, and merchandise orders to the main office in La Coruña, Spain. When the well-made, affordable apparel quickly arrives in the stores, it flies off the shelves, and sales continue to grow.

### THINK CRITICALLY

1. List as least three elements that make Zara unique among retail stores.
2. How does in-house production of all the apparel impact the delivery of goods to the stores?

# INFORMATION, PLEASE

## GOALS

**Describe** bases of segmenting target markets.

**List** ways to collect marketing information.

## The Latest Style

Luxury retailer Coach targeted a younger, more feminine customer when it rejuvenated its stores and products. Coach leather bags, brief cases, and luggage are known worldwide and compete with designer brands like Prada.

In the late 1990s, Coach was seen as a boring, uninteresting brand of products with falling sales. A revamped marketing plan was developed to promote the new product line and redesign the stores. Promotion included a new catalog to help announce the expanded line. Coach added colors, fabrics, and styles to its limited line of tan-only bags and luggage. Customers liked what they saw, as proven by increased sales. Coach was on target for the new customer segment.

Work with a group. Discuss why Coach changed its image to target a younger customer. What information would help Coach stay focused on its customers?

# WHO IS THE CUSTOMER?

**MARKETING-INFORMATION MANAGEMENT**

Business activities generally fall into one of four categories: production, marketing, finance, or management. Fashion marketers make decisions based on marketing plans that cover all four business activities. The plans are based on data or information focused on a target group of customers. Gathering and utilizing the information is known as marketing-information management.

## MARKET SEGMENTS

To get to know customers better, marketers group people by common characteristics. Customers can be divided into target segments based on **demographic information**, including age, gender, ethnic group, nationality, education, and income. Other customer segments are based on lifestyle and psychographics. **Psychographics** uses characteristics such as ideology, values, attitudes, and interests to group people. Knowing the demographics and psychographics of customers helps fashion marketers understand what people buy.

Wal-Mart® has become the largest company in the United States by targeting the low- to mid-income customer. Originally, Wal-Mart's apparel was carefully selected to appeal to a penny-wise shopper who works hard but lives from paycheck to paycheck. To continue to grow, Wal-Mart began targeting a more affluent customer using pricier products. Wal-Mart® customized products by location to meet the needs of this new segment of customers, with the goal of increasing the size of the average sales transaction. About the same time, Wal-Mart, for the first time ever, sent press releases to fashion and beauty magazines touting its ability to offer trendy styles at affordable prices. Wal-Mart will know if it has succeeded by the sales information on the new, pricier items.

## THE TARGET CUSTOMER

In the United States, care must be given to grouping people by race, since fashion appeals across racial groups. Marketing to people grouped by lifestyle and demographics such as age and income is more effective. A fashion marketer must, of course, decide who the target customer is early in the product-planning process. Before designing or buying products to market to middle-income teens ages 16 to 19, a smart fashion marketer will research all information available about this group. The information should include where they currently buy, how much they spend, and what motivates them to buy.

## TRY IT ON

**Describe the difference between demographics and psychographics in relation to marketing information.**

_____

_____

_____

## MANAGING INFORMATION

**MARKETING-INFORMATION MANAGEMENT**

**S**uccessful marketers know what the next trend will be, who is buying what, and what is selling well. They find out what customers think and then direct fashion marketing to provide what customers want. Collecting information about consumer groups, focusing on the consumption habits of target groups, and analyzing how the group is acting toward the merchandise is all part of managing marketing information. It is all about keeping a _marketing concept_ at every stage. Successful fashion businesses always keep customer needs in mind during design, production, and distribution of products.

**CYBER MARKETING**

*Vogue Magazine*'s web site, **www.vogue.com**, formed a partnership with **www.Net-a-porter.com** to open an online shop on the *British Vogue* web site. Net-a-porter is a London-based online boutique that sells high fashion, with an average online sale of $450. Items offered at the online boutique are hand-picked by *Vogue* editors. The offerings are updated every two weeks and the profits split between the two companies. The partnership will add *Vogue* readers to Net-a-porter's potential customer base.

**THINK CRITICALLY**
Visit a fashion web site and look for links to other businesses. What are the benefits for the two businesses in joining together?

## WHAT THE CUSTOMER WANTS

Successful fashion marketing can be described in deceptively simple terms—ask customers what they want and then exceed their expectations. In reality, learning what customers want requires research. Firms that specialize in marketing research for the apparel industry use a multitude of techniques to gather information from potential consumers. Marketing research can take the form of meeting with a focus group, conducting surveys, observing fashion trends, or studying competitors.

Information is gathered every time someone makes a purchase, especially if the purchase is made online. Data about who customers are and what they have purchased are recorded electronically in many stores. For example, whenever a purchase is made at a Talbots store, the customer is asked for a zip code. Knowing the area in which a person lives provides approximate income of families living in the area, allowing the marketing-information manager to group the purchaser by lifestyle.

## GLOBAL MARKETS

As global markets grow, marketers must increase their knowledge of cultures, collect information about the needs and wants of the diverse customers, and please them. One way to collect data about the next trend is to visit places where trend setters are and observe what they are wearing.

The Internet has made the exchange of data instant and has increased the speed at which fashion marketers must respond. Manufacturers can find out what people in a trendy restaurant in Italy are wearing via the Internet and can begin production of a garment to make it available for sale the following week. Information is critical to beat the competition to market and to maximize sales while a trend is "hot."

## TRY IT ON

**Name ways information about fashion trends is collected.**

## UNDERSTAND MARKETING CONCEPTS

Circle the best answer for each of the following questions.

1. Marketing-information management means
   a. gathering and using information to make marketing decisions.
   b. providing the retailer with the right merchandise.
   c. creating and maintaining satisfying exchange relationships.
   d. none of the above.

2. Grouping customers based on age, race, and gender is grouping based on
   a. distribution.
   b. demographics.
   c. ethnicity.
   d. advertising.

## THINK CRITICALLY

Answer the following questions as completely as possible. If necessary, use a separate sheet of paper.

3. **Communication** Discuss with a partner how you feel about marketers gathering information about you. Briefly describe the methods you would prefer they use to gather information about your likes and dislikes in clothing.

   _____

   _____

   _____

   _____

4. If you knew that 50 percent of the salespeople in a large retail chain buy and wear the brand of clothes you manufacture, how could you use that information to improve your manufacturing business? Write a narrative on the action you would take based on that information.

   _____

   _____

   _____

   _____

   _____

# CHAPTER 3
## Lesson 3.2

# THE RIGHT PRODUCT, THE RIGHT PLACE

**Describe** the development of fashion products.

**Explain** the channels of distribution for fashions.

## The Latest Style

The sister retail stores, Ann Taylor and Ann Taylor Loft, target two different customers. The Loft stores provide dressy-casual and business-casual women's wear. Loft prices are considered upper-moderate with the value-to-price ratio being very good. *Value-to-price ratio* is the relationship between the perceived quality and expected satisfaction with the garment and the price. Loft stores occupy about 5,500 square feet of space and are generally located in "B" grade malls.

Ann Taylor customers are employed in higher-level professional positions and have a higher income level than Loft customers. Ann Taylor offers more suits and fitted business apparel at 20 percent to 30 percent higher prices. Ann Taylor stores are located in "A" grade malls and average 4,000 to 5,000 square feet. The corporation is beginning to put both stores in some "A" grade mall locations.

Work with a group. Discuss why the company would want both stores in some locations. Which store might this help? Which store might this hurt?

## FROM A CATWALK TO A CLOSET

**PRODUCT/ SERVICE MANAGEMENT**

Fashions take many paths to a consumer's closet. Models walk down narrow runways called *catwalks* wearing high-fashion, designer originals during seasonal fashion weeks in New York, Paris, and Milan. Fashions for sale at mass retailers take a different path. Product development starts with information about trends and customers.

### PREDICTING FASHION

Information management leads to ideas for garments. The products are developed by merchandisers based on what the marketing information indicates will sell. A **merchandiser** plans the styles, prices, and number of garments to be produced based on the information, and finally the garments are manufactured. The common themes of fashion collections, including fabrics, colors, and silhouettes, are all featured in clothing seen at the malls based on decisions in some cases made more than a year in advance. Stores like Zara that control the product development process from start to finish can react within weeks to provide a new, specific style or color, but it takes longer to develop an entire season's collection.

**Forecasters** predict trends and decide on the colors and details that make the next season's fashions different and exciting. Forecasters usually make predictions about 18 months in advance of clothes hitting the stores. A chain with its own brand may begin planning as soon as information about trends, colors, and fabrics is available.

# TRY IT ON

**What is the job of fashion forecasters?**

_____

_____

_____

# THE FASHION CHANNELS

**D**elivering the right product to the right place is a critical step in marketing fashions. **Channels of distribution** are the paths and businesses involved in moving the product from the idea stage to the consumer. *Indirect channels of distribution* require intermediaries who help get the product to the consumer. The intermediaries add value to the product by making it available to the consumer where they need it or making the consumer aware of the product and related items. Companies that use *direct channels of distribution* are involved in both producing the goods and selling them directly to the consumer.

## DISTRIBUTED FASHION

Some companies, such as Zara, are called *manufacturing retailers*. They manage, finance, and market garments, but contractors are hired to actually produce the garments. *Contractors* are businesses that provide the equipment and labor to cut and sew the garments. Zara has the advantage of direct distribution combined with economy of scale. **Economy of scale** means the price per garment is low due to large-volume production. This occurs because one-time costs, such as setting up equipment for a specific product, can be spread over more garments and because large quantities of the same fabric can be purchased for less.

When companies perform more than two of the business activities, such as managing, financing, and marketing, it is called **vertical integration**. A

Korean-Americans are the largest immigrant group in the apparel industry on the west coast of the United States. They set the standard for fast production time in junior-size clothing. Using a very lean staff, they have held their prices down and have a large volume of business.

In 1941, the Board of Trade in England issued a ruling that impacted fashion design. Due to material and labor shortages during World War II, the amount of material used in garments was strictly limited and no trim was allowed to be made or imported. This left manufacturers of low-end garments no way to cover up the poorly designed, shoddy clothes they had been mass producing. The Board of Trade commissioned London fashion designers to produce dress patterns with good style that met the simple standards. The garments were called "utility" clothes and were rationed to the public through a system where an individual received 20 coupons twice a year. The coupons, in addition to money, were required for clothing purchases, with a suit requiring 18 coupons and a dress 12 coupons. For the first time in English history, the masses were exposed to well-tailored clothes for a reasonable price.

**THINK CRITICALLY**
**Discuss with a group the way world events can impact the distribution of fashion.**

trend toward consolidation of the industry into a few large corporations is creating more vertical integration and more direct channels of distribution.

When garments are distributed internationally from the United States, they are *exported*. Some countries block garment exports from the United States by increasing the costs with fees called *tariffs*. Tariffs make the item too expensive for people to buy. In turn, U.S. laws impact garments made in other countries and imported to the United States.

## WHAT'S IN A NAME?

PRODUCT/
SERVICE
MANAGEMENT

**Private labels** identify a line of garments produced for only one retailer. For example, evening dresses with a Neiman-Marcus label are found only at Neiman-Marcus stores. Private labels are ordered to meet exact retailer specifications and provide the customer a consistent value and price line.

**Brand names** identify the product for consumers. Extensive advertising can help build a brand loyalty that is associated with a particular quality and price line targeted at a consumer group. Once a brand is established, the manufacturer or designer may sign licensing agreements to allow others to use the brand name. A *licensing agreement* is a legal contract in which a manufacturer agrees to produce garments with the brand name and pay the original brand name owner a percentage of sales called a *royalty*. This allows wider distribution of the name brand with no additional investment on the part of the original owner.

## TRY IT ON

**What is a manufacturing retailer?**

## UNDERSTAND MARKETING CONCEPTS

Circle the best answer for each of the following questions.

**1.** When a fashion company is vertically integrated, it is
   **a.** a manufacturer with economy of scale.
   **b.** a retailer of chain specialty stores.
   **c.** a contractor who makes quality garments.
   **d.** involved in more than two of the business activities.

**2.** Private labels
   **a.** identify a line of garments produced for only one retailer.
   **b.** are ordered to meet exact specifications.
   **c.** provide the customer a consistent value and price line.
   **d.** do all of these.

## THINK CRITICALLY

Answer the following questions as completely as possible. If necessary, use a separate sheet of paper.

**3.** What is meant by economy of scale? Why would costs be impacted by the quantity of a garment that is produced?

_____

_____

_____

_____

_____

**4.** **Economics**  Write a paragraph about why channels of distribution are impacted by the world economy.

_____

_____

_____

_____

_____

_____

# THE RIGHT PRICE

## GOALS

**Explain** fashion pricing.

**List** and define the categories of price ranges used in fashion marketing.

## The Latest Style

**W**al-Mart® has been known as a discount or budget-priced retailer, with an average price point on clothing of $10 and an upper price point of $20. A *price point* refers to a specific price within a specified price range. For example, shirts are sold at $10, $12, and $20, rather than at many different prices. Wal-Mart recently moved up its top price point, hoping to increase its average sale. Wal-Mart's plan includes working with its suppliers to give them a specific profit and sales quota to meet. Wal-Mart provides information to suppliers that is kept secret by many other retailers. The information, including sales data, provides a unique opportunity for the suppliers to mini-manage their businesses with Wal-Mart.

Work with a group. Discuss why Wal-Mart might want to move up the top price point of its clothing. What difference will this make in sales?

## THE PRICE IS RIGHT

PRICING

**W**hen a consumer buys a garment, price plays an important role in the decision-making process. The process includes assessing the quality and the value-to-price ratio of the garment. The *value-to-price ratio* is the relationship between the perceived quality and expected satisfaction with the garment and the price.

### SETTING THE PRICE

Retailers buy from manufacturers and resell to consumers. When a manufacturer sells to a retailer, the manufacturer is called a *vendor*.

**Wholesale** is the manufacturer's price to the retailer. The price a vendor charges is at least partially based on the demand for the product and the supply available. A hard-to-find, hot-selling item will sell for considerably more than an item that is readily available or low in demand.

**Retail** is what the final consumer pays for a garment. The retailer must set prices to cover the cost of the fashions, the operating expenses of the store, and the desired profit, with allowances for returns of merchandise by customers and markdowns. A **markdown** is taken when the original retail price is reduced to speed up sales. Markdowns occur when a buyer overestimates the demand for a product. To move the unsold merchandise, the price is reduced. Salaries, advertising, and building maintenance are part of the *operating expenses*. Operating expenses also include the cost to cover damaged or stolen merchandise that cannot be sold and the cost of security systems to protect from losses.

The difference between the selling price and the cost of the fashion items is called the **margin** or **gross profit**. The balance left after the operating expenses are paid is called the **net profit**.

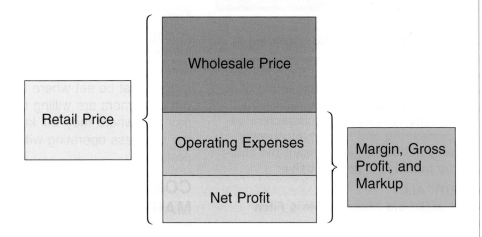

The formula to calculate net profit is

Selling price − Cost of items − Operating expenses = Net profit

The retail price at which a garment actually sells is based on many factors, including the wholesale costs and the markup. **Markup** is the amount added to the cost to cover the operating expenses and desired profit. The percentage of markup is usually figured as a percentage of retail price. For example, a shirt selling at retail for $100 might have a wholesale cost of $48, making the markup $52 or 52 percent. The formulas for calculating retail markup dollars and the markup percentage are

Retail $ − Cost $ = Markup $

$$\text{Markup \%} = \frac{\text{Retail \$} - \text{Cost \$}}{\text{Retail \$}}$$

A manufacturer or retailer sets a percentage of markup to cover all expenses and allow for a profit. Profits in a well-run company can average four to six percent. Manufacturers and retailers usually mark up items from 30 to 50 percent above their costs to achieve the desired profit.

# TRY IT ON

**What is meant by markup?**

_____

_____

_____

_____

Abercrombie & Fitch, known for appealing to college fraternities, quickly withdrew T-shirts after Asian-Americans protested the controversial printing on the shirts. In a marketing blunder that made national news, the retailer had printed cartoons of retro-Asian characters depicted in demeaning and stereotypical ways. The company indicated that it meant the characters to be humorous, not offensive.

**THINK CRITICALLY**
**1.** What mistake did Abercrombie & Fitch make with these shirts?
**2.** How could its management have prevented this blunder?

# PRICING POLICIES

**F**or a manufacturer or retailer to make proper decisions about pricing policies, it must know its customers. Price ranges and price points within a range must be set where target customers are willing to pay and where they will keep the business operating with a profit.

## COMPETITION AND MARKET SHARE

The *competition*, or other businesses that are selling similar items, is seeking business from the same customers. The percentage of the total market represented by customers in a target group is referred to as **market share**. If you set prices too high, your competition may attract a larger percentage of the available market share.

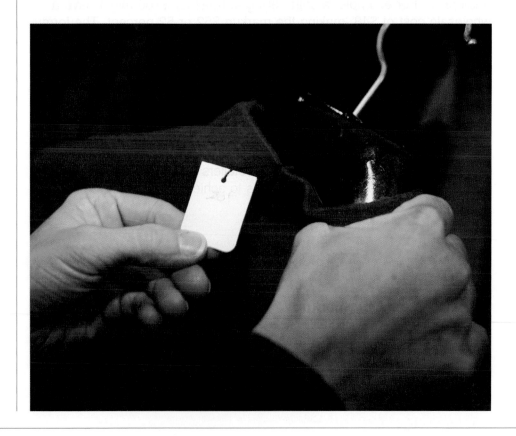

## CATEGORIZING THE PRICE

The price-line image a manufacturer or retailer has with customers influences the price that is set for an item. Customers expect expensive items in high-end stores.

*Price ranges* can be used to identify the quality of fashions and are described as discount, budget, value-priced, moderate, better, bridge, designer, and couture.

R. SCOTT FRENCH

- *Discount* is the low-end price line and usually represents closeouts or high-volume sales items.
- *Budget* items are those garments sold at below-average prices by stores like Wal-Mart.
- *Value-priced* garments have an excellent value-to-price ratio. A value-priced item may be good quality, but not high fashion.
- *Moderate* refers to middle-priced items.
- *Better* is defined by middle-to-high prices and is generally sold in specialty shops or department stores.
- *Bridge* is at the low-price end of a designer line of fashions.
- *Designer* is at the high-price end and carries a brand name that has an image allowing the prices to be high.
- *Couture* refers to original, luxury, designer garments. These garments are made with the highest standards of the highest quality fabrics, and they carry a very high price. A price point for couture garments can be more than $15,000.

Choosing the right price for a fashion item is a complex decision. When an item is priced too high, it will not sell, and when it is priced too low, it will not cover expenses.

## TRY IT ON

**List the eight price ranges for fashions.**

_____

_____

_____

_____

## UNDERSTAND MARKETING CONCEPTS

Circle the best answer for each of the following questions.

**1.** Net profit is
  **a.** what is left after the cost of goods and operating expenses are paid.
  **b.** the price lines charged by retailers.
  **c.** the margin made by wholesalers.
  **d.** the cost of the goods and operating expenses.

**2.** Some of the ways garments are categorized by price line include
  **a.** chain, specialty, and department store.
  **b.** retail, wholesale, and service selling.
  **c.** discount, budget, value-priced, and moderate.
  **d.** denim, silk, cotton, and nylon.

## THINK CRITICALLY

Answer the following questions as completely as possible. If necessary, use a separate sheet of paper.

**3. Communication**   Write a paragraph about why correct pricing is so critical to a business and to its customers.

_____

_____

_____

_____

**4. Marketing Math**   A garment costs a retailer $22.50 at wholesale and sells for $46.00. Calculate the markup percentage, and list two expenses that the markup must cover.

_____

_____

_____

_____

_____

_____

_____

# THE RIGHT PROMOTION = SALES

## The Latest Style

The fashion magazine *Glamour* and the College Television Network (CTN) formed a partnership for a multi-tiered cross-promotion. CTN is a broadcast TV network available at 1,800 colleges and universities. A *multi-tiered cross-promotion* is one that uses several forms of media, such as TV, billboards, print media, and giveaways, and the two businesses promote each other. The partnership promotion included a short TV program that CTN aired several times a week called *Glamour on Campus*. Special advertising in the magazine touted the event sponsors, and *Glamour* gave away gift bags and hosted fashion shows on campuses.

Work with a group. Make a list of the benefits of a cross-promotion between two businesses. Make an additional list of different kinds of businesses that might partner to cross-promote fashions.

**GOALS**

**Identify** the components of the promotional mix.

**Explain** the interdependence of selling and promotion.

## THE RIGHT COMBINATION

A fashion business could have the most wonderful product developed, but if no one knows about it, it will never sell. Promotion is the marketing function that provides information to customers about the company and its products and encourages them to buy.

### THE COMPONENTS

PROMOTION

Promotion has four components—advertising, public relations, publicity, and personal selling—which combined are called the **promotional mix**.

*Advertising* is the paid communication of information about products and services between the seller and possible buyers. The purpose of advertising is to generate sales, sales leads, or increased customer traffic. *Traffic* refers to the number of people who visit a store. Effective advertising stands out from other ads and encourages action, such as suggesting that consumers "order today."

*Public relations (PR)* involves creating and maintaining beneficial relationships between the business and the public. A business may participate in community programs or sponsor special events in order to develop good relations with the public and enhance its image. Effective PR can generate a positive image for a company, but cannot cover up bad news. PR frequently emphasizes a third-party endorsement of the business. For example, a representative of the Chamber of Commerce cutting the ribbon at a new store opening generates a positive image.

The Chamber of Commerce is an organization of businesses in the community that is seen as endorsing the new business.

*Publicity* is a component of public relations that is not paid for by the business and, thus, is not controlled by the business. A firm might issue news releases to announce an upcoming event in hopes of attracting media coverage. A newspaper or TV station may then choose to cover the event. Since the business does not control the coverage, it may be negative, but it can be positive and free of cost. Good public relations with the media can improve chances of positive publicity.

*Personal selling* is the individual, one-on-one effort made by a representative of a company to persuade a customer to purchase goods or services. E-commerce and other forms of nonpersonal selling cannot take the place of the interaction between two people that happens during a sale. A salesperson is able to read the customer and respond immediately to meet the customer's needs.

The two marketing functions of promotion and selling are very interdependent. Promotion is needed to provide awareness and information about the product, and selling is needed to provide the personal touch that can close the sale.

## TRY IT ON

**How are advertising and public relations different?**

_____

_____

_____

# PROMOTIONAL PLANNING

The components of promotion—advertising, public relations, publicity, and personal selling—are combined to form a promotional mix. People employed in fashion promotion combine the right amounts of the four components to reach the desired result—sales.

### THE PLAN

There is no exact recipe for the promotional mix, as each company and situation requires a slightly different combination. A promotional plan should include

- Goals and objectives for the campaign so that the purpose is clear. This will help determine how much of each component is needed.
- A clear statement of the target customer.
- The media to be used for each component, such as TV or billboards.

• The budget for the campaign since this affects the sales price of the garments.

Careful planning can help make a promotion successful and bring in sales.

## THE SALE

**SELLING**

After making customers aware and creating a desire to buy, the next step is to make the sale. The salespeople who interact with the all-important customer must be included in promotional planning and provided with knowledge of the product features, product benefits, and special pricing that is available. Product information, especially that provided in advertising, must be shared with the sales staff to prepare them. They should know more than the customer about the product.

*Sales knowledge* must be provided through training. The beauty advisors at the Estée Lauder cosmetics area and the consultants at the Clinique cosmetics counter provide excellent examples of personal sales methods that work. The salespeople receive as many as 150 hours of training as well as uniforms to wear. They are taught

• to build rapport with the customer to assure repeat business

• to link products such as lip liner and lipstick for extra sales

• to hand products to the customer so that they start to take ownership

**CYBER MARKETING**

**Luxury accessory items seem to be easier to sell online than ready-to-wear items. The www.hermes.com site was launched to sell silk scarves, ties, and fragrances, but not the designer apparel for which Hermès is known. The web site shows locations of Hermès' stores around the world as well as beautiful photographs of Hermès' products.**

**THINK CRITICALLY**
**1.** Visit **www.hermes .com** and determine why Hermès uses horses in its advertisements.
**2.** What information is available about the neckties that are offered for sale?

- to assume a customer's objections to a price is a sign of interest
- to empathize and then list a product's benefits for the customer

The excellent training pays off as shown by the fact that these beauty products businesses tend to weather downturns in the economy better than other areas of the fashion industry.

# TRY IT ON

## What should salespeople know about a product?

### TREY LAIRD

The founder of Laird + Partners, an advertising agency, has an impressive list of clients, including Gap and designer Donna Karan. Trey Laird attracted the much-sought-after clients because of his extensive experience in advertising. Laird began his career with a large New York advertising firm where he worked on the Donna Karan account. He later worked for an Italian apparel designer for about a year before moving on to do in-house advertising for Donna Karan. When Laird opened his own agency, Donna Karan moved the approximately $23-million account to Laird's new agency.

Millard Drexler, Gap Inc. president and CEO, invited Laird to make a proposal for reviving Gap. Gap had been losing mar-ket share and needed new ideas. Laird worked with Gap's in-house marketing department to turn Gap around. According to *The Wall Street Journal*, Laird planned "to remind consumers that Gap is an American icon." In a Gap Inc. news release, Millard Drexler stated, "Trey's creativity and understanding of the Gap brand will help us talk to our customers in new ways."

### THINK CRITICALLY

**1.** What would you recommend to Trey Laird to increase sales at a store like Gap?

**2.** How can Gap reach its target customer? What is the best media to use?

**3.** Would the use of celebrities be a good idea? If yes, which ones should it use?

## UNDERSTAND MARKETING CONCEPTS
Circle the best answer for each of the following questions.

1. The promotional mix components are
   a. planning, distribution, price, and place.
   b. discount, budget, bridge, and designer.
   c. advertising, public relations, publicity, and personal selling.
   d. petite, small, medium, and large.

2. Publicity is a part of public relations and
   a. is part of pricing.
   b. is independent of design.
   c. is driven by the customer.
   d. is free.

## THINK CRITICALLY
Answer the following questions as completely as possible. If necessary, use a separate sheet of paper.

3. Describe the promotional mix you might use to advertise a new style of shorts designed to flatter a slender, young woman. How would you seek publicity for the new item?

_____

_____

_____

4. **Marketing Math** If you had $15,000 to spend on advertising, which television station would you choose to make sure the most people saw your ad, assuming the rates were as follows?
   - At Station XYZ, the ad will run once a day for three days during a show with 5,000 average viewers at a cost of $5,000 each time shown.
   - At Station CGO, the ad will run twice a day for two days during shows with 4,000 average viewers each at a cost of $7,500 per day.

_____

_____

_____

_____

# CHAPTER 3 REVIEW

## REVIEW MARKETING CONCEPTS

**Write the letter of the term that matches each definition. Some terms will not be used.**

_____ **1.** Someone who plans the styles, price points, and number of garments based on marketing information

_____ **2.** Paths and businesses involved in moving the product from the idea stage to the consumer

_____ **3.** A low per-garment cost due to the production of a large volume of garments

_____ **4.** When companies perform more than two business activities, such as managing, financing, and marketing

_____ **5.** The amount added to the cost to cover the operating expenses and desired profit

_____ **6.** A combination of advertising, public relations, publicity, and personal selling

_____ **7.** Customer data such as age, gender, ethnic group, nationality, education, and income

_____ **8.** Characteristics such as ideology, values, attitudes, and interests used to group people

_____ **9.** A line of garments produced for only one retailer

**a.** brand names
**b.** channels of distribution
**c.** demographic information
**d.** economy of scale
**e.** forecasters
**f.** gross profit
**g.** margin
**h.** market share
**i.** markdown
**j.** markup
**k.** merchandiser
**l.** net profit
**m.** private labels
**n.** promotional mix
**o.** psychographics
**p.** retail
**q.** vertical integration
**r.** wholesale

**Circle the best answer.**

**10.** Fashion marketers need information about customers including
   **a.** income and education level.
   **b.** what they think of the product.
   **c.** how they would improve the product.
   **d.** all of these.

**11.** A manufacturing retailer may
   **a.** design and sell garments directly to the consumer.
   **b.** advertise only other products.
   **c.** create channels of distribution.
   **d.** contract for all business activities.

# THINK CRITICALLY

**12.** With a group, spend five minutes discussing the difference between brand names and private labels. Why do customers look for brand names? Why might brand names cost more?

_____

_____

_____

_____

_____

**13.** Why is the marketing concept of always keeping your customer in mind so important?

_____

_____

_____

**14.** List three or more factors to consider when determining a retail selling price.

_____

_____

_____

_____

**15.** Describe the kind of data included in marketing information about customers and how it might be collected.

_____

_____

_____

_____

_____

CHAPTER 3 REVIEW

# MAKE CONNECTIONS

**16. Marketing Math**   Your store has promised investors a net profit of 4%. Your selling price is $40. You expect to sell 1,000 items that cost $22.50 each, and you expect total operating expenses of $17,000. How much will you need to lower operating expenses in order to achieve the desired profit?

_____

_____

_____

_____

**17. Ecology**   Why would a cosmetics company like Kiehl's Since 1851 and a designer like Todd Oldham spend time and money to help the Amazon Conservation Team preserve the Amazon jungle? This is an example of which component of the promotional mix?

_____

_____

_____

_____

_____

**18. Technology**   How does technology impact marketing-information management? What changes has the Internet brought to the collection of marketing information?

_____

_____

_____

_____

_____

_____

# RETAIL MARKETING RESEARCH EVENT

The retail clothing industry depends heavily upon research to determine trends and customer needs. You are challenged to develop a strategic plan for increasing the level of customer satisfaction and loyalty for an existing clothing store. Your assignment involves

- selecting an actual, local business operation
- designing and conducting a marketing research study
- analyzing the results of the study and preparing a strategic plan for increasing the level of existing customer satisfaction and loyalty
- presenting the design, findings, and conclusions of the study, and the resulting strategic plan

**www.deca.org
/publications/HS_
Guide/guidetoc.html**

This assignment can be completed in small segments that are combined as the complete project. The parts of your written paper are the Summary Memorandum (one-page description of the plan), Introduction, Research Methods Used in the Study, Findings and Conclusions of the Study, Proposed Strategic Plan, and Bibliography.

You will have ten minutes to explain your plan, and the class will then have five minutes to ask questions.

# PROJECT: The COLLECTION POINT

A manufacturer wants to offer a selection of jean styles to fit teenage girls but is not sure what styles to offer. Your firm has a contract to conduct the research and determine the right selection of styles.

**Work with a group and complete the following activities.**

**1.** Determine the information you need about the target customer.

**2.** Create a spreadsheet using software. In the rows, list style options for cut, fit, and fabric, such as straight leg, flared leg, low rider, and washed denim. Have the group brainstorm the options. Include an "other" row for possibly overlooked styles.

**3.** Over several days or a week, each member of the group should spend a few minutes observing the clothing worn by the target customer in your school or at malls.

**4.** In the headings of the columns of the spreadsheet, list the dates and locations of the observations. Record each observation of the listed styles. Make a note of related ideas while observing.

**5.** Write a one-page report that explains your chart and makes a recommendation of the styles that should be offered.

# CHAPTER 4

# FASHION ECONOMICS

## LESSONS

### 4.1 SUPPLY AND DEMAND

### 4.2 THE COMPETITION

### 4.3 FINANCIAL RECORDS

### 4.4 SOURCES OF MONEY

# WINNING STRATEGIES

## THE ARMANI GROUP

**W**ith reported sales in the billions of dollars, The Armani Group has made founder and sole owner, Giorgio Armani, one of the few billionaires in fashion. The Armani Group is one of the world's leading companies that design, manufacture, distribute, and retail high-end men's and women's ready-to-wear clothing. The Italian-born Armani has established the company as the standard for wearable elegance and luxury in fashion. Brands include Giorgio Armani, Armani Collezioni, Emporio Armani, Armani Jeans, Armani Exchange, Armani Junior, and the home collection, Armani Casa.

Founded in 1975 in Milan, Italy, the company started with a phenomenally successful collection of men's wear. Over the next four years, the fashion house added several new lines, including a line of women's wear. By the turn of the century, the company was worth over $2 billion and included hundreds of retail stores located throughout the world, as well as manufacturing plants, distribution centers, and plans to continue growing.

Giorgio Armani believes that to protect the excellent brand name and image, the company must control worldwide manufacturing and distribution of its fashions. His long-term strategy to reach that goal is to bring all manufacturing and distribution in-house and to improve the company's profits. The Armani Group is one of the few fashion houses with the financial resources required to grow while maintaining individual ownership.

### THINK CRITICALLY

1. List at least three elements that make The Armani Group successful.

2. Why would it financially benefit The Armani Group to control manufacturing and distribution of its fashions?

# SUPPLY AND DEMAND

**CHAPTER 4**

**Lesson 4.1**

**Describe** the laws of supply and demand.

**List** factors that impact demand.

## The Latest Style

**W**hen a designer's brand name has reached a high level of fame and success, manufacturers want to sign licensing agreements to manufacture the brand. The licensing agreements usually allow the original owner to maintain some control over the quality of garments, price lines, and type of stores where the garments will be sold.

If a brand name is sold at discount stores, it loses its prestige and few upscale shoppers will want to pay full price for the brand at trendy stores. Calvin Klein, Inc. licensed its jeans to apparel maker Warnaco Group, Inc. The two companies later had a very public dispute over Warnaco allegedly selling too many of Calvin's jeans at warehouse clubs. Calvin Klein, Inc. feared its brand name would be cheapened and would lose its appeal.

Work with a group. Discuss why Warnaco would want to sell Calvin Klein jeans at discount stores and warehouse clubs.

## WANTS, NEEDS, AND SCARCITY

**P**eople's needs and wants will always exceed the available resources. Once people have the minimum clothing needed for protection from the elements and the minimum coverage society requires (which satisfies their *needs*), then they wish to own more (to help satisfy their *wants*). *Scarcity* is the economic situation that occurs when unlimited needs and wants cannot be met due to limited available resources.

### THE DEMAND GOES ON

**PRICING**

During the introductory phase of a fashion cycle, the quantity of a garment style available for sale may be less than the number of customers wanting to buy it. When a product is scarce, prices may rise, but when a product becomes readily available, prices may drop as demand is diluted. **Demand** is the quantity of a product that customers are willing and able to buy. If every store has the item, then consumers can shop for the lowest price, causing prices to drop further. Stores left with unsold merchandise have to mark down the item to try to stimulate demand.

In addition to price and availability, demand is stimulated by needs and wants. When a fashion-conscious person sees a trend setter who looks good in an outfit, the person would like to own the same or a similar outfit. Wanting to buy the garment may be a wish, but reality may be limited by the amount of money available to spend on clothing. When economic times are difficult, however, people may tighten optional spending on apparel. However, upscale shoppers may still have plenty of disposable income. **Disposable income** is the money that is left after needs are met and bills are paid. Many high-end fashion vendors can weather the storm caused by a sluggish economy because their customers have enough disposable income to continue buying.

## THE AVAILABLE SUPPLY

**PRODUCT/ SERVICE MANAGEMENT**

In a free enterprise system such as that found in the United States, individuals are free to own businesses and develop fashion items to supply to consumers. **Supply** is the quantity of a product that the producer is willing and able to make available. Profit is the motive for production and consequently drives the supply that is available for sale. When the supply of an item is low and the demand high, the price will be high, causing the manufacturer to want to produce more.

With fashion items, the time period in which consumers seek a style can be very short. Clothing manufacturers with fast reaction time can profit during a short fashion cycle by quickly increasing the supply of a specific item. Often, other producers will react to a fast-selling item by providing similar items for the consumer.

Producers carefully look at marketing information when determining the quantity of a garment to make. If they produce too few, they miss sales, but if they produce too many, they have to sell them at a reduced price. Retail stores like Marshalls and Burlington Coat Factory buy manufacturers' **overruns** when the manufacturer has produced too many of an item. The garments are then sold at low prices to consumers.

## Fashion Flashback

In 1967, Ralph Lauren designed a line of wide silk men's ties to replace the skinny ties men had been wearing for years. The $7.50 ties sold so well that Lauren was offered a contract to develop a men's clothing line, which he named Polo. Lauren was given a $50,000 investment to form a company. Eight years later, in 1975, the company was worth $1.9 million with sales of $65 million. By 1997, when the company made the initial public offering of its stock, it was estimated to be worth about $4 billion. In 2001, Ralph Lauren celebrated 35 years of success as a brilliant businessman.

### THINK CRITICALLY
**1.** Why has Polo Ralph Lauren been successful for 35 years?
**2.** What will the company have to do to continue its success?

## TRY IT ON

**How does price impact demand?**

# SUPPLY MEETS DEMAND

**PRICING**

**S**ince companies are in business to produce a profit and consumers have limited resources with which to buy, the price of a garment influences the quantity that will be produced and sold. The **market price** is the price at which consumers are willing to buy enough of the fashions for the producer to make a profit. Other factors that influence supply include governmental regulation, consumer action, and promotion.

## INFLUENCING SUPPLY

When governments are involved in stabilizing the price of a product through laws or regulations, supply can be impacted. Textile mills in the United States have been drastically impacted by the import of low-cost textiles from foreign producers. In some textile-producing countries where the standard of living is lower than in the United States, wages are kept low. Low wages reduce the cost of producing goods, which lowers the selling price. In an effort to maintain textile producers and jobs in the United States, Congress provides *direct-payment subsidies* (grants of money) that cover the difference between foreign and U.S. prices. Thus, U.S. producers can offer textiles to clothing manufacturers at prices that compete with the low-cost imports.

Bad publicity can also impact demand and supply. Consumers who believe that manufacturers are using disreputable practices, such as child labor, can gain publicity for boycotting the products and can influence demand.

Promotion can have a positive impact on demand and supply. When consumers learn about a product through advertising, they are motivated to try the product. When consumers see trend setters wearing a style, the demand is increased and manufacturers rush to meet the demand by increasing the supply.

# TRY IT ON

**Why would Congress allow low-cost imports and, at the same time, maintain textile producers in the United States?**

_____

_____

_____

## UNDERSTAND MARKETING CONCEPTS
Circle the best answer for each of the following questions.

1. What customers are willing and able to buy is called
   a. distribution.
   b. demand.
   c. decline.
   d. supply.

2. What manufacturers are willing and able to produce is called
   a. demand.
   b. wholesale.
   c. retail.
   d. supply.

## THINK CRITICALLY
Answer the following questions as completely as possible. If necessary, use a separate sheet of paper.

3. Why does scarcity of a product influence its selling price?

   _____

   _____

   _____

   _____

4. **Economics** Discuss with a group the pros and cons of the government providing subsidies to a U.S. industry that cannot compete with foreign producers due to low wages. Summarize your conclusions here.

   _____

   _____

   _____

   _____

   _____

   _____

# THE COMPETITION

**GOALS**

**Explain** how to respond to competition.

**Describe** how international marketing affects the fashion industry.

## The Latest Style

Nakane Reiko has blown away the competition in the Tokyo suburbs. In one day, she led her branch of the Egoist fashion chain to score a sales record of more than $90,000. In one month, the store sold more than $1.9 million in apparel and accessories.

Nakane attracts customers with a unique combination of her current, offbeat look and charisma with customers. Young teens flock to Nakane to see what she is wearing and how she has applied her makeup. She is willing to listen and offer advice to shoppers as if they were her close friends. The shoppers are taking her advice and buying like crazy.

Work with a group. Discuss other ways a fashion store could beat the competition by providing superior service.

## COMPETITIVE BENEFITS

In economic systems where the government controls what is produced and who can buy it, there is little or no competition. Without competition, there is little incentive to improve goods or please customers. Competition assures that multiple sellers offer the best products for a consumer's money. If a company is the only producer of a garment that is in high demand, then it has no competition and can charge high prices. With competition, prices will be lower, and multiple vendors will work to improve efficiency and offer the best possible products.

### BRING ON THE COMPETITION

**MARKETING-INFORMATION MANAGEMENT**

If a company is successful at marketing a line of apparel, it can assume that someone is going to try to offer a similar product. Fashion marketers spend time researching what their competitors are doing right. In many cases, they will use this marketing information as inspiration for their own, similar item in an attempt to gain market share. Influential

French designer Coco Chanel is credited with using men's wear as an inspiration for women's work apparel and liberating women from restrictive, ornate fashions of the early 1900s. This look was quickly copied by early mass producers in the United States and throughout the world.

Because fashion is cyclical in nature and can quickly go out of favor, companies must continually look for new items that will please consumers.

## FASHION PRODUCTIVITY

SELLING

Being competitive requires efficient productivity. In retail fashion stores, **productivity** is measured by the dollar amount of apparel and accessories sold per square foot of store space per year. Sales per square foot is one key measure of a retail store's success. The industry average is about $237 per square foot. Larger stores can increase sales per square foot by encouraging the purchase of related items that are carried in the additional space.

A store can move merchandise more quickly to achieve productivity levels needed for a profit if located near other highly productive stores. This combined increase in productivity is referred to as **synergy**. A stand-alone store does not have this advantage. A store that does not achieve profitable productivity levels within the first two years will usually close. Becoming productive requires beating the competition at pleasing customers and professionally managing the store.

SmartBargains Inc. is an online, off-price retailer for whom fashion and apparel are about 25 percent of the business. The company reports that online sales increased by six times and customer traffic by ten times within the first 18 months of business. These increases were attributed to marketing deals with Yahoo!, MSN, and AOL. SmartBargains' positive performance helped secure a second round of financing needed for additional growth of the company.

**THINK CRITICALLY**
**1.** Make a list of stores that would compete with the online site, **www. SmartBargains.com.**
**2.** What does SmartBargains offer that helps it beat the competition?

# TRY IT ON

**What are the benefits of competition?**

# WORLD TRADE

**B**uying and selling apparel and accessories on an international basis is a common practice. A quick look at a clothing label reveals the country of origin. Many garments sold in the United States are made in other countries. Some garments are made in the United States from imported fabric or are made in another country from fabric produced in the United States. Fashion companies seek vendors throughout the world that produce the quality garments they require for the lowest possible price. Vendors compete with each other and move production to countries where the standard of living does not cause wages to be too high for vendors to remain competitive.

## THE WORLD TRADE ORGANIZATION

To help alleviate some of the complexity of international trade, the **World Trade Organization (WTO)** was formed. The WTO fosters trade and provides a forum for the 144 member countries to negotiate and handle trade-related disputes. The WTO is the only global organization dealing with trade between nations. The WTO is a type of **trading bloc**, an organization whose members agree to remove trade barriers between the member nations while imposing barriers on countries that are not members. Membership brings both privilege and obligation to the member countries, which must open their markets and abide by the rules of the WTO. Textiles and garments are two of the product classifications covered by the WTO agreements.

Through a WTO agreement effective in 2005, countries that produce large quantities of textiles, such as China, India, and Indonesia, will no longer be subject to restrictions on the export of textiles to the United States or to European Union (EU) members. The EU is a trading bloc and more. The EU is currently made up of 15 European countries that share a common currency, called the euro, and are merging their economies.

China is the third largest supplier of textiles and apparel to the United States and was admitted to the WTO in December 2001.

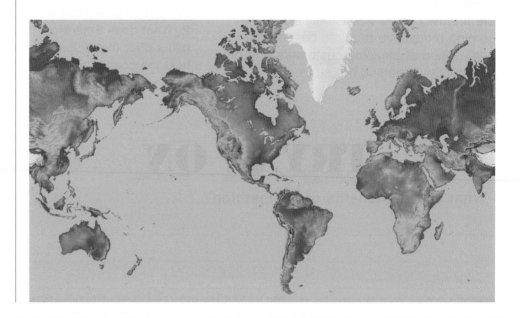

## DEVELOPING NATIONS

**PRODUCT/ SERVICE MANAGEMENT**

Businesses want to conduct trade with companies in other countries when the potential for profit exists. Countries in Southeast Asia have become very competitive in the textile and garment business due to the low cost of wages, the high quality of textile manufacturing equipment, and the knowledge and skill of management. Southeast Asian countries, including China, have caused a major shift in the textile and clothing industry away from Europe and the United States. These developing nations are very competitive because they can leverage the advantage of low-cost labor to produce clothing and hold down prices. In 2000, the hourly wages for textile and clothing workers in India, Indonesia, and China ranged from $0.24 to $0.42 per hour, while workers in EU countries earned from $4.50 to $23.00 per hour.

Textile production can take advantage of improved technology to remain competitive, since wages account for about 40 percent of the costs of producing textiles. Clothing construction requires a great deal more human labor, with about 60 percent of the cost of clothing attributed to wages. Faced with brutal competition from low-wage countries, the manufacturers remaining in the United States and Europe will need to stay at peak performance to remain in business. U.S. workers who have a high standard of living and high wages are some of the most productive workers in the world. The reasons include working conditions, technology, equipment, training, and pay incentives.

# TRY IT ON

**Why must fashion marketers in the United States buy and sell internationally?**

**Final Fit**

## UNDERSTAND MARKETING CONCEPTS

Circle the best answer for each of the following questions.

**1.** A trading bloc is
   **a.** small squares used as currency in Asia.
   **b.** a group of nations that agree to remove trade barriers.
   **c.** a group interested in apparel.
   **d.** an economic tariff.

**2.** The amount of apparel and accessories sold per square foot of store space is a measure of
   **a.** promotion.
   **b.** profit.
   **c.** products.
   **d.** productivity.

## THINK CRITICALLY

Answer the following questions as completely as possible. If necessary, use a separate sheet of paper.

**3. Research**   Think about clothing stores in an area near you that have gone out of business. Speculate about why they might have closed. How long did they stay open? What other stores were in direct competition with them? Were there any nearby stores to create synergy?

_____

_____

_____

_____

**4.** How does the standard of living in a foreign country impact fashion marketing in the United States?

_____

_____

_____

_____

_____

# FINANCIAL RECORDS

## The Latest Style

**W**hen fashion marketers project sales for the coming season, they use economic forecasts as part of the information on which to base the projection. Usually when the economy is up, sales are up, but when lipstick sales are really up, the economy is usually down. Historically, women keep buying lipstick when they are not buying other fashion items.

After September 11, 2001, when terrorists attacked the United States, MAC, one of the Estée brands of cosmetics, ran extra shifts to produce more lipstick. By November, sales were up more than 12 percent from the previous year. Other brands showed similar increases. Sales for most other fashion items were down by six percent or more during the same time period.

Work with a group. Discuss why strong sales of lipstick might be a bad economic sign. Can you think of other items that might be heavily influenced by the state of the economy?

**GOALS**

**Describe** budgets and financial statements.

**Discuss** the importance of accurate record-keeping in fashion marketing.

## PLANNING

FINANCING

**M**ost businesses do not make a profit the first year of operation, and one out of every seven stores does not ever make a profit. Many fail due to poor financial planning, poor recordkeeping, and the owner's lack of knowledge about finances. A **financial plan** is a major part of a complete business plan and consists of summary statements of financial data that make up a complete budget.

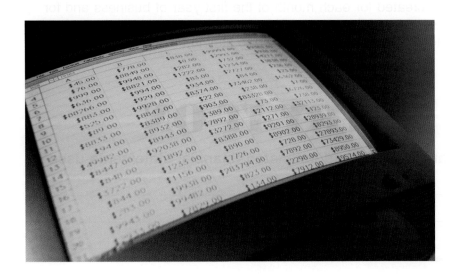

## BUDGETS AND ESTIMATED FINANCIAL STATEMENTS

A **budget** is a plan that helps a business determine what revenues and expenses to expect. The budget can be produced for the total business and broken down into *cost units*. For example, promotional expenses can be a cost unit with a separate budget figured for all advertising.

**Estimated financial statements** are used to project the potential for a new business. They are based on estimates made after a great deal of research and include startup costs and expected cash flows.

**Startup Costs**   Startup costs or one-time costs, such as those needed to open or move a retail apparel store, would include store fixtures and equipment, legal fees, licensing fees, and utility deposits for phones, water, and electricity. The items are listed along with their estimated costs and are referred to as the *startup cost statement*. Accurately determining startup costs lets the owners and potential lenders or investors know how much money is needed and can prevent overspending.

**Cash Flows**   Estimated *cash flow statements* show the flow of operating expenses (funds going out of the business for day-to-day costs), revenue (the money coming into the business), and the difference between the two. To estimate revenue, a *sales forecast* is developed. The sales forecast is an estimate of what will be sold and the selling price.

It generally takes customers five trips to a new store to feel comfortable about the store and its merchandise, and in the meantime, expenses continue. Even if nothing sells the first month the store is open, the bills for the apparel offered for sale, rent, utilities, payroll, insurance, and other operating expenses must be paid. Failure to pay in a timely manner can damage the credit rating of the business and result in termination of services.

During the first year of a business, the *net cash flow*, the difference between the revenue coming in and the operating expenses going out, may be negative. Less money may be taken in than is spent, meaning that the business will have a *negative cash flow*. A strong business should have a *positive cash flow*, with revenue exceeding operating expenses by the end of the first year of business. A cash flow estimate should be created for each month of the first year of business and for the full second and third years. This estimate will provide information to determine how much cash is needed to stay in business.

When Evelyn Gorman moved her sleek, chic, designer apparel store called "Mix: Modern Clothes" to a 50-year-old, 3,000-square-foot building that had been a Stop 'N Go, she had startup costs that included an architect's fee to redesign the space and the actual renovation costs. The costs were kept down by using common building materials in innovative ways, such as lacquered Baltic birch as an inexpensive hardwood for the floors.

## TRY IT ON

**How are budgets and estimated financial statements used?**

_____

_____

_____

# KEEPING TRACK

FINANCING

**F**ailure to keep accurate financial records can lead to failure of a fashion business. Statements generated from the records are the income statement, balance sheet, and personal financial statement(s) of the owner(s).

## INCOME STATEMENT

The **income statement** is used to determine if the business has earned a profit. Like the cash flow statement, the income statement reports on revenues and expenses. However, the income statement is different from the cash flow statement in that it includes transactions for which cash has not changed hands. For example, it may show money that is due but has not yet been paid, such as for items bought or sold on credit. The amount of a credit sale will be included on an income statement as earned revenue, but will not show up on a cash flow statement until cash actually changes hands.

Major fashion players, including Liz Claiborne, May Department Stores, and Coldwater Creek™, stopped using Arthur Andersen as their financial audit firm. The list of firms dropping Arthur Andersen grew as Andersen's involvement as the audit firm for Enron, a collapsed energy trading company, became public. Investors do not want their company allied with an accounting firm that is associated with possible unethical activity.

**THINK CRITICALLY**

**1.** What impact can unethical behavior have on a company's reputation?

**2.** How might the integrity of the accounting firm auditing a fashion business's financial statements influence its credit rating?

Lakeesha Williams' Boutique
Income Statement
For the Period Ending April 30, 20XX

| | | |
|---|---|---|
| Revenues: | | |
| Gross sales | $500,123 | |
| Less returns | − 456 | |
| Net sales | | $499,667 |
| Cost of garments sold | | −389,050 |
| Gross margin | | $110,617 |
| Operating expenses: | | |
| Rent | $ 16,000 | |
| Credit card fees | 1,500 | |
| Equipment | 3,400 | |
| Insurance | 1,500 | |
| Salaries/benefits | 25,635 | |
| Supplies | 800 | |
| Advertising | 13,500 | |
| Total operating expenses | | −62,335 |
| Net income | | $ 48,282 |

## BALANCE SHEET

A **balance sheet** reports the amount of assets, liabilities, and capital of the business as of a given time. The *assets* are what the business owns, such as equipment, cash, and inventory. The *liabilities* are what the business owes, such as amounts due to suppliers for purchases of garments to be resold. The *capital*, also called value or net worth of the business, is the difference between the assets and the liabilities. Note that the total of the assets and the total of the liabilities and capital must be equal. Thus, the two sides of the statement are balanced, and hence the name "balance sheet."

### Tom Sanders Fashions
### Balance Sheet
### June 30, 20XX

| Assets | | Liabilities | |
|---|---|---|---|
| Current assets: | | Current liabilities: | |
| Cash | $ 85,000 | Accounts payable | $ 42,000 |
| Accounts receivable | 26,300 | Rent payable | 5,000 |
| Garment inventory | 152,000 | Loans payable | 25,000 |
| Total current assets | $263,300 | Taxes payable | 12,300 |
| Long-term assets: | | Total liabilities | $ 84,300 |
| Equipment | $ 55,000 | | |
| Less depreciation | | **Capital** | |
| of equipment | − 2,560 | Owner's equity | 231,440 |
| Net long-term assets | $ 52,440 | Total liabilities | |
| Total assets | $315,740 | and capital | $315,740 |

## PERSONAL FINANCIAL STATEMENTS

Creditors or investors require a **personal financial statement** that includes a list of the owner's assets and liabilities, personal net worth (the difference between the owner's assets and liabilities), bank references, and past credit history. A person's house or car is an asset, but the amount owed on the house or car is a liability. Business credit is often given based on the personal assets and credit history of the owner, not just on the business merit or idea. A company is generally not considered for loans on its own merit until it reaches a level of $10 million of sales and above. People who manage their own money responsibly are likely to manage a company's money responsibly and are trusted with credit and loans.

## TRY IT ON

**How are financial statements used?**

Final Fit

## UNDERSTAND MARKETING CONCEPTS
Circle the best answer for each of the following questions.

**1.** Balance sheets are
   **a.** a type of bed linen.
   **b.** another term for couture fashions.
   **c.** a financial statement that reflects net worth.
   **d.** a public record of sales.

**2.** An income statement shows the difference between
   **a.** revenues and expenses.
   **b.** costs of advertising and promotion.
   **c.** salaries and costs.
   **d.** net sales and costs.

## THINK CRITICALLY
Answer the following questions as completely as possible. If necessary, use a separate sheet of paper.

**3.** What is a sales forecast and how is it used?

_____

_____

_____

_____

**4.** Name three financial statements and the purpose of each. Why are financial records important to a fashion business?

_____

_____

_____

_____

_____

_____

_____

_____

# CHAPTER 4
## Lesson 4.4

# SOURCES OF MONEY

# GOALS

**Develop** credit policies to be used as a marketing strategy.

**Identify** sources of financial assistance.

## The Latest Style

**P**rada is an Italian, ultra-high-end fashion business. Originally known for luxury leather goods, the brand has risen to cult status with nylon and leather backpacks and has expanded to include women's apparel and men's wear.

Prada grew quickly by acquiring other, smaller labels and opening retail stores. Prada assumed a debt estimated at over $1 billion during what was described as an "acquisition binge." To lower its debt, Prada intended to raise funds by selling as much as 30 percent of the company through shares of stock in an initial public offering (IPO). Prior to the IPO, the economy slowed, making the success of an IPO risky. Twice Prada postponed the IPO and sold specific acquisitions, such as the Fendi label, to raise funds. Additionally, Prada issued $624.1 million in bonds, allowing investors to exchange the bonds for shares of the company if the IPO took place within 3 1/2 years.

Work with a group. Discuss why a privately owned company might want to sell shares of stock to the public. What might investors consider before buying shares of a company?

# CREDIT

FINANCING

**P**eople who start their own businesses are called **entrepreneurs**. To start a fashion marketing business requires money. Very few people personally have all the required funds. Most entrepreneurs must either borrow the money or find partners who can also invest in the business.

After a business begins to grow, additional money is frequently needed to fund major expansions, but the financing may be difficult to obtain.

## OBTAINING CREDIT

To grant credit means to trust someone with the expectation of future payment. Fashion marketers obtain credit to expand their businesses and extend credit to their customers as a strategy to encourage sales.

When a buyer for a retail store selects garments to offer for sale, the manufacturer requires that the store establish credit before the purchase order is accepted. Transactions between retailer and wholesaler are usually paid 30 to 60 days later. To stay in business, the wholesaler must have proof that the store management can be trusted to pay for garments at the end of the agreed-upon time. The proof for small retailers is often based on the credit history of the store owner, not the business itself. Stores that do not pay their bills are quickly denied credit by their vendors.

## BENEFICIAL CREDIT

A small business establishes credit based on the owner's personal financial statement and the owner's history of not violating the trust of creditors. The amount of credit approved for an individual is sometimes short of what is needed to successfully operate until the business is big enough to qualify for credit on its own.

Purchasing on credit allows a store to buy more garments to sell, while leaving its cash for other bills. This allows time to receive and sell the garments before having to pay for them. For a small business, this can be a major way to increase the potential for profit.

Credit allows a store to replenish with new merchandise, thus improving sales. Another way for a store to increase sales is to offer credit to retail customers. People are more likely to make larger purchases when they can charge them, rather than having to pay cash.

**CYBER MARKETING**

In the past when a retail merchant accepted a check for a purchase, the merchant was taking a chance that the check would be returned due to insufficient funds in the writer's account. Additionally, checks had to be manually handled and deposited into the merchant's bank account. Most banks charged the merchant a per-check fee for depositing the checks. Using new technology, TeleCheck can make check acceptance mirror a credit card transaction. Called Electronic Check Acceptance®, the process begins when a merchant accepts the check from the customer and provides a printed receipt for signature. The signature allows TeleCheck to electronically present the transaction to the customer's bank for payment and then deposit the money electronically in the merchant's account. If the check does not clear the customer's account, TeleCheck is responsible, not the merchant.

**THINK CRITICALLY**
How does TeleCheck make money?

## CONSUMER CREDIT

A wholesaler or retailer can offer credit to customers by accepting major credit cards or by establishing its own credit plan. Large businesses offer their own credit plans, with fees and interest serving as an additional source of revenue. Interest is charged if the total amount is not paid within the specified time. Some stores offer special discounts to users of the store's credit card as a way to increase sales and traffic in the store.

A *credit policy* must be set up with clear guidelines for offering credit. The policy should include

- Characteristics of a creditworthy customer, such as credit history, current assets, and financial references
- Application process and approval
- Total amount of credit to be offered and fees or interest charged to the customer
- Length of time for payment to be due
- Collection procedures for customers who do not pay

Most retail and wholesale businesses accept major credit cards from customers due to the potential for increased sales. To accept major credit cards such as VISA and MasterCard, a business sets up a *merchant processing account* with a credit card acquirer affiliated with a large bank or an independent sales organization. If a transaction is approved by the processor, the merchant is paid for the sale and will not suffer the loss if the bill goes unpaid.

## CHECKS

Accepting checks as a form of payment from customers can increase the amount of sales compared to a cash-only business. A merchant can ensure safety by using a check-approval company such as TeleCheck. If TeleCheck approves a check, then it pays the merchant the face value, even if the check is later rejected by the writer's bank. Without a check-approval process, a fashion business may be stuck with the cost of the goods and owe its own bank a returned-check fee.

# TRY IT ON

**Name three things a credit policy should include.**

_____

_____

_____

# RAISING CAPITAL

**A**fter a business reaches a certain size, there may be a need for large sums of additional money for capital expenses. A fashion business may want money to open a second location, to renovate or expand the existing location, or to buy another, similar store. Finding friends or family with the funds available and who are willing to loan money may be out of the question. Other sources for funding must be found.

## SEEKING INVESTORS

A new building or major new equipment is considered a long-term **capital expense**. To find sources for the large sums of additional money needed for capital expenses, a business may have to seek partners or offer shares of stock to the public.

**Partners**   Partners may take the form of venture capitalists. **Venture capitalists** provide funds to start or expand a company in exchange for part-ownership. The investment contract may require the original owners to relinquish some control and decision making to the new part-owners.

**Initial Public Offering (IPO)**   The point at which a business moves from private ownership to public ownership by selling shares of the company on the stock market is called the **initial public offering (IPO)**. Depending on the percentage of ownership represented by the stock sold to the public, the original owners may be relinquishing control of the business. A board of directors sets policies for a public company based on what is good for the shareholders. Many large companies in the fashion industry are traded on the New York Stock Exchange, including Wal-Mart®, Warnaco, Jones Apparel Group, and Polo Ralph Lauren. Ralph Lauren offered his IPO

in 1997 for $26 per share, but the stock immediately opened at $32.12 per share.

The benefits of "going public" are the availability of funding and the opportunity for the original owners to reap the benefits of becoming a financial success. The downside for the original owners is giving up control of the business to a board of directors who may or may not agree with the ideas held by the individuals.

## TRY IT ON

**What is an initial public offering (IPO)?**

_____

_____

## TrendSetters

### SUSAN SILVERSTEIN

The number-one stock picker in the textiles, footwear, and apparel industries loves to shop and earns her living doing it. Susan Silverstein is a New York-based analyst for Banc of America Securities LLC, a unit of Bank of America Corporation in Charlotte, North Carolina. Ms. Silverstein is the Managing Director and Senior Research Analyst, and her job is to know exactly what is happening financially in the fashion marketing industry. She visits many stores to see what is selling for full price or being marked down, and she visits regularly with retail buyers in New York City manufacturers' showrooms. From her research, she makes predictions about what will sell and which companies will have the best sales figures.

For three years in a row, her fellow institutional investors rated Ms. Silverstein as number one at picking the fashion companies that are the best investments. Her picks have consistently offered the best returns to shareholders. She is frequently quoted in *Women's Wear Daily, Footwear News,* and *The Wall Street Journal.* Her stock picks have been consistently right on target.

### THINK CRITICALLY

**1.** Why would Susan Silverstein look at what people are wearing to make market predictions?
**2.** Why are stock market predictions important to the fashion marketing industry?

## UNDERSTAND MARKETING CONCEPTS
Circle the best answer for each of the following questions.

**1.** A credit policy should include
   **a.** the collection procedures for customers who do not pay.
   **b.** the application process and approval.
   **c.** the length of time for payment to be due.
   **d.** all of these.

**2.** A person or company that exchanges money for part-ownership is
   **a.** an entrepreneur.
   **b.** a store buyer.
   **c.** a wholesaler.
   **d.** a venture capitalist.

## THINK CRITICALLY
Answer the following questions as completely as possible. If necessary, use a separate sheet of paper.

**3.** Why might a fashion store check on the creditworthiness of someone applying to be a store manager? Why is it important in business for an individual to have a good financial standing and pay bills on time?

_____

_____

_____

**4.** What are two sources of funding for expanding a fashion business? What are the positive and negative aspects of the two sources?

_____

_____

_____

_____

_____

_____

# CHAPTER 4 REVIEW

## REVIEW MARKETING CONCEPTS

**Write the letter of the term that matches each definition. Some terms will not be used.**

_____ **1.** The quantity of a product that customers are willing and able to buy

_____ **2.** The quantity of a product that a producer is willing and able to make available

_____ **3.** The garments left when a manufacturer produces too many

_____ **4.** The dollar amount of apparel and accessories sold per square foot of store space per year

_____ **5.** A plan that helps a business determine what revenues and expenses to expect

_____ **6.** Reports the amount of assets, liabilities, and capital of the business as of a given time

_____ **7.** Fosters trade and provides a forum for negotiation and trade-related disputes

_____ **8.** Summary statements of financial data that make up a complete budget

**a.** balance sheet
**b.** budget
**c.** capital expense
**d.** demand
**e.** disposable income
**f.** entrepreneur
**g.** estimated financial statements
**h.** financial plan
**i.** income statement
**j.** initial public offering (IPO)
**k.** market price
**l.** overruns
**m.** personal financial statement
**n.** productivity
**o.** supply
**p.** synergy
**q.** trading bloc
**r.** venture capitalist
**s.** World Trade Organization (WTO)

**Circle the best answer.**

**9.** People who start their own businesses are called
  **a.** marketers.
  **b.** entrepreneurs.
  **c.** financial officers.
  **d.** competitors.

**10.** Money left after an individual pays bills is
  **a.** net income.
  **b.** gross income.
  **c.** purchasing.
  **d.** disposable income.

# THINK CRITICALLY

**11.** Why are trading blocs formed between nations? Does this benefit the fashion industry? Why or why not?

POINT YOUR BROWSER

fashion.swlearning.com

_____

_____

_____

_____

_____

**12.** What are the benefits to a fashion business that is able to buy on credit? How does a small business establish credit?

_____

_____

_____

_____

**13.** What influences the supply of a specific line of garments that a manufacturer is willing to make available? How does government regulation impact the supply of garments?

_____

_____

_____

_____

**14.** Why would a retail fashion business want to offer customers credit? How can credit be used as a marketing strategy to increase sales?

_____

_____

_____

_____

_____

## MAKE CONNECTIONS

**15. Marketing Math** Someday you would like to open a retail store, and you want to apply for credit with vendors. You figure you need a net worth of $60,000 to start. Your net worth is the difference between your assets and your liabilities.

Your assets are
- A car that is worth $18,000
- A certificate of deposit that is worth $5,000
- A home worth $155,000
- Furniture and electronics worth $8,000
- A checking account of $3,500 and a savings account of $2,500

Your liabilities are
- A principal balance of $12,400 owed on your car
- A principal balance of $120,000 owed on your home mortgage
- A sound system on which you still owe $600

Use spreadsheet software and complete a personal financial statement listing your assets, liabilities, and net worth based on the information provided. How much do you need to save to reach the $60,000 goal?

_____

_____

_____

_____

_____

**16. Economics** Why is the financial health and credit rating of the individual owner considered before making a business loan?

_____

_____

_____

**17. Accounting** What are some financial records that are important for a business to keep? Why is accurate recordkeeping important?

_____

_____

_____

_____

www.deca.org
/publications/HS_
Guide/guidetoc.html

## CUSTOMER SERVICE ROLE PLAY

You are the customer service clerk for a well-known department store. Your store has always been concerned about shoplifting and other scams that cause profits to go down and consumer prices to rise.

Your store has a policy that all returned merchandise must be accompanied by a receipt in order for the consumer to get a refund or exchange. Reduced-price merchandise will only be exchanged for store credit equaling the sale price. Since there has been an increase in the amount of shoplifting, your company has given you strict guidelines to follow when customers bring in returns. If you suspect that a customer is trying to return stolen merchandise, you must contact store security immediately.

Some scam artists have been stealing merchandise from a competitor, removing the price tags, and then trying to get a refund on the merchandise at your store. One of your best customers has a designer shirt that he wants to return. The customer tells you that he received the shirt as a gift and wants to return it since it is not his style. The customer indicates that he wants a cash refund instead of different merchandise. He does not have a receipt or the original tags since the shirt was received as a gift.

You have been given strict orders by management to closely follow the return policy and detain customers who you think are trying to get a refund for stolen merchandise. You want to handle this situation in a manner that follows management's guidelines and yet maintains good relations with this regular customer. You must explain the store policy to the customer and devise the best possible solution for this situation.

PROJECT: The COLLECTION POINT

You have been hired to develop a credit policy for a fashion manufacturer, Anita Hinojosa. Her business designs junior-sized shorts and shirts and sells them to small retail stores. She has the funding to offer credit to customers that are creditworthy. She is concerned about how to determine who gets credit and what to charge. She would also like to accept major credit cards for purchases.

**Work with a group and complete the following activities.**

**1.** List the information you need to know to write the credit policy.

**2.** Create a credit application using a word-processing program.

**3.** Write a one-page credit policy that covers how the business will offer its own credit plan.

**4.** Search the Internet for information about how Anita can begin accepting national credit cards. Visit **www.firstdata.com** and find out how to open a merchant account to accept credit cards.

# CHAPTER 5

# THE CENTERS AND THE DESIGNERS

## LESSONS

### 5.1 AMERICA'S FASHION CENTERS

### 5.2 EUROPEAN FASHION

### 5.3 ASIAN AND OTHER EMERGING CENTERS

# WINNING STRATEGIES

## VERA WANG

Known as the bridal designer to celebrities, Vera Wang started her fashion career as an editor at *Vogue* magazine. After 16 years with *Vogue,* she became a director for an American designer. In 1990, she started her own business, opening a boutique in New York and making a name for herself in bridal designs.

There are two Vera Wang boutiques located on Madison Avenue in New York. The flagship store specializes in bridal and ready-to-wear apparel and is located in The Carlyle Hotel. The second boutique focuses on bridesmaids' apparel. Vera Wang currently does about $80 million per year in retail business in the two stores. Additionally, there are Vera Wang boutiques within major retailers such as Barney's and Saks Fifth Avenue.

The Vera Wang fashion collections include evening-wear, evening and bridal shoes, and bridal gifts. She has plans for adding other bridal-related items, from accessories to tableware. Waterford Wedgwood USA, the luxury china and stemware company, has signed a first-ever licensing agreement to offer the Vera Wang by Wedgwood Collection, a natural association with the bridal business. Wang also plans to add jewelry, lingerie, bathing suits, and prom dresses.

Wang, the daughter of Chinese immigrants, was born in New York, attended Sarah Lawrence College, and studied at the Sorbonne in France. She is married and is the mother of two daughters. Her strong artistic sense combined with an understanding of business has led to an internationally recognized fashion business.

### THINK CRITICALLY

1. If Vera Wang were to consider opening a boutique in another city, where should she consider locating the boutique and why?
2. Why does Vera Wang license her accessories and gift lines?

# CHAPTER 5

## Lesson 5.1

# AMERICA'S FASHION CENTERS

## GOALS

**Discuss** the major fashion centers in America.

**Name** well-known and new designers.

## The Latest Style

Eastside is an eclectic retail venture for Los Angeles-based designer, Estevan Ramos. It offers Ramos's designs as well as those of other designers. Ramos sees the retail store as a chance to be creative, rather than catering to what buyers for retail stores think will sell. Ramos has designed a line of women's and men's wear with a Mexican-American couture look. His designs are also available at Saks Fifth Avenue, Nordstrom, and Dillard's. The designs are very trendy and always reflect his culture.

Deemed one of the most talented students ever to attend the Fashion Institute of Design and Merchandising, Ramos was awarded the Outstanding Student Design Scholarship. After graduating, he was twice selected as a "Rising Star" by the Hispanic Designers Association. His designs top $1.6 million in sales per year.

Work with a partner. Discuss why Ramos's designs appeal across ethnic lines.

## AMERICAN CENTERS

**DISTRIBUTION**

In the United States, New York City is considered the dominant fashion center due to the large number of fashion-related businesses and the reputation of the city as a fashion hub. Other U.S. fashion centers that continue to grow include Los Angeles, Chicago, Atlanta, and Dallas. Fashion is also a significant industry in Canada, Mexico, and other countries of Central and South America. Designers and manufacturers in the countries north and south of the United States find creative ways to make their apparel available to fashion markets in their regions.

### NEW YORK, NEW YORK

The people and products needed to create fashion, including textile and apparel manufacturers and apparel wholesalers, are found in the area of New York City known as Manhattan Island. The center of the fashion area is located between 35th Street and 40th Street, west of 5th Avenue and east to 9th Avenue. It is 7th Avenue that gives

the area its name. About half of the fashion people in the 7th Avenue area are employed in the apparel wholesale business. The number of people employed in the fashion industry in New York dropped dramatically during the 1990s and early 2000s. The most significant drops were in manufacturing employment.

The New York fashion area has about 4,000 manufacturers. Most are small businesses that offer apparel, accessories, and related items for sale in about 5,100 showrooms. The vast majority of fashion businesses within the center have fewer than 20 employees. Wholesale businesses offering the same type of apparel tend to locate near each other to facilitate ease of planning for buyers. For example, moderate to bridge outerwear and sportswear showrooms are primarily located in the 500 block of 7th Avenue.

Fashion weeks in New York are sponsored by designers who are members of the Council of Fashion Designers of America (CFDA). CFDA is made up of more than 250 designers who formed a corporation called 7th on Sixth, Inc. to centralize the **runway shows** in the United States, where designs are worn by live models. Prior to CFDA, the New York fashion shows had previously been held in many locations and at varying times that were inconvenient for the fashion editors and buyers to attend. Shows are referenced by the primary sponsor's name, such as the Mercedes-Benz Fashion Week, and they are held in tents in nearby Bryant Park.

In addition to the runway shows, manufacturers from the United States and around the world have permanent showrooms in the area to show their garments to buyers from retail stores. Fashion weeks happen throughout the year, with women's wear fall/winter buying in February, holiday buying in May/June, and spring buying in September/October. Fall men's wear is purchased in January, and spring lines in August.

New York remains an attractive market for upscale buyers because many of the best lines do not show at any of the other regional market centers. Most of the permanent showrooms are open weekdays all year long, not just during show weeks, although the majority of buyers do tend to come during fashion weeks when the new lines are first available.

Skechers USA, Inc. is a lifestyle footwear design and marketing corporation based in Manhattan Beach, California. The Children's Advertising Review Unit (CARU) of the Council of Better Business Bureaus, Inc. asked Skechers to modify TV ads for its 4Wheelers™ roller skates. CARU safety guidelines state that ads should not portray children in unsafe situations without proper safety equipment. CARU noted that the teens in the Skechers ad were skating and performing a stunt without the use of safety gear. Skechers contended that the skaters were not using the skates in an athletic manner, but rather as a fashion item and an alternative to walking. Skechers appealed the CARU recommendation, noting that it includes a safety pamphlet with every pair of 4Wheelers™ sold.

### THINK CRITICALLY

**1. Do fashion apparel companies have an obligation to promote safety?**
**2. Do you think Skechers should have changed the ad?**

## MOVING WEST

Los Angeles has rivaled the New York market in size for a number of years. CaliforniaMart in downtown Los Angeles is the largest fashion and textile facility in the United States. Over 1,200 permanent showrooms in CaliforniaMart and additional spaces nearby in The New Mart host a Los Angeles fashion week five times per year. A junior show is held twice a year, and textile shows are held twice a year. An 82-block business district is home to a complete scope of fashion-related businesses, including designers, wholesalers, manufacturers, and patternmakers.

Los Angeles employs 173,000 people in the fashion industry, surpassing New York. In spite of competition from businesses in other countries, L.A. manufacturing has remained stable due to the quality of construction and the ability to meet production deadlines.

Regional market weeks are held throughout the United States, with Los Angeles serving most of the West Coast, Dallas and Chicago serving the central states, and Atlanta serving the southeast. The International Apparel Mart in Dallas showcases a complete line of women's wear as well as all major manufacturers of boots, hats, and western apparel. The Atlanta-based AmericasMart offers a premiere show that features new and edgy contemporary lines. Many retail buyers have expressed pleasure in being able to buy lines that were traditionally shown only in New York in a less hectic setting.

## HEADING NORTH AND SOUTH

Canada, Central America, and South America have smaller versions of the fashion centers found in the United States. Canada hosts fashion weeks in both Montreal and Toronto to showcase primarily Canadian designers. Canada's Peter Nygård is one of the most successful manufacturers of women's better and bridge designs.

Latin American, Caribbean, and Canadian fashion talent is showcased each year at the Fashion Week of the Americas held in Miami, Florida. Designers from North, South, and Central America show their collections for an audience of international buyers, media, and celebrities.

When the Fashion Week of the Americas originated in 1999, little-known designers were showcased, and it was more of a media event than a buying event. In later years, the event has focused on more established designers, such as Carolina Herrera, and the commercial opportunities available to businesses affiliating with them. Retail buyers are always interested in checking out promising, upcoming designers with new ideas in clothing, but want to commit most of their "open-to-buy" to fashion businesses that have a proven record of quality products delivered on time. **Open-to-buy** is the amount of money the buyer has available to commit to the purchase of new apparel for a given period of time.

New designers in other countries without their own U.S. showrooms find it difficult to attract U.S. buyers. Firms like Talent Ensemble International represent such designers in a showroom in New York, and the owner, Theissy Mahecha, assists them in developing their business. Many designers from the Americas travel to U.S. markets for access to the large numbers of buyers from the United States and other countries.

**TIME OUT**

Buyers looking for colorful, comfortable, lightweight island wear can find it from designers who know the beach resorts best, like Claudia Pegus of Port of Spain, Trinidad. Pegus apprenticed with couturiers in England, France, Germany, and Spain before returning to her native Trinidad to open her couture and ready-to-wear business.

# TRY IT ON

**Why do fashion-related businesses group together geographically?**

_____

_____

_____

_____

# AMERICAN DESIGNERS

**PRODUCT/ SERVICE MANAGEMENT**

**A**merican designers have not always been internationally known. In the Americas, manufacturers' names were once better known than the designers' names. European designers' captured more media attention. But for the past 50 years, American designers have flourished to create names that are recognized throughout the world.

## THE MEGABRANDS

A few American designers have managed to turn their fashion labels into megabrands known and purchased throughout the world. Each has managed to make the business a success in his or her own style. In addition to Ralph Lauren, others who have reached this level of fame and size include Tommy Hilfiger, Calvin Klein, and Donna Karan.

**Tommy Hilfiger**  Tommy Hilfiger's style represents the all-American boy. He has turned the men's tailored clothing design business into an urban fashion legend. He started with a small store in upstate New York before eventually creating his own line of clothing. Hilfiger remains the principal creative designer, and in 2001 was the highest-paid fashion executive in the United States, making in excess of $26 million.

**Calvin Klein**  Calvin Klein is known for ads that push the limits of acceptability and for turning jeans into an affordable designer item. He was born in New York, attended the Fashion Institute of Technology, and wanted to design clothes for most of his life. He launched his jeans line in 1980 with a TV campaign featuring Brooke Shields. Klein is thought to be a marketing genius and the master of "minimalistic chic."

**Donna Karan**  Donna Karan is an American designer who became famous for her upscale, cozy women's and men's suits and sportswear designs under the Donna Karan and DKNY labels. Additionally, she has licensing agreements for beauty products, watches, children's clothing, hosiery, and the operation of her retail stores throughout the world. Donna Karan has relinquished financial control of her business by selling it to the French luxury-goods conglomerate, LVMH.

## A NEW GENERATION

While the megabrands fight to stay on top and not dilute their brand names, new designers try to establish a place for their designs in as

many *doors* as possible. A **door** is fashion jargon for a retail store. Thousands of new designers enter, but few move beyond the starting line. Some names to watch include Peter Som, Daphne Gutierrez, and Sean Combs.

**Peter Som**   Peter Som is destined to be one of the next great designers. His elegant, classic designs were propelled to fame after being worn on one of HBO's hottest TV shows. In addition to a no-nonsense approach to fashion, Som is paying close attention to properly running his business, which he knows is as important as designing.

**Daphne Gutierrez**   Daphne Gutierrez is one-half of the design team credited with the label Bruce. After Gutierrez won an award from the Council of Fashion Designers of America for best new talent, tickets to the fashion week showing of the Bruce label became hard to find. By designing flattering clothing for women, Gutierrez is building a fashion business catering to a confident and sophisticated customer.

**Sean Combs**   Sean Combs, already known as a music executive and rapper, launched his Sean Jean boys' and men's wear line in 1999. Able to capitalize on his celebrity status, Combs' line propelled itself into $100 million of sales per year in the first two years. The line is sold in "shop-in-shops" at Bloomingdale's and Macy's.

# TRY IT ON

**Why do designers need to understand the business side of fashion?**

## UNDERSTAND MARKETING CONCEPTS

Circle the best answer for each of the following questions.

1. The amount a retail buyer has available to spend on new apparel during a given time period is
   a. designer fees.
   b. open-to-buy.
   c. product costs.
   d. supply.

2. Fashion jargon for retail stores is
   a. tops.
   b. bottoms.
   c. doors.
   d. houses.

## THINK CRITICALLY

Answer the following questions as completely as possible. If necessary, use a separate sheet of paper.

3. Why might a designer want to have a business in New York or Los Angeles?

_____

_____

_____

_____

4. **Marketing** How can a little-known designer attract the attention of buyers from major retail stores?

_____

_____

_____

_____

_____

_____

# EUROPEAN FASHION

## GOALS

**Describe** the European markets of the fashion industry.

**Identify** prominent European fashion designers.

## The Latest Style

**W**hen the international press covered her runway show at her graduation from design school featuring famous models like Naomi Campbell, she was off to a spectacular start. It didn't hurt to have apprenticed with design firms, starting at age 15 and including firms on Savile Row in London, before going to design school. A London native and daughter of ex-Beatle Sir Paul and Linda McCartney, Stella McCartney's fast ascent to fame as a designer was aided by her family's celebrity status, but is firmly based on her talent.

McCartney is known for combining sharp tailoring with femininity. After launching her own fashion line, she worked as creative director for Chloé and propelled its sales back into positive territory. In April 2001, she resigned from Chloé to manage her own line under a partnership with the Gucci Group. She agreed to work with Gucci only after gaining control of design and material. A staunch animal rights advocate, McCartney refuses to use leather or fur in her designs.

Work with a group. Discuss what Stella McCartney might need to know to stay at the top of the fashion business.

## GLOBE TROTTING

PROMOTION

**F**ashion is a global business with hundreds of fashion trade shows held all over the world. There are apparel, accessories, textile, or findings shows throughout Europe and Asia almost any day of any month, except mid- to late December and early January. The most famous of the shows are the Milan and Paris runway shows. The packed international show calendar offers something for everyone. Show organizers struggle to schedule the events so as to attract the maximum number of buyers and media representatives, thus providing supreme exposure for exhibitors.

Traditionally, the designer runway shows start in New York and then move to London, Milan, and finally Paris. The runway shows are expensive, glamorous, dramatic productions staged to attract attention to the designer's collection. The shows are by invitation only—buyers, celebrities, and

R. SCOT___NCH

media representatives receive the invitations. Tickets to the hottest designers' shows are highly sought-after commodities.

## THE UNITED KINGDOM

**DISTRIBUTION**

Behind the glamour of the runway is the hard-working fashion industry. In the United Kingdom, fashion is one of the largest industries, with about 220,000 people employed nationwide. Britain's footwear industry employs more than 10 percent of the fashion-related employees and is the fifth-largest footwear producer in the European Union.

London fashion weeks are miniature when compared to those of New York, Paris, or Milan. About 50 to 60 designers show on an official schedule set by the British Fashion Council. London is a place where new designers are discovered, but many find it difficult to achieve financial success in Britain. A number of British designers got their start in London and then moved to Milan or Paris to expand their careers.

## ITALY

Beginning with production of luxury woolen fabric in the 1880s, Italy has long been known as the country of quality, luxury fashion apparel. The care that is given to high-end garment tailoring and beautiful fabric has driven this longstanding image.

About 50 percent of Italian women's wear is exported, primarily to other European countries. Germany and France are the two largest consumers of Italian apparel. Italy imports many fashion-related supplies from France and China. Italy has a large textile industry based in the cities surrounding Milan, such as Como, Torino, and Biella. A large supply of skilled people keeps the industry running.

**Moda pronta**, Italian ready-to-wear apparel, is shown primarily in Milan and Florence. The officially scheduled shows in Milan are sponsored by the Camera Nationale della Moda Italiana, the governing body of Milan fashion designers.

## FRANCE

France is known as the creative center of fashion. All of the elements needed for a successful fashion industry are present in France, including designers, skilled garment makers, textile and findings suppliers, government support, business know-how, and buyers who flock to the shows and markets. The industry originated as a creative center based on the talent of a few designers whose word was law. The industry has changed to focus on commercially viable fashion businesses where customers rule.

**PROMOTION**

**Fashion Weeks in Paris** The prêt-à-porter shows take place two times each year. The **collection opening** is the first opportunity for buyers to view new fashions. The shows are the grand finale following showings in New York, London, and Milan. The shows, called Prêt À Porter Paris®, are portrayed in advertisements as "a must for all women's wear professionals" and attract more than 40,000 visitors from 30 countries to 1,100 exhibitors. The trade fair is divided into segments based on the type of women's wear offered by the exhibitors, ranging from well-known

The British Fashion Council graciously agreed to lead off the 2003 spring collection shows. The move from the traditional date of the London fashion week allowed New York-based CFDA to avoid an original show date of September 7–13 in New York. The original date would have conflicted with services marking the first anniversary of the terrorist attacks in the United States.

Cristobal Balenciaga was a Spaniard who became a leading French fashion designer. As early as age 13, he was enthralled with fashion and began designing and constructing clothing. He was unique in that, according to Coco Chanel, he was the only true couturier able to cut the fabric, assemble a creation, and sew the garment himself. Balenciaga's career spanned from the late 1930s to the late 1960s, and he left his imprint on each period in which he designed. His designs included several influential pieces, one of the most famous being Jaqueline Kennedy's pillbox hats. He refused membership in the Chambre Syndicale and showed his line a month after other houses. Balenciaga was determined to never license his products or allow retail sales of his designs. He abruptly closed his fashion house in 1968 and died four years later. Despite his efforts, the Balenciaga name does live on in ready-to-wear lines and licensing agreements.

### THINK CRITICALLY
**1.** What would happen to designers today who showed their line a month late?
**2.** Why would Balenciaga resist ready-to-wear apparel and licensing?

brands to designers of international fame. Ready-to-wear fashions are shown at the trade fair before being mass-produced.

In addition to the trade shows, French and other European fashions are offered in showrooms throughout the year and at regional trade shows throughout Europe.

**Haute Couture**   The haute couture shows have retained some of the glamour of the French designer era. The live runway shows take place in January for spring collections and July for fall collections. The shows are a significant publicity opportunity for the French and world designers who participate.

The couture houses are a minimal part of the fashion industry in France, but the shows attract major media attention. Some designers will show outlandish costumes to get media coverage, and then show reasonable, salable apparel in ready-to-wear shows.

**LVMH**   Louis Vuitton Moët Hennessy (LVMH) is a French luxury-goods corporation that owns about 50 brands. Christian Dior SA is the parent company of LVMH, with brands that have included Pucci, Donna Karan, Givenchy, Céline, TAG Heuer, and De Beers—all considered high-end brands. Companies like LVMH buy and sell brands based on the potential for profit.

# TRY IT ON

**Why do designers spend time and money on runway shows?**

# EUROPEAN CREATORS

**M**ost of the well-known European fashion houses are named after founding designers who have since retired or are deceased. Their names remain on the businesses due to the advantages of association with past success. Major corporations like LVMH have purchased financial control of the fashion houses.

## BRAND NAMES

Designers whose names are known in Europe may have started their careers in other parts of the world, but have made their brands viable in Paris or Milan. Some of these names include Donatella Versace, Tom Ford, and Miuccia Prada.

**Donatella Versace**   Donatella Versace provides the creative side of the Versace family business based in Milan. Donatella was propelled into the international business after the tragic death of her brother, Gianni. She has made the Versace name a continued commercial success.

**Tom Ford**   Texan Tom Ford is the creative director for Paris-based Gucci and Yves Saint Laurent (YSL). Ford brought both back from the brink of disaster to commercial viability. His success is partially due to moving YSL from 167 unrelated licensing agreements to just 15 agreements and reacquiring control of the brand.

**Miuccia Prada**   Miuccia Prada, granddaughter of Prada founder Mario Prada, entered the business in 1978 and is credited with making the Italian brand what it is today. Muiccia added women's wear to the mostly leather handbag lines. The Miu Miu line, her namesake, is expected to grow, especially in Asian markets.

## CYBER MARKETING

**Who's Next** is a fashion trade show for new designers. Held in Paris, the show provides exposure for new street styles, especially in sportswear and juniors. The show's web site at **www.whosnext.com** is fascinating and divides the clothing into catagories such as fresh, fame, juli, fast, and hot, with a different insect representing each.

**THINK CRITICALLY**
**1.** After visiting **www.whosnext.com,** what impression do you have regarding who should attend this show?
**2.** Make a list of stores familiar to you that might want to buy at this show.

# TRY IT ON

**Why do fashion houses keep the names of deceased designers?**

_____

_____

_____

_____

## UNDERSTAND MARKETING CONCEPTS

Circle the best answer for each of the following questions.

**1.** A collection opening is
   **a.** money owed.
   **b.** a party for designers and manufacturers.
   **c.** the findings for a collection.
   **d.** an opportunity for buyers to view new fashions.

**2.** The prêt-á-porter shows take place
   **a.** once a year.
   **b.** twice a year.
   **c.** three times a year.
   **d.** every month.

## THINK CRITICALLY

Answer the following questions as completely as possible. If necessary, use a separate sheet of paper.

**3. Research**   Are European brands popular with students in your school? Ask five students what French or Italian brands they can name and if they have ever purchased the brands. Make a list from the results of your research. Combine your list with those of other students in your class. Reach a conclusion about the results.

_____

_____

_____

_____

**4.** Why would Parisians want to have their fashion week last on the schedule of the big four fashion weeks?

_____

_____

_____

_____

_____

# ASIAN AND OTHER EMERGING CENTERS

## The Latest Style

**V**illa Moda is a 75,000-square-foot luxury boutique in Kuwait City, Kuwait. Villa Moda is the creation of retailer and Kuwaiti prince, Majed Al-Sabah. It opened in April 2002 and houses in-store shops for designer brands such as Gucci, Prada, Ferragamo, Stella McCartney, and Fendi.

Shopping is a major pastime in Kuwait. The oil-rich, Middle Eastern nation is about the size of New Jersey, has a population of about two million, and has a very high average income per person. The fashion-conscious Kuwaitis want the trendiest clothes available, and they purchase new items weekly. Kuwaiti women are freer to wear Western clothing than women in most other Islamic countries and are not required to cover their faces in public. Many Kuwaiti women rarely wear the same garment twice.

The highest volume of sales at Villa Moda occurs when large shipments of apparel arrive from favorite designers. Customers are invited to help open the shipments, and they immediately buy the clothes.

Work with a group. Discuss the elements that make Villa Moda a success. Why would a fashion retailer allow customers to unpack newly arriving apparel? Would that strategy work in other retail settings?

**GOALS**

**Identify** and **describe** the fashion markets in Asia.

**Identify** emerging fashion markets and designers.

## ASIAN MARKETS

DISTRIBUTION

**A**sian and other emerging fashion markets hold a potential for growth that is beyond most American and European markets. The growth can be derived from increased sales to the consumer as well as increased production and distribution. Developing nations such as Madagascar, Korea, Vietnam, and China continue to expand their manufacturing and consumer bases. Japanese and Singaporean consumers have a voracious

As the average annual income in China has increased, young Chinese women have become more fashion conscious. In addition to having more income to spend on clothing, fashion is now more readily available in stores within China. A huge rise in materialism has accompanied the growth in the Chinese economy, with fashion marketers reaping the benefits.

appetite for fashion, but they are **mature markets** in that they have reached their full potential, with steady demand but not much room for continued growth.

## CHINA

Admitting China to the World Trade Organization (WTO) unleashed a Chinese fashion boom with a growth rate in international distribution that does not seem to slow. The Chinese textile and manufacturing trade show's attendance swelled once the tarriffs associated with non-WTO membership were lifted.

Apparel makers from the United States and other countries are quickly recognizing the opportunities for profitable fashion marketing in China. China has an enormous population with a pent-up demand for fashion and a huge potential workforce. U.S. and global firms are rushing to sign licensing agreements with retailers such as the Hempel Corporation, the retail arm of a Chinese apparel conglomerate.

**Hong Kong**   The former British colony of Hong Kong used to be a major clothing manufacturing center. As the standard of living rose, manufacturers moved most moderate- to budget-priced production to less expensive areas within mainland China. Hong Kong, long a shopper's haven, is now evolving into an international trade center for fashion with its own developing designers.

Hong Kong's fashion week features local manufacturers, designers, and brands, as well as those of other Asian countries. The Asia Pacific Leather Fair is a major event held in Hong Kong featuring leather footwear and apparel. Buyers from around the region find the Hong Kong fashion fairs a convenient place to buy. Additionally, the Hong Kong Trade Development Council promotes local designers by sponsoring their shows at other major market fairs, such as those in New York and Tokyo.

**Guangdong**   Located in southern China, Guangdong has attracted much of the manufacturing base that left Hong Kong. Its focus has been on garment production outsourced from companies outside of China. A new focus is on increasing recognition of locally initiated brands. The industry is promoting the growth of a fashion infrastructure made up of designers and marketers that will support this effort.

## JAPAN

Fashion in Japan is centered in Tokyo and includes more than just apparel. Fashion is thought of as a lifestyle that appeals to a large number of people.

Fashion journalist Shoko Hisada serves as the chairperson of the Tokyo Fashion Designers' Association. She was instrumental in founding the association, which has grown to about 50 members and promotes both new and experienced fashion designers. It is one of several organizations in Tokyo that promote the fashion industry.

The International Fashion Fair is one of a number of trade shows that are held in Tokyo and attract buyers from all over the region. It is held in late July/early August and shows women's, men's, and children's wear, shoes, and accessories. A sportswear show called Active Collection is held in September.

## TRY IT ON

**Why is China becoming a major player in the fashion industry?**

# EMERGING CENTERS AND DESIGNERS

**DISTRIBUTION**

**G**lobal sourcing involves working with manufacturers throughout the world. Fashion marketers must consider the risk of global sourcing when placing orders with new apparel producers in developing nations. Reliable, timely delivery of quality apparel is critical to retailers. Retailers plan promotions up to a year in advance and must commit open-to-buy and advertising budgets based on the requested delivery date of the apparel. Having apparel arrive late or not at all can be a costly disaster for a retailer. If ads run for products that are not available, it alienates customers who will blame the retailer, not the manufacturer. Dealing with businesses in countries that do not have political or economic stability can be more than challenging. The price may be right, but the experience may be too costly.

## MADAGASCAR

Madagascar is an island nation off the coast of Africa that should be benefiting from the U.S. Congressional Trade and Development Act of 2000. The Act was intended to create incentives for U.S. apparel importers to use sub-Saharan African sources for apparel production and, consequently, improve economic conditions in these poor countries. Political unrest in Madagascar, however, has made it difficult for the fashion industry to take advantage of the incentives. At one point, the Groupe Socota Industries, headquartered in Madagascar, was successful in winning orders, but then had difficulty in fulfilling its commitments due to the lack of fuel needed to dye fabric.

Another difficulty in working with developing African nations is that many of the garment factories are owned by Asian investors who employ African people at very low wages, and then take the profits back to their home countries rather than benefiting the local economies. The treatment of garment workers in African countries is of continuing concern.

## VIETNAM

Vietnam is a member of the Association of Southeast Asian Nations, which is a trading bloc with other Asian nation members. Vietnam is attempting to expand its economy by opening its business community to international interests. The International Textile and Garment Industry Exhibition is held in Hanoi, and exhibitors from other nations are solicited. Vietnam has a huge potential labor pool for garment manufacturing that could also become a consumer market if jobs are developed.

## KOREA

Korea is known for its low-priced fashions and fabrics. Improvements in the economy have helped spur the development of more middle-priced textile and apparel manufacturing. The improvements in income and employment have also increased the demand for fashions consumed by the Korean population and have raised the interest in developing unique Korean fashions.

Korea has developed a small high-end fashion business that represents less than one percent of all Korean apparel purchases. Korean designer garments are almost totally purchased by government officials and their spouses to wear at formal public government events. The wearing of non-Korean-made garments by government officials would not be acceptable.

## ASIA'S FASHION PEOPLE

It has been difficult for Asian designers to establish a successful brand in Asia. Most Asian designers find that they must go to New York, Paris, or Milan to make an international name for themselves, but a few designers have managed to remain in their homeland and find success. Some of the designers in China, Japan, and India who have been successful in their own region are Flora Cheong-Leen, Sabyasachi Mukherjee, and Rei Kawakubo.

**Flora Cheong-Leen** Flora Cheong-Leen is based in Hong Kong, but has lived all over the world. She uses her background as inspiration for her fashion line—Tian Art. Cheong-Leen describes her fashion as "highlighting the clash of East and West" rather than combining them. In addition to showing her line in Hong Kong, she has at times shown her line in Paris.

**Sabyasachi Mukherjee** Sabyasachi Mukherjee is well known in his native India as a fashion designer. The British Council awarded him the Femina Miss India 2001 Most-Promising-Designer-of-the-Year award. Mukherjee's fashions have been featured at a number of events, including bridal shows and Miss India pageants.

**Rei Kawakubo** Rei Kawakubo has been a designer in Tokyo for many years. Her label is Comme Des Garcons, which translates from French to mean "like a boy." Kawakubo's designs are considered architectural or sculpture-like and feature unusual silhouettes. She also designs graphics, packaging, and furniture.

## CYBER MARKETING

Robinsons is a chain of upscale department stores in Southeast Asia that was founded in 1857 in Singapore. Robinsons has always stayed on the cutting edge of marketing, finding ways to sell to distant customers. In the 1860s, Robinsons merchandise was sent by ship with travelling representatives to Malaysia, Borneo, and Siam. More recently, Robinsons has gone online with links from **www.Yahoo.com** to offer fashions and other products to distant customers. Robinsons customers can send gift vouchers denominated in the currency of the country in which the recipient lives. The GloboGift vouchers can be used at major retailers elsewhere in the world, such as Macy's in the United States. Robinsons has also developed e-commerce capabilities that tie to major suppliers, enabling them to instantly communicate needs.

**THINK CRITICALLY**
What are some reasons that Robinsons has stayed in business for so many years?

# TRY IT ON

Why is it difficult to work with manufacturers in developing nations?

_____

_____

_____

## TrendSetters

### SCOTT FRENCH

R. Scott French is the second successful, multimillion-dollar fashion business opened by Scott French. His first successful business was French Jenny, a lingerie collection. The R. Scott French collection includes both men's and women's sportswear. French has a knack for spotting what is missing in available fashions and filling that niche. "I just get in there and design a product that sells," states French. His first line was called Happy Clothes. Barney's, a New York landmark specialty store whose web site states "We're gaga for emerging designers," bought all the pieces French made and displayed them in its front window.

Scott French was taught to sew by his grandmother and her quilting circle. He believes that quilting influenced his understanding of the geometry of design. The designs of his sportswear collections reflect this beginning. The success of his businesses reflects his wide range of experiences in retail, wholesale, and production.

The R. Scott French collection attracted attention when every-day men rather than professional models were chosen to show the collection. Building on the success of men's sportswear, a collection of women's sportswear in an accessible price range was added in the third year of the business. The collection was titled "The Purity of the Diagonal," and had strong, almost architectural lines. R. Scott French uses sources from throughout the world for ideas and materials, but manufactures the garments in the United States.

Scott French is a member of the Council of Fashion Designers in New York and takes his business seriously. He believes that humility is a needed virtue in the fashion industry. "Get over yourself! After all, you are making and selling garments, not saving lives," says French, who knows how to design, package, and merchandise fashion that sells.

### THINK CRITICALLY
**1.** Why do you think Scott French has been a success?
**2.** What ideas do you have for inexpensive ways to promote a new fashion line?

## UNDERSTAND MARKETING CONCEPTS

Circle the best answer for each of the following questions.

**1.** A mature market is one that
   **a.** is for people over 50.
   **b.** is in an old building.
   **c.** is in need of money.
   **d.** has reached full growth potential.

**2.** A concern in sourcing with a developing nation is
   **a.** political unrest.
   **b.** missed timelines.
   **c.** loss of revenue.
   **d.** all of the above.

## THINK CRITICALLY

Answer the following questions as completely as possible. If necessary, use a separate sheet of paper.

**3.** How might politics influence the fashion industry?

_____

_____

_____

_____

_____

**4.** How might wealthy countries assist poor countries in developing their fashion industry? Why would it be in both parties' interests?

_____

_____

_____

_____

_____

_____

_____

# REVIEW

## REVIEW MARKETING CONCEPTS

**Write the letter of the term that matches each definition. Some terms will not be used.**

_____ **1.** The first opportunity for buyers to view new fashions

_____ **2.** Working with manufacturers throughout the world

_____ **3.** A fashion show using live models

_____ **4.** A steady market that has reached full growth potential

_____ **5.** Italian ready-to-wear apparel

_____ **6.** The amount of money a buyer has available to commit to the purchase of new apparel for a given period of time

**a.** collection opening
**b.** door
**c.** global sourcing
**d.** mature market
**e.** moda pronta
**f.** open-to-buy
**g.** runway show

**Circle the best answer.**

**7.** Regional U.S. fashion centers are located in
   **a.** Dallas.
   **b.** Chicago.
   **c.** Atlanta.
   **d.** all of these.

**8.** Newly emerging fashion centers include
   **a.** Madagascar and Vietnam.
   **b.** Kuwait City and Tokyo.
   **c.** Hong Kong and Singapore.
   **d.** all of these.

**9.** The big four international fashion weeks are held in
   **a.** Los Angeles, Dallas, Chicago, and New York.
   **b.** London, Paris, Rome, and Tokyo.
   **c.** New York, London, Milan, and Paris.
   **d.** Singapore, Hong Kong, New York, and Paris.

**10.** China is becoming a major player in the industry because of
   **a.** its admission to the World Trade Organization.
   **b.** its large available workforce.
   **c.** its potential consumer base.
   **d.** all of these.

# THINK CRITICALLY

**11.** Why is the fashion industry in New York losing employment and the Los Angeles industry growing?

_____

_____

_____

_____

_____

**12.** Why does Paris retain its reputation as the fashion center of the world?

_____

_____

_____

_____

**13.** Why do designers from all over the Americas come to the United States to do business? Where do they go within the United States and why?

_____

_____

_____

**14.** Why is fashion considered an international business?

_____

_____

_____

_____

_____

# MAKE CONNECTIONS

**15. Marketing Math**  You are a buyer for Vanderver's Department Store in Tulsa. You plan to attend the fashion week shows in New York, London, Milan, and Paris. You need to spend four days in New York, two days in London, three days in Milan, and four days in Paris to complete your buying trip. You have the following information:

| Destinations | Airfare one way |
| --- | --- |
| Tulsa to New York | $425 |
| Tulsa to London | $850 |
| New York to London | $550 |
| London to Milan | $236 |
| Tulsa to Paris | $890 |
| Tulsa to Milan | $876 |
| Milan to Paris | $266 |

| Location of Shows | Dates of Shows | Hotel per night | Food per day |
| --- | --- | --- | --- |
| New York | 9/12 to 9/17 | $255 | $135 |
| London | 9/18 to 9/22 | $150 | $ 98 |
| Milan | 9/23 to 9/29 | $112 | $120 |
| Paris | 9/30 to 10/6 | $200 | $156 |

Plan a trip itinerary resulting in the most efficient use of time and money. You want the least expensive trip possible, and you do not want to waste any more days than necessary. Note that the airfares given are for one-way travel in either direction between the two destination cities listed. Complete a trip expense report, using a spreadsheet with columns for date, destination, airfare, hotel, and food costs for each day between 9/12 and 10/6. Calculate the total costs of the trip.

_____

_____

_____

_____

_____

**16. Geography**  Locate Madagascar on a global map. List nearby countries. Research information on the Internet about the current economic and political conditions in Madagascar. Write a paragraph about how these conditions might impact the fashion industry.

_____

_____

_____

_____

# CREATIVE MARKETING PROJECT

You work for a consulting firm that provides marketing research for fashion businesses and recommends improvements based on the research. Select a clothing store (or any fashion-related business) in your area and assume you, with a group of associates, have been assigned that store as your client. You are challenged to plan and conduct research for the store in order to improve marketing activities. Your research may be aimed at increasing the trading area of the store, finding new markets for local products, increasing sales, or solving other problems or challenges affecting the marketing process. You will design a survey, develop a budget for your research, conduct the survey with a target market, and report your recommendations to the business.

Work as a group. This project consists of a written document and an oral presentation. The written creative marketing project must not exceed 30 numbered pages including the appendix. The paper will consist of a Summary Memorandum, Introduction, Procedure and Research Methods Used, Findings and Conclusion, Recommendations, Bibliography, and Appendix.

www.deca.org
/publications/HS_
Guide/guidetoc.html

# PROJECT: The COLLECTION POINT

You have been hired to assist a new retail buyer, George Sudds, who needs information to prepare for his first buying trip. Sudds is a new buyer of men's wear. He is attending the next women's wear fashion week in Dallas and wants information to make his trip efficient and effective.

**Work with a group and complete the following activities.**

1. Visit **www.dallasmarketcenter.com** for information about the Dallas apparel mart.

2. Make a list of services provided for new buyers by the Dallas Market Center.

3. Outline the admission requirements for the market.

4. Make a list of suggestions for trip preparation, including information on nearby hotels and restaurants.

5. Use presentation software to develop a five-minute presentation that you could use to acquaint Sudds and other new buyers with the Dallas Market Center.

6. Present your findings to the class as if they were a group of new retail buyers.

CHAPTER 6

# PROMOTING A FASHION IMAGE

## LESSONS

### 6.1 ADVERTISING FASHION

### 6.2 PROMOTING THROUGH EVENTS

### 6.3 SELLING FASHION

# WINNING STRATEGIES

## NICOLE MILLER

**N**icole Miller is often quoted as saying, "All those male designers get so much more press," but Miller knows how to "get press" herself. Miller is a designer of cocktail dresses, sportswear, accessories, and men's ties, to name a few of her lines, and is adept at gaining her own publicity.

Miller opened a store at 125th Street and Fairway, the main shopping area in Harlem, an upper-Manhattan neighborhood in New York City with a predominantly African-American population. The opening kicked off with a charity reception that raised more than $20,000 for the Harlem Week Educational Scholarship Fund. The Harlem store was Miller's third store in New York. Manhattan Borough President C. Virginia Fields stated, "Many of us who live in Harlem wear Nicole Miller's clothing, and it's about time to have more stores open there like this."

Miller has taken other opportunities to gain publicity by supporting worthy causes. She has partnered with the National Football League to support the Susan G. Komen Foundation in the fight against breast cancer by designing a special print that combined NFL icons with the Komen Foundation pink ribbon. The NFL used extensive national advertising during 26 in-game spots, 48 daytime spots, and 55 ESPN spots to publicize the effort, with Miller's name included in each. She was also interviewed during a Monday night game at halftime. Miller's name brands benefit from her efforts to support causes, and the results are tremendous publicity that money could not buy.

### THINK CRITICALLY

1. Why would Nicole Miller tie a charity event to her new store opening?

2. Why is it effective publicity to be associated with positive causes?

# CHAPTER 6
## Lesson 6.1

# ADVERTISING FASHION

## GOALS

**Identify** and **explain** the components of the promotional mix.

**Define** and **describe** fashion advertising.

## The Latest Style

**M**ost fashion and beauty items have a fleeting moment in the spotlight and then vanish, but a few classics live on. Few beauty items have had the long life of Chanel No. 5 perfume. It premiered in 1921 by designer Coco Chanel and continues to attract new generations of users. Much of its popularity can be attributed to advertising.

Chanel No. 5 ads use up-and-coming models rather than established stars and stick to one approach—simplicity. Over the last 40 years the ads have been updated, but they continue to reflect the simplicity that has become Chanel's trademark.

Work with a group. Make a list of fashion or beauty brands used by your parents' generation. Are any of them popular with your age group? Why or why not?

## ADVERTISING THE PRODUCT

PROMOTION

**P**romotion is one of the seven marketing functions. The components of the promotional mix are advertising, public relations, publicity, and personal selling. A promotional plan contains all four components, but advertising is what keeps the fashion message fresh in consumers' minds.

### WHAT IS FASHION ADVERTISING?

**Fashion advertising** is the paid communication between the product maker or seller and the audience or customer about a fashion item. Advertising is a nonpersonal communication with a large group of people, even if it is targeted to a specific audience.

### EFFECTIVE ADVERTISEMENTS

Advertising is expensive and needs to provide a payback for the company. Effective advertising should be a significant part of the promotional plan for a fashion business. The effectiveness should be measured to determine if an ad accomplished its intended purpose. If the purpose is increased sales, then the quantity of sales at the end of the ad campaign is the data used to evaluate the ad.

## TARGETING A CUSTOMER

**MARKETING-
INFORMATION
MANAGEMENT**

Understanding exactly who the customer is and what the customer wants helps focus the advertisement. Knowledge of customers and their habits directs the type of ad and the media used to convey the message. People can be targeted by the TV shows they watch or the magazines they read.

Nike was spending about $1 billion per year on ads for Air Jordan shoes and related merchandise. The campaign used Michael Jordan in frequently aired TV commercials to successfully sell the shoes. A different style of campaign was developed when Nike launched a new line of sneakers called Presto. Nike spent only $15 million on advertising. Focusing on teens, Nike produced humorous TV, radio, and print ads for Presto shoes. The ads ran on MTV and Comedy Central and in *YM* magazine. Sales of Presto shoes soared in the first year the shoes were offered.

## BUILDING A BRAND

**Brand building** is establishing an identity or image for a line of apparel. Branding requires the use of a consistent advertising message that conveys the image to the consumer across every type of media used. A brand helps customers shop by providing a consistency of quality and price lines.

In an effort to break through the clutter of advertising messages bombarding consumers, some fashion brands have resorted to attention-getting shock tactics. Benetton went so far as to use shock ads to convey messages about its political and social opinions. Benetton caused major waves with a campaign titled "We, on Death Row," that sympathetically showed death row inmates. The controversial ads drew protests from victims' rights groups and law enforcement agencies, as well as legal suits from states over the commercial use of the inmates. Benetton wanted to spark debate about the death penalty, but victims' families felt the ads were trivializing those who were murdered. According to *USA Today*, Sears "pulled the plug on its exclusive Benetton USA line" due to pressure from those who were offended.

**THINK CRITICALLY**
**1.** Do shock ads attract consumers to apparel? Why or why not?
**2.** Why do most apparel marketers avoid controversial topics in their advertisements?

## RELEVANT REASONS TO BUY

With messages bombarding people from every direction, advertising must appeal to the target customer or it will be ignored. **Persuasive language** is relevant to the potential customer. The message must be in "you" language, not "me" language. *Copy*, the words in a print ad, must persuade the customer to act now, not later.

**Product features** are benefits to the customer and should be presented that way. The message should tell the customer what the product would do for them, not how it works or what the technical aspects are. An ad can tell the reader that the style will make them look thin and elegant, rather than telling them it is washable and won't fade.

**TIME OUT**

Maria Barraza is the owner of Barraza Associates Ltd., a clothing design and manufacturing company. Publicity found her business in a big way and at no cost to her. Barraza simply agreed to allow American Express to use her small, minority-owned business in its commercials. As a result, she received publicity in the *New York Daily News* and *The Wall Street Journal*, as well as TV coverage and a national speaking engagement.

## TRY IT ON

**What is persuasive language?**

_____

_____

_____

# PRODUCING THE AD

**PROMOTION**

**S**ince multiple businesses are involved in actually creating and selling a garment, it is to textile and garment manufacturers' benefit to cooperate with retailers in advertising the garment to consumers. With **cooperative advertising**, a vendor may share the cost with a retailer and pay as much as 50 percent of the cost of advertising the merchandise. The amount is based on a percentage of the dollar volume the retailer purchased from the vendor and is called an **advertising allowance**.

## BUDGETING FOR ADS

There are two major costs for advertising—the cost of producing the ad and the cost of the media for distribution of the ad. Two factors affecting media cost include the size or length of the ad and the number of consumers exposed to the ad. Advertising during a TV show with a large audience is much more expensive than advertising in the middle of the night when few people are watching. Major fashion businesses commit to advertising budgets and buy print space or TV time as much as a year in advance. When advertisers buy a large quantity of ad space for a given period of time, the media source may offer a quantity discount.

## SELECTING THE MEDIA

**MARKETING- INFORMATION MANAGEMENT**

Fashion advertisers select the media for ads based on the most current marketing information about the target customer group, including where, when, and how often they see or hear each type of media. The media can include print, broadcast, direct mail, or the Internet.

**Print Media**  Print media are most frequently used in fashion advertising and include magazines, newspapers, billboards, and outdoor posters on taxis and buses. Fashion magazines are chosen based on their readership. A fashion business chooses the magazines in which to advertise to help build its brand and reinforce the image of its line. Some magazines insert special ad pages in a regional edition directed at a specific geographic location. The placement of the ad impacts visibility and the cost of the ad. For example, the back cover of a magazine is a prime spot that is in view almost as often as the front cover and therefore costs more than interior-page ads.

**Broadcast Media** Broadcast media include television and radio, which can be regional or national. Because of the number of TV stations available, the selection of the station and time of day for the fashion ad to air is dependent on available data about the viewers. The cost of the ad is directly related to the number of viewers. Radio is not used as frequently as television to advertise fashion products because of the lack of visual appeal.

**Direct Mail Media** Direct mail ads such as postcards, statement enclosures, and catalogs are considered extremely effective fashion advertising media. Consumer response to direct mail is very high when targeted to the right group.

**Cyber Media** Cyber media include web sites, e-mail, and online ads. Online fashion media have tremendous growth potential for the teen market. Annemarie Iverson, editor-in-chief of *Seventeen*, was quoted by *Women's Wear Daily* as saying, "My readers are online eight hours a day."

## CREATING THE AD

Once the customer has been targeted, the ad's message and theme must be tailored to the media most likely to reach that customer group. With messages flying at people from all directions, attracting attention is difficult and must be done without violating customer values. Shocking ads may get the customers' attention, but may cause some to avoid, rather than buy, the product. Each set of target customers requires a different approach with an ever-changing appeal.

Japanese consumers of pop culture will be able to place online orders for T-shirt styles that change weekly. The web site is a partnership between Itochu Corp. and Yahoo! Japan. The consumer will be able to see the total number of T-shirts of the style that is being ordered. The orders will be filled when the number ordered exceeds 30 shirts. The price will start at about $23 for each shirt and drop lower as the demand increases. Sales for the T-shirts are projected to exceed $1.2 million during the first year.

**THINK CRITICALLY**
Would this sales promotion work in other cultures? Why or why not?

# TRY IT ON

**Why must care be given to the selection of media for fashion ads?**

## UNDERSTAND MARKETING CONCEPTS

Circle the best answer for each of the following questions.

**1.** Fashion advertising is
  **a.** purchasing and distributing fashions.
  **b.** paid communication about a fashion product to a targeted mass audience.
  **c.** the exchange of goods and services.
  **d.** none of the these.

**2.** Cooperative advertising is when
  **a.** a vendor and retailer share the cost of an ad.
  **b.** a customer acts on an ad.
  **c.** the media gives a discounted price.
  **d.** multiple media are used.

## THINK CRITICALLY

Answer the following questions as completely as possible. If necessary, use a separate sheet of paper.

**3. Communication**  Look at two print media ads for fashion items. Read the messages and write a paragraph about the way the products' benefits are described. Are the benefits described in technical terms or in terms relative to the consumer? Who is the intended consumer?

_____

_____

_____

_____

**4.** You have been hired to help a retailer market a new line of teen apparel. Choose two types of media in which to advertise. Describe why the selected media are the best for reaching the target customer.

_____

_____

_____

_____

# PROMOTING THROUGH EVENTS

## The Latest Style

**F**ashion advertising is about gaining the attention of customers and causing them to act. Finding new ways to accomplish this purpose takes creativity. The use of celebrities to promote fashions is not new, but Marvel Comics and Karin Models have given the use of celebrities a new twist. Karin Models is an international modeling agency that represents famous models like Liliana Dominguez, the YSL model.

Karin Models signed Marvel Comics' virtual superhero Elektra Natchios as a model. Elektra, the female star in the *Daredevil* comic book series, was hired to represent a variety of fashion industry clients. This promotional event was scheduled to tie in with the release of an Elektra comic book, a *Daredevil* movie opening, and the release of movie-related apparel items. Elektra was treated like a top model, complete with a portfolio containing her appearances in comic books and special drawings created by Marvel artists for specific fashion industry clients.

Work with a partner. Discuss fashion brands best suited to use Elektra as a model. Why would Elektra be a good match?

**Describe** the use of special events for promotion.

**Describe** how to obtain publicity through special events.

## SHOWING OFF

PROMOTION

**P**romotional activities that are out of the ordinary are **special events**. The fashion industry is well-known for producing special events, the most familiar of which is the fashion show. A fashion show can range from a very complex, expensive production by a designer to a simple, informal showing in a store. Fashion shows are one way to obtain publicity that results in stories written or broadcast about the events.

### ORGANIZING THE SHOW

Designers and retail stores hold fashion shows as media events to attract attention. The steps for organizing a show remain similar, no matter how simple or complex the show.

- *Determine the purpose.* The purpose of a fashion show can vary from connecting the viewer with the retail store to gaining publicity for a designer's collection. Many stores host fashion shows in connection with civic or nonprofit groups. For example, the American Cancer Society may ask a department store to host a fashion show as a fundraiser. Both the store and the organization benefit from the publicity that is generated.

- *Determine a theme.* Gather ideas for the theme and the event from key people. The designer, buyer, or special events coordinator at the store will have ideas based on the purpose of the event. The ideas will form a theme around which planning can be based. The purpose will determine the audience for the show, and all ideas will be geared toward attracting the audience.

- *Develop a written plan, including a timeline.* A plan can be developed on a spreadsheet. The column headings might be titled "Action," "Person Responsible," and "Due Date." All of the steps needed for the show can be listed under the Action column. One way to assure organization is to have everyone know who is responsible for an action step and when it must be completed. Holding status meetings to check progress will help action steps get completed on time.

- *Schedule a location, date, and time.* A fashion show can take place in an auditorium, a museum, a tent, or almost anywhere depending on the purpose and theme. The location, date, and time should be convenient for the audience. For a formal fashion show, the location should accommodate the models' walk down the runway. Also called a *catwalk*, it is a long, narrow stage that projects out into the audience so they can get a close look.

**MARKETING- INFORMATION MANAGEMENT**

- *Develop a guest list.* The guest list is critical to a fashion show. Retail stores use marketing information to create a list of current or potential customers to invite. If the event is in connection with a civic or social organization, the organization will add its membership to the invitation list. When designers spend $50,000 or more to host a fashion show in a tent at Bryant Park in New York City, they need to make sure the right people are in attendance. Designers generally want to attract the media, such as fashion journalists from *Women's Wear Daily* and *The New York Times*, in hopes of getting publicity. Additionally, designers invite celebrities for two reasons. A celebrity's presence will attract media attention in and of itself, but if the celebrity also wears the designer's clothing, it will attract even more attention to the style being promoted. Celebrities are generally paid and given designer garments to wear.

- *Find sources for the components—models, hair, makeup, music, lighting, sound system, and props.* A fashion show is made up of models that need to have hair and makeup done by professionals, if possible. Most designer shows use professional models to show the clothing to the best advantage. A show may feature nonprofessional models as well, such as members of a club sponsoring the event. To save money, co-sponsors can sometimes be found. For example, a cosmetics or shoe manufacturer may provide makeup or shoes for the models in exchange for acknowledgment (publicity) in the invitation and program. The props and music should be selected with the theme and audience in mind. A DJ is hired to spin the music, which must be cleared for use under copyright laws.

- *Develop and send invitations.* Since fashion editors get hundreds of invitations to shows, the invitation must grab the attention of the receiver. It should be creative, provide the needed information about the

event, and provide a compelling reason for the guest to attend. There may be a need to know how many people will attend so that seating can be arranged and an adequate supply of refreshments provided. If so, guests should be asked to R.S.V.P, which is the abbreviation for the French words "répondez s'il vous plait," meaning "please reply to say you are coming or not coming." Usually a phone number or an e-mail address is provided for the reply.

- *Develop a promotional plan.* The plan should include all four components of the promotional mix—advertising, publicity, public relations, and personal selling. The budget will determine the amount of advertising. Publicity can be gained by having a great purpose and clever theme to attract the media. By putting together a **press kit** that includes an invitation, a typed news article, and information about the best time to take photos, the event might receive some news coverage. Depending on the initial response to the invitations, personal selling might be needed to attract an audience.

- *Develop a script and program.* A script details what will be said to introduce each fashion, the order in which the selected garments will be shown, which model will be wearing each garment, and the music and lighting details. A program is a printed guide with a brief description of the garments, the models' names, and acknowledgment of the sponsors. The program lets the audience know what to expect and gives them a place to make notes about what they are seeing.

- *Schedule and rehearse.* Schedule dates and times for models to be fitted in the clothing selected for the show. Schedule a rehearsal one or two days in advance of the show to assure everyone knows where to be and when. Establishing a clear division of responsibilities in the planning stage will help everyone know what to do when things go wrong at the last minute and will minimize anxiety and tension.

- *Make the audience welcome and comfortable.* If the audience enjoys the experience, they will be more likely to take the wanted action of providing publicity or purchasing from the store or designer. Furthermore, a happy audience will look forward to the next event.

Prior to the 1930s, fashion journalists did not collaborate with the fashion industry to promote brand names. Fashion writers and women's magazines covered fashions but did not provide information about their origins. Fashion editors learned to work with ready-to-wear manufacturers and retail buyers in the 1930s, and all found advertising and fashion articles beneficial to their business. The editors worked behind the scenes to learn in advance what was new for the next season and where to get the garments. The manufacturers and retailers in turn bought space to advertise in the magazines. This process first developed in the United States, but quickly spread to Europe and is continued today. With the collaboration of the media, manufacturer, and retailer, what the customer sees as fashion promotion is aligned for the benefit of the industry.

**THINK CRITICALLY**

**1.** Why is it beneficial for fashion manufacturers, journalists, and retailers to collaborate?

**2.** How might the collaboration impact consumers?

**MARKETING-INFORMATION MANAGEMENT**

• *Gather data and evaluate the effectiveness of the show.* Fashion shows take time and money to produce. The sponsors should collect data about the number of people in attendance, the sales that take place, and the news articles that are published or broadcast after the show. This information can be used to determine the value of the show compared to the expense.

# TRY IT ON

**Why are fashion shows presented?**

_____

_____

_____

Sales of the fall collection exceeded $1.9 million following a trunk show for Ralph Lauren's women's collection, according to *Women's Wear Daily* in June 2002. The event was held at the Rhinelander Mansion, which serves as the flagship store for Lauren. One of the best-selling items was a $3,795 black dress worn by Penélope Cruz, which was also shown on the cover of *Town & Country* and inside *Elle* magazine's July issue.

# OTHER SPECIAL EVENTS

**PROMOTION**

Trunk shows, fundraisers, fashion awards, and infomercials are additional special events that are used to promote fashions and gain publicity. By hosting events for organizations, retail stores have the opportunity to attract new customers and gain loyalty from their current customers.

## TRUNK SHOWS

A **trunk show** is an informal fashion show that is held in a retail store as a way of promoting one individual designer's collection. In some cases, the designer will actually be at the show, which attracts more media attention and customers, especially if the designer is a celebrity. Big-name designers may host trunk shows for collection openings at their own retail boutiques. In multi-store chains, the trunk show is usually held in the flagship store, or it may travel from store to store. With trunk shows, live models are used to show the clothing, but a catwalk is generally not used due to lack of space.

Invitations are sent by the store to current customers who frequently buy the featured brand, and they are provided special seating at the show. Potential customers may also receive special treatment. The happy customer is likely to order some of the garments following the show.

Showing a collection on the road at trunk shows is a way of getting orders, but it can be very expensive and tiring for designers. Little-known designers generally do not attract a crowd large enough to justify the cost and time.

## FUNDRAISERS

Whether it is a party to support an AIDS foundation or an art museum, the fashion industry uses fundraisers to promote causes it believes in and to positively portray its brands. Including the brand name as part of the event name draws attention to both the cause and the promoter.

Creating an item to be sold for charity is another way the fashion industry supports favorite causes. For example, Kiehl's Since 1851, a beauty product company, made a three-year commitment to donate 100 percent of the proceeds of a best-selling product to YouthAIDS.

## FASHION AWARDS

The American Fashion Awards is an annual publicity event that honors the best fashion design talent. Since 1981, the event has been held by the Council of Fashion Designers of America (CFDA) with the assistance of financial sponsors. In past years, DuPont LYCRA® has been a sponsor. Both Hollywood and fashion-world celebrities attend the glamorous media event, and as they have a chance to present or receive awards, they "plug" the sponsor. For example, Vera Wang, the bridal-wear designer, is credited by DuPont in a news release from the awards event as saying, "I live for LYCRA®. LYCRA® has been part of my life for as long as it's existed. I don't think clothing would be the same today without LYCRA®. LYCRA® is the present and the future." Such news releases are sent to major newspapers and broadcast media.

## INFOMERCIALS

The fashion industry is learning to use television and other broadcast media to its full advantage. **Infomercials** are commercials that are the length of a regular hour or half-hour TV show and feature information about the sponsor's products in a show format. Indeed, at times it is difficult to tell the difference between a TV show and the commercials.

The fashion industry has been using this method of advertising for many years. In 1994, a weekly program called "Main Floor" began airing on broadcast stations. The show presents information about fashions and beauty trends with sponsors paying for two- or three-minute segments.

Infomercials have significant viewer ratings, making them a valuable promotional tool. The natural tie between showing brand-name fashions and running real commercial breaks featuring the retail stores that carry the brand is a form of promotional collaboration that is effective.

**What is a trunk show?**

_____

_____

_____

## UNDERSTAND MARKETING CONCEPTS

Circle the best answer for each of the following questions.

**1.** Three types of special events are
   **a.** buying, advertising, and selling.
   **b.** design, construction, and distribution.
   **c.** manufacturing, designing, and retailing.
   **d.** fashion shows, trunk shows, and fundraisers.

**2.** A press kit includes
   **a.** a typed news article.
   **b.** information about photo opportunities.
   **c.** an invitation.
   **d.** all of these.

## THINK CRITICALLY

Answer the following questions as completely as possible. If necessary, use a separate sheet of paper.

**3.** What is the purpose of fashion award events? Who might sponsor this type of event?

_____

_____

_____

**4. Communication**   Write a short paragraph about your opinion of a one-hour TV show that features one company's products. Is it a TV show or an advertisement, and why?

_____

_____

_____

_____

_____

_____

_____

_____

# SELLING FASHION

## The Latest Style

**M**ass retailers like Sears, Wal-Mart®, Target, and JCPenney have made significant moves into what has been an exclusive junior market. The mass retailers are attempting to attract teen girls away from junior specialty retailers and gain market share.

One success has been a partnership between Wal-Mart and *Seventeen* magazine to develop an in-store video campaign. The 12-minute video runs on monitors in the stores and features music and fashion-forward looks available at Wal-Mart. The campaign to sell teens on Wal-Mart is thought to be successful because teens believe *Seventeen* offers fashion advice with authority.

Target has attracted teens with its exclusive Mossimo label, and making a "Target run" has become popular with teen shoppers. Sears and JCPenney have used special events, celebrities, and contests to successfully attract more teen shoppers.

Work with a group. Discuss what you believe is important to teens in choosing a place to buy clothing. Make a list of your ideas and share them with the class.

**Explain** the keys to being a successful salesperson.

**Discuss** the steps in making a sale.

## MAKING A SALE

SELLING

**S***elling* is one of the seven functions of marketing and is a personal, direct way of communication with the customer to assist with the decision to buy. In a free-enterprise system, consumers are free to buy what they choose, but selling can provide them with the information they need to make the right choice. Selling must be customer focused.

### THE KEYS TO SUCCESS

A well-informed salesperson is the most successful selling tool available to the fashion industry. In fashion and in all consumer goods industries, nothing can happen until someone makes a sale. The textile manufacturer is soon out of business if the fabric does not sell, and a designer must have buyers in order to thrive. Finding the keys to making a sale is an art, and keeping loyal, repeat customers is the way to make a fashion business succeed.

The retail sale of high-fashion items to an individual is a very personal sales transaction. Salespersons in high-fashion stores are sometimes given special titles, such as fashion coordinator or personal shopper. They are usually paid based on a percentage of what they sell, called a **commission**. The salespeople are extensively trained and spend a considerable amount of time getting to know their merchandise and their customers. The outstanding salespeople at stores like Neiman-Marcus and Saks Fifth Avenue can make salaries in excess of $100,000 per year.

Training is important to all salespeople. Fashion manufacturers sometimes send sales specialists to assist in training salespeople who will work in the departments where their brand is sold.

Knowing the customer is a critical part of being a professional fashion salesperson. The professional salesperson keeps a record of the customer's size, color preferences, favorite brands, previous purchases, and important events coming up in the customer's life, like a wedding or party. This information can be used to personalize sales and provide quality service. Often, professional relationships develop with the clients who are provided trusted recommendations about the right fashions for them. In short, the customer is treated as an individual in a comfortable and welcoming environment.

CYBER MARKETING

Some girls dread trying to find the perfect pair of jeans. They imagine visiting multiple stores to find the right brand, color, pocket arrangement, and leg shape, only to find their size missing. For those for whom this search sounds like punishment, Lands' End online has a perfect fit. Lands' End Custom™ uses technology to customize jeans to the purchaser's specifications. Customers answer questions and make choices on the web page. The information is stored so the customer can reorder without re-entering all of the information.

**THINK CRITICALLY**
**1.** What customer might be most attracted to this web site?
**2.** Why would Lands' End provide this service?

# TRY IT ON

**Why is sales an important function of marketing?**

_____

_____

_____

_____

# THE STEPS

SELLING

**S**uccessful fashion salespeople know the special features of the garments available and stay current on what is being shown in fashion magazines. They help their customers look good for every occasion in garments and colors that flatter their body types and skin tones.

## ANATOMY OF A SALE

The sales process can be broken down into steps that can be practiced ahead of time.

- **Preapproach**  Before making contact with the customer, the fashion salesperson must have knowledge of the clothing for sale and the intended potential customers. Are they looking for value, or do they want the latest fashion with no regard for price?

- **Approach**  Approaching a customer with the same old question, "May I help you?," assures a negative answer. However, no single comment is appropriate for every customer. Some people need time to look, so a salesperson must judge when to make the approach. Acknowledging the person with a greeting is one place to start.

- **Determine the Need**  Customers make themselves available to salespeople for a reason. The advertising or display of merchandise has drawn the customer into the store, but now human contact is needed. Listen for signals of the customer's needs.

- **Demonstrate**  This is the time to show benefits of the product to the customer. Some garments require information and assistance, such as how to tie a wrap blouse so it looks great on the customer. This is a salesperson's chance to personalize the product features for the consumer. Having customers try on garments, adding the right accessories to finish the look, and letting customers see themselves in a three-way mirror can move the sale toward closure.

- **Answer Questions**  The customer may want to clarify information provided about the specific product. This is a time when the salesperson can gain the confidence of the customer.

- **Close the Sale**  The salesperson has an opportunity to make it easy for the customer to buy the product, but not pressure the customer, by asking if the customer will be paying with a credit card.

- **Suggest**  An offer of additional related items, called **suggestion selling**, can improve the customer's satisfaction and increase the size of the sale. This is the time to offer additional items, such as the accessories shown during the demonstration.

- **Follow Up**  A contact after the sale can bring customers back when they are ready to buy again. Customers can be mailed thank-you notes and notified when new items of their favorite brands are on sale.

Retailers are seeking ways to make sure they have the right sales approach for minority shoppers, a growing segment of the population in the United States. Pamela Macklin, fashion director of *Essence Magazine,* believes African-Americans buy clothing to show they are part of a lifestyle and have the income to support it. Research by Cotton Inc.'s Lifestyle Monitor™ found that minorities rated sales associates as a major influence when buying clothes.

True selling is much more than merely taking orders or operating a cash register. Selling assists customers in finding satisfaction with their purchases and provides them a level of comfort that will assure their return.

# TRY IT ON

**Why would a salesperson follow up with a customer after a sale?**

_____

_____

_____

## TrendSetters

### MARY WELLS LAWRENCE

As the first female chief executive officer of a company listed on the New York Stock Exchange, Mary Wells Lawrence is an advertising legend. In April 2002, *Women's Wear Daily* headlined an article about Wells entitled "The Queen of Madison Avenue." Madison Avenue is a street in New York City where many major advertising agencies are headquartered.

After college, Lawrence started her career as an advertising copywriter at department stores and moved on to Doyle Dane Bernbach (DDB), a major Madison Avenue advertising firm. While working at DDB, she quickly rose through the ranks by developing very successful ad campaigns. Five years later, she joined Jack Tinker and Partners agency and helped send that firm to the top with her famous ads.

Lawrence is most famous for literally making Braniff Airlines fashionable. She hired Italian designer Emilio Pucci to use fashions to remake the image of its flight attendants. Pucci designed high-fashion wardrobes that were layered, and the flight attendants shed layers during flights. Other designers were hired to decorate the planes and the airline terminal areas. Lawrence is credited with moving a stuffy, boring airline into a marketing success.

After being told that a woman could not be president of Tinker because the world was not ready for it, Lawrence quit and opened her own agency, Wells Rich Greene. It reached a level of $100 million in accounts within five years. Lawrence is credited with revolutionizing advertising.

#### THINK CRITICALLY
**1.** Could Mary Wells Lawrence have succeeded if she had started her own company right after college? Why or why not?
**2.** What personal characteristics made Lawrence successful?

## UNDERSTAND MARKETING CONCEPTS
Circle the best answer for each of the following questions.

**1.** Suggestion selling is
   **a.** a way of advertising.
   **b.** offering additional related items.
   **c.** a type of style.
   **d.** a luxury item.

**2.** When a salesperson is paid a percentage of sales, it is called
   **a.** distribution.
   **b.** information.
   **c.** a commission.
   **d.** planning.

## THINK CRITICALLY
Answer the following questions as completely as possible. If necessary, use a separate sheet of paper.

**3.** Contact a local retail store manager and ask about the training provided to sales staff at the store. Write a paragraph about the information you obtain and share it with the class.

_____

_____

_____

_____

_____

**4.** Why is it important for sales staff to know details about the merchandise before the customer arrives in the store?

_____

_____

_____

_____

_____

_____

# CHAPTER 6 REVIEW

## REVIEW MARKETING CONCEPTS

**Write the letter of the term that matches each definition. Some terms will not be used.**

_____ **1.** Payment as a percentage of sales

_____ **2.** Establishing an identity or image for a line of apparel

_____ **3.** An informal fashion show held inside a store to promote one brand of clothing

_____ **4.** Paid communication between the product maker or seller and the customer

_____ **5.** Offering additional related items

_____ **6.** A percentage paid to retailers by vendors for cooperative ads

_____ **7.** Includes an invitation, a typed news article, and information about the best time to take photos

**a.** advertising allowance
**b.** brand building
**c.** commission
**d.** cooperative advertising
**e.** fashion advertising
**f.** infomercials
**g.** persuasive language
**h.** press kit
**i.** product features
**j.** special events
**k.** suggestion selling
**l.** trunk show

**Circle the best answer.**

**8.** Two of the costs of advertisements are
   **a.** selling and buying.
   **b.** production and media.
   **c.** promotion and purchasing.
   **d.** none of these.

**9.** In a free-enterprise system,
   **a.** consumers are free to buy what they choose.
   **b.** prices are fixed.
   **c.** sellers decide what is sold.
   **d.** planning is centralized.

**10.** An infomercial is a
   **a.** type of finance.
   **b.** method of distribution.
   **c.** planning tool.
   **d.** commercial the length of a regular TV show.

**11.** Fashion special events include
   **a.** trunk shows and fundraisers.
   **b.** fashion awards and infomercials.
   **c.** fashion shows.
   **d.** all of these.

# THINK CRITICALLY

POINT YOUR BROWSER

fashion.swlearning.com

**12.** In pairs, discuss why establishing brands is important to fashion marketers. Write a list of the advantages to the fashion marketers and a separate list of advantages to consumers.

_____

_____

_____

_____

**13.** In pairs, discuss a theme for a fundraising event for a food bank. The event will be held in conjunction with the opening of a new fashion boutique. Write down at least three potential themes to attract three different target groups.

_____

_____

_____

_____

**14.** Describe the difference between a commercial advertisement and an infomercial.

_____

_____

_____

**15.** In a group, brainstorm ideas for what to say to a customer during the sales approach in a retail store. Write down the list and share it with the class.

_____

_____

_____

_____

# MAKE CONNECTIONS

**16. Marketing Math**  You have an advertising budget of $6,000 to advertise a new brand of shorts and T-shirts for people over age 40. You want to advertise on television. A 30-second ad costs $200 appearing at 9:00 a.m., $1,000 appearing at 6:00 p.m., and $800 appearing at 10:00 p.m. The number of viewers over age 40 at each time slot is 5,000, 40,000, and 20,000, respectively. What combination of 30-second time slots will you use and why? How many viewers in the target group will see the ad?

_____

_____

_____

_____

**17. Sociology**  Write a paragraph on how you feel about fashion marketers using ads to promote social causes.

_____

_____

_____

_____

_____

_____

_____

**18. Technology**  In pairs, make a list of ways to attract teens to fashion web sites. Share the list with the class.

_____

_____

_____

_____

_____

_____

_____

## FASHION MERCHANDISING PROMOTION PLAN

www.deca.org
/publications/HS_
Guide/guidetoc.html

You are challenged to create a promotion plan for a fashion merchandising store. Working with a group, you must organize and prepare a budget for promotional events throughout the year. Your plan must include double-spaced, outlined promotional fact sheets. You will sell the plan to the store's owners (i.e., your classmates) in an oral presentation. They will vote on which plan is the best for use by the store.

The body of the written plan must be limited to ten numbered pages, not including the title page. The oral presentation will be a maximum of 20 minutes (15 minutes for presentation and defense of the promotion plan and five minutes for a question-and-answer period). Participants will be evaluated for communication, analytical and critical thinking, production, time management, and budgeting skills. Fact sheets must include

1. Description of the store
2. Objectives of the promotional campaign
3. Schedule of events (promotional activities)
   a. special events (fashion shows, demonstrations, etc.)
   b. advertising
   c. displays
   d. publicity
   e. other in-store activities
4. Responsibility sheet (assigned positions and activities)
5. Budget
6. Statement of benefits to the retail establishment

# PROJECT: The COLLECTION POINT

Plan a fashion show as a fundraiser in collaboration with a retail store and a local nonprofit group. The show may be either formal or informal. You will either sell tickets or ask for donations from those who attend. Members of the class or others in your school, including teachers and the principal, can be asked to model. Also consider asking local celebrities, such as the mayor or a local sports hero, to model.

**Work with a group and complete the following activities.**

1. Reread and follow the planning steps found in Lesson 6.2.
2. Create a spreadsheet to use as the planning tool for the show.
3. Be creative in thinking of ways to get the audience to attend.
4. Try to get all materials and components donated, so any funds raised can go to the nonprofit cause.
5. Write an evaluation of the effectiveness of the project and what you would do differently next time.

# CHAPTER *7*

# USING TECHNOLOGY IN FASHION MARKETING

## LESSONS

7.1 PRODUCTION PROCESSES

7.2 RESEARCH AND TECHNOLOGY

7.3 DISTRIBUTION TECHNOLOGY

# WINNING STRATEGIES

## LECTRA

Lectra is a global technology company that provides software and equipment to apparel, textile, and home furnishing manufacturers and retailers. Lectra uses computer-aided design (CAD) and computer-aided manufacturing (CAM), 3-D technology, and the Internet to provide complete solutions for apparel producers and marketers.

Lectra was founded in France in 1973 and within 15 years became one of the world's leading CAD/CAM equipment producers for the apparel industry. The company has four divisions: e-design, e-sales, e-manufacturing solutions, and LectraOnline Exchange. Each division is set up to meet the needs of a particular business activity, from design to sale of apparel.

The e-design division allows designers to virtually create a garment without having to make a prototype (model of the garment) out of fabric. The e-sales division can make virtual presentations of fashion collections to help sell the garments prior to production. The e-manufacturing solutions division addresses automation of production, inventory, and ordering. LectraOnline Exchange allows manufacturers to connect with all of the companies and individuals involved in production, no matter where in the world they are located.

### THINK CRITICALLY

1. Why might a designer want to make a virtual garment instead of a fabric prototype to see how it will look and fit?
2. How might technology help designers and manufacturers save time and money?

# CHAPTER 7
## Lesson 7.1

# PRODUCTION PROCESSES

**List** the steps of garment production, from design to finished product.

**Identify** the impact of technology on apparel production.

## The Latest Style

A California state agency, the Employment Training Panel (ETP), is working with Santa Monica College to support local fashion manufacturing. Participating companies send their employees to train on knitting machines in classes offered through the community college, while the ETP pays the instructors' salaries and purchases class supplies. A local custom knitwear company, French Rags, provides access to knitting machines that are used for the training. The skilled knitwear operators who learn how to program the machines earn salaries between $75,000 and $100,000 per year.

The joint effort to train more skilled employees is intended to boost the apparel industry in California. California has lost manufacturing business of low-priced, mass-produced garments to other countries with lower standards of living and low wages.

Work with a group. Discuss why it would be beneficial for the fashion industry to work together to train more high-skilled employees. Make a list of possible benefits to the industry.

## GARMENT PRODUCTION

Creating apparel, from the original design to the finished product, is a complex process even with today's technology. Clothing construction is a labor-intensive process because it means turning two-dimensional fabric into a form that fits a three-dimensional, nonuniform body. The mass production of garments must also meet a quality level that coincides with the price point of the garment.

### STEP BY STEP

The design, price point, fabric, and certainly the quality and quantity of the garment that is being produced all affect the path that it will follow. The manufacturing steps detailed here are a general guide for a moderately priced, mass-produced garment.

**MARKETING-INFORMATION MANAGEMENT**

**Research** Using marketing information, wise apparel designers will know what target customers are currently buying and have purchased in previous seasons, and they will use this and other data to project trends. Trends for moderately priced garments do not change dramatically overnight. They head in a direction not far from the previous season's trends, but with a new touch.

**Design** A manufacturer can choose to modify an existing style. A garment that has been a best-seller can reappear with a few modifications in fabric, color, or detail. The manufacturer can also choose to go with an entirely new design. It is expensive and time-consuming to create a new design, and it is also more risky.

**Cost** The price point, function, and size range for target customers will influence the quality of fabric, findings, and construction. An estimate of the cost to produce the garment will determine if the design is cost-effective for mass production. The production manager and the designer must come to agreement on quality and cost specifications, and some compromises may have to be made. Once the garment specifications are finalized, a more accurate **bill of materials** will list the component parts of the garment and their costs.

**Source** *Sourcing* means selecting the provider of materials and the contractors who will mass produce the garments. Seldom can a designer handle all of the production processes in house. Businesses that specialize in production are hired to do the work.

**Prepare** To prepare for production, a model of the garment, called a **prototype**, is developed. A **fit model**, a person who is representative of the target customer, tries on the garment for the designer to see the final look and fit. A **production pattern**, the pattern shape of each piece of a garment, is then prepared for mass production. The detail of the technical specifications, construction techniques, stitching, and sizing of the garment are determined. A *size and measurement table* is developed that specifies the exact measurements for each garment size to be produced.

A **marker** is the plan that shows how the pattern pieces will be placed on the fabric for its most efficient use—the goal being to use the least amount of fabric possible. Pattern placement can be a quality and cost struggle. If the pattern is laid off slightly to save fabric, a design on the fabric may run crooked or the garment may hang unevenly.

While all of this is taking place, there must be communication with *downstream* key personnel to track the progress of the garment and notify people of any changes in plans or timing. Having all of the materials arrive just when they are needed is the goal. If they arrive too soon, storage costs will add to the expense of the garment. Late arrival can cause wasted time and, ultimately, lost sales.

The Tommy Hilfiger web site, **www.tommy.com**, has more than 3.2 million unique visitors each year, of which 440,000 are registered users who belong to the CLUB-tommy fan club. The web site features a live chat room where Hilfiger occasionally appears, a fashion horoscope called "style-scope," and photos of people who attend events sponsored by Hilfiger.

**THINK CRITICALLY** Who besides the designer might be featured in a designer's live chat room to attract visitors?

**Produce** Actual production of garments begins with spreading the fabric. **Spreading** is layering fabric on a table so that the marker can be placed on top. There may be as many as 500 layers of fabric that are spread, depending on the type of fabric, quantity of garments, and cutting process to be used. After cutting around the pattern pieces, the pieces are bundled and sent to assembly areas.

*Assembly* is the actual sewing of the garment and may take place in several different locations or countries. The labels are sewn in, and the garments are inspected for quality. Other steps may take place, such as *wet processing*, which includes prewashing or bleaching as in the case of jeans. Pressing the garment and trimming the threads are the final steps of assembly. Reputable manufacturers will do a final quality inspection before packaging and shipping.

## TRY IT ON

**Why is it necessary for fashion marketers to know what target customers are currently buying?**

_____

_____

_____

# TECHNOLOGY IMPACTS

**PRODUCT/ SERVICE MANAGEMENT**

Technology impacts every step of apparel production. Leading-edge garment manufacturers and support companies are developing technological advances every year that cut the time it takes to manufacture and deliver garments. Delivering garments to the retailer in a timely manner is critical to maintaining a low cost of production and to hitting the retail store before peak selling time has ended.

## MASS PRODUCTION

Garment manufacturers use technology throughout the production process.

**CAD** Instead of hand sketching garments, designers use *computer-aided design (CAD)* systems. A previously used design that has been a best-seller can be updated electronically. Virtual prototypes are created with CAD software to show new design details or a new fabric and color. The design is converted by the system into a pattern for a prototype, and pattern pieces are developed for a real sample garment to be shown to buyers for retail stores. These steps, which previously required days, now take only hours or minutes.

**Cost Control** Cost control is critical to the life of a garment manufacturer. The most competitive pricing sources can be found and compared using software designed for apparel producers. Utilizing this technology in the planning stages can help a designer balance creativity with costs.

**Communication** Communication with sources and contractors can happen instantly with the Internet and software developed for the production process. All of the people involved in the development process, inside and outside of the company, can share information and technical specifications as well as track progress. This kind of communication helps improve productivity as well as control quality throughout the process, especially when key people are spread around the globe.

**Production** Garment production has become highly automated. As many as 500 layers of cloth can be cut accurately with today's advanced *computer-aided manufacturing (CAM)* systems. Computer-guided lasers cut the fabric while vacuum tables use suction to hold the fabric in place. CAM equipment can also print bar-coded labels and place them on the cut pieces. Optical readers scan the labels during the sorting and bundling process, thus eliminating errors.

## CUSTOMIZATION

Technology has increased productivity tremendously for mass-produced apparel items. Technology has also made it efficient to customize apparel. Small quantities of a garment can be produced because quick and efficient adjustments can be electronically made for special orders. Small runs of garment construction were not previously cost-effective. Now when a store needs a dozen shirts in blue, it can have them instead of having to order a hundred.

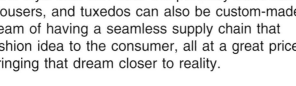

Custom-made clothing may seem like a flashback to a previous time, but digital tailoring brings the process to today's market. At Brooks Brothers in Manhattan, a computer scans more than 200,000 points on a man's body to take precise measurements. The information is captured to create a three-dimensional picture used to design a custom-made suit. For about $100 more than an off-the-rack suit, a man can select the fabric, color, and style and can wear the perfectly fitted suit within 15 days. Shirts, trousers, and tuxedos can also be custom-made.

Fashion marketers dream of having a seamless supply chain that moves quickly from a fashion idea to the consumer, all at a great price. Today's technology is bringing that dream closer to reality.

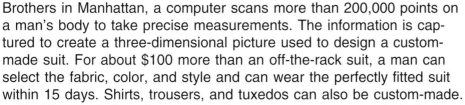

**Name three ways technology has improved apparel production.**

_____

_____

_____

_____

## UNDERSTAND MARKETING CONCEPTS

Circle the best answer for each of the following questions.

**1.** The major steps in apparel production are
 **a.** style, pricing, quality, and category.
 **b.** fabric, findings, stitching, and detail.
 **c.** spreading, prototype, sourcing, marker, and assembly.
 **d.** research, design, cost, source, prepare, and produce.

**2.** The software system used by designers to create drawings of apparel is
 **a.** CAD.
 **b.** CAM.
 **c.** spread.
 **d.** marker.

## THINK CRITICALLY

Answer the following questions as completely as possible. If necessary, use a separate sheet of paper.

**3. Research** Visit the web site for the Garment Industry Development Corporation at **www.gidc.org**. Write a brief description of this organization based on information found at the web site.

_____

_____

_____

_____

_____

**4. Economics** Why does it cost more to produce apparel in the United States than in Mexico or China?

_____

_____

_____

_____

_____

_____

# RESEARCH AND TECHNOLOGY

## The Latest Style

Sneaker freaks are people obsessed with collecting sneakers, and they are the subjects of research by major sneaker makers like Nike, Adidas, and Puma. Revivals of past styles and limited releases of special colors have created a demand by collectors for high-priced sneakers ranging from $125 to $590.

Nike does sneaker freak research at Kbond in Los Angeles and Alife Rivington Club in the Lower East Side of Manhattan. Both are tiny boutiques that cater to the "couturization" of a common product. More than 10,000 people visit the Niketalk web site at **www.niketalk.com**, which operates like a fan site for Nike. Using data gathered at the site and the boutiques, Nike has become a fashion-oriented business.

Research has shown that customers react more favorably to fashion over function. Consequently, the sneaker makers have shifted their emphasis from athletic functionality to the pop-styling of their products. Adidas hired designer Yohji Yamamoto to design its line of chic shoes, and Puma hired Jil Sanders.

Work with a group. Discuss how manufacturers can stay ahead of teen trends. Suggest ways that a manufacturer can obtain feedback from teens.

**GOALS**

**Describe** research trends in fashion marketing.

**Explain** the importance of emerging technologies in inventory management.

# ELECTRONIC LINKS

**MARKETING-INFORMATION MANAGEMENT**

Technology has changed the way research and data collection for marketing information are completed. In the past, retail buyers depended on manual counts of merchandise and intuition about what might sell. Today, with fierce competition for consumers' purchasing power, buyers use data gathered instantly from every retail transaction.

## RESEARCH AND PROJECTIONS

Part of a retail buyer's job is to obtain research data on what has sold in order to make projections for what needs to be purchased for the future or marked down now to gain sales. The quantity of garments sold is not nearly enough information. The complete picture of what is selling needs to include colors, sizes, styles, vendors, and price lines. Using bar-coded tags, data is collected upon receipt of items into the store and again at the point of sale.

In Federated Department Stores during the early 1970s, price tags were coded with data about the garment by numbers and holes punched into the tag. The series of numbers and corresponding holes provided information that included the vendor, the style, the season the garment was brought into the store, the color of the garment, and the department in which it was sold. The tags were divided in half, with identical information on the top and bottom halves. One-half of the tag was torn off at a perforated line when the garment was sold. The tags were collected from the sales floor and sent to a data-processing department where the holes were read by a computerized system and the data was printed into a report. The reports, which came back weeks later, were used to analyze sales. The data was slow in arriving, inaccurate and inadequate, and did not take returned items into account. Since this was all that was available, buyers continued to rely on physical counts of a particular item to see if it had sold.

**THINK CRITICALLY**
How has technology changed the availability of data in the past 30+ years?

**Bar codes** are the optically scanned lines that contain the garment's Uniform Product Code (UPC). The code provides information about the garment, including the vendor and the vendor's production number. The bar codes, in many cases, are used instead of a retailer's own separate stock-keeping units (SKU) number. This allows the garment to be priced by the manufacturer so that it is ready to sell the instant it arrives at the store.

Standards for bar codes and other product specifications allow suppliers and retailers to transmit data to each other, which speeds the reaction time for forecasting and replenishing merchandise. As the use of information technology increases, there is a constant need across the fashion industry to standardize the way data is collected and reported, making it easier to share between suppliers and retailers.

## INFORMATION TECHNOLOGY

Capturing, analyzing, and disseminating information about consumers is a major use of technology in fashion marketing. Making complete use of the information to plan, forecast, and manage customer relations is a challenge of technology yet to be fully developed.

When Sears purchased Lands' End, it gained access to Lands' End's upscale customer database in addition to its clothing and accessories. The companies both used the same web-imaging technology, so merging the *back-end* activities, such as ordering and receiving, was simple.

Privacy concerns remain a source of controversy in relation to the collection of customer data. Customers tend to rebel against the use or sale of data collected about their purchasing habits. Technology makes it easy to capture customer behavior and then use the information to target advertising messages, but the collected data must be used carefully or customers could be scared away from the business.

Using technology to obtain, analyze, and then act on data has become much easier. Using the research to make good decisions still requires the intuition of a savvy marketer with the experience to properly interpret the information.

# TRY IT ON

**How has the use of bar codes increased efficiency in the fashion industry?**

_____

_____

_____

_____

# INVENTORY CONTROL

**PRODUCT/
SERVICE
MANAGEMENT**

The process of selling out old stock and bringing new garments into a retail store is called **inventory turnover**. With today's technology, retailers can have real-time, two-way inventory data exchange with suppliers, providing for a constant flow of new merchandise as items are sold. Finding ways to share data with suppliers is critical to the process and calls for collaboration. Sharing information can help improve and accelerate inventory turnover.

## THE BASICS

Most fashion styles have a short life cycle, making reordering unusual. However, a few basic apparel items, such as underwear and socks, have long life cycles and are reordered constantly. Styles of basics sometimes last for years and are restocked on a regular basis, similar to items in a grocery store. Retailers are under considerable pressure to increase margins per square foot of selling space, and being out of stock on basic items can lead to lost sales.

Maintaining stock levels can be simplified with the use of technology that connects the inventory and point-of-sale (POS) data to the supplier. This connection allows the use of **just-in-time inventory**, meaning that garments are received at the time they are needed, not early or late. Early arrivals must be stored and moved by people who could be doing more productive activity. Late-arriving merchandise can make customers unhappy, which can lead to reduced sales.

There is a trend toward **vendor-managed inventory** by many retailers. Under this system, the manufacturer decides how much of a product the retailer needs based on POS data. Vendor-managed inventory is currently used by many grocery stores and mass merchandiser for items that have long life cycles, but it will require a change in thinking on the part of fashion retailers and vendors.

The Electronic Retailing Association has a code of ethics for its members. The members pledge that they will be honest and fair in dealing with customers, suppliers, employees, and fellow members. The specifics of the code include complying with all laws, honoring warranties and addressing customer complaints, making accurate statements, fulfilling contracts, refraining from offensive conduct such as discrimination, staying informed about legislative changes, and supporting free enterprise. The code is followed voluntarily by members.

**THINK CRITICALLY**
**1.** Why would an association of retailers develop a code of ethics?
**2.** Why would members comply?

The variations in clothing sizes, and consequently returned items, are a major problem for online fashion merchants. Customers cannot try on clothing ahead of time, and returns are estimated at 10 to 50 percent of sales as a result of items not fitting properly. Some products, such as men's ties or socks, aren't subject to size problems, but many clothing sizes are not fully standardized.

## MARKDOWNS

SELLING

According to the National Retail Federation's web site at **www.nrf.com,** the percentage of sales that comes from markdowns has increased from 8 percent to 20 percent in the past 30 years. Reducing the price of a garment in order to increase sales can be expensive. Most retailers lose from 5 to 30 percent of potential revenue to markdowns. Improving that number can make a big difference in profits.

The decision of when and by how much to mark down an item must be based on accurate data. Markdowns of true fashion items with short life cycles create a real dilemma for the retailer. Marking the items down too soon results in a loss of potential revenue, but letting them grow stale ties up funds and eats up inventory space. **Markdown optimization** is a process that involves careful analysis of what is being marked down by vendor, style, size, and color in order to limit the need for future markdowns. The process can be quickly accomplished with software programs designed for this purpose.

## SCAN IT

Shoppers at mass retailers that have centralized checkout stands can have their items quickly scanned by a hand-held device used by a sales associate. Customers at the upscale Prada store in Manhattan can have sales associates check to see if a specific size is in stock by using

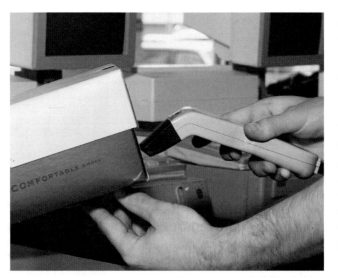

hand-held devices to scan a garment's tags. Apparel tags may also be scanned as a shopper enters the dressing room, allowing the customer to check out other sizes or matching accessories on a touch screen within the dressing room. This technology brings new convenience to customers.

## TRY IT ON

**Why must the percentage of markdowns be controlled?**

_____

_____

_____

_____

## UNDERSTAND MARKETING CONCEPTS

Circle the best answer for each of the following questions.

1. When the manufacturer makes the decision about how much of a product the retailer needs to stock, it is called
   a. markdown optimization.
   b. just-in-time inventory.
   c. vendor-managed inventory.
   d. inventory turnover.

2. Selling out old stock and replacing it with new merchandise is known as
   a. inventory turnover.
   b. markdowns.
   c. vendor-managed inventory.
   d. retailing.

## THINK CRITICALLY

Answer the following questions as completely as possible. If necessary, use a separate sheet of paper.

3. Why do customers have privacy concerns about data collected by fashion marketers?

   _____

   _____

   _____

   _____

4. **Communication** Write a paragraph about the technology changes of retail stores in your area. Discuss your ideas with a small group of students and compare your thoughts.

   _____

   _____

   _____

   _____

   _____

# CHAPTER 7
## Lesson 7.3

# DISTRIBUTION TECHNOLOGY

## GOALS

**Explain** the need for standards in the fashion industry.

**Describe** the impact of emerging technologies on fashion marketing.

## The Latest Style

**B**lue Nile, Inc. doesn't have brick-and-mortar stores, and it only has 10,000 square feet of warehouse space. Even so, it had over $1.1 million in operating profit in its second year of operation! Blue Nile sells fine jewelry entirely online. The average sales price for Blue Nile products is more than $1,000, but the costs for shipping and handling are small.

Blue Nile capitalizes on some men's anxiety about making large jewelry purchases, such as engagement rings, and caters to that hesitation. Customers can spend all the time needed shopping the web page and can even call and talk to customer sales representatives who are low key and don't work on commission.

There are only 80 people employed by Blue Nile. Because of its low operating expenses, the company can offer tremendous prices that are 20 to 40 percent below that offered in a retail jewelry store.

Work with a group. Discuss why small, expensive fashion items might sell well using the Internet. Make a list of other fashion products that might do well online.

# ZIPPING THROUGH

**DISTRIBUTION**

**Q**uickly moving fashions from the production process to the consumer's closet increases the potential for profit across the industry. Fashion marketers are always seeking efficient processes that will shorten the apparel pipeline. This effort has brought about industry improvements, including standardization of information and protocols for data exchange and collaborative communication between suppliers and retailers.

## CLASSIFICATION STANDARDS

Standards for product classification codes are necessary to help identify the products for suppliers, retailers, and the U.S. Customs Service. If a product is to be imported, it must be classified by the U.S. Customs Service to determine the tariff rate under which it will enter the United States. A **tariff** is a tax on goods being brought into or exported out of the United States. Garments are generally classified at the preparation stage so that delivery to the retailer is not delayed. The exact specifications, including a sketch of the garment and a photo of the fabric, are sent electronically to the U.S. Customs Service. This information is used to assign the tariff classification based on current laws and tariffs. This technology-enhanced process speeds up distribution.

## VOLUNTARY STANDARDS

Product standards systems have been developed by the *Voluntary Interindustry Commerce Standards (VICS) Association*, a nonprofit organization with members from textile, manufacturing, and retail fashion businesses. VICS states its mission as "improvement of the flow of product and information about the product throughout the entire supply chain in the retail industry." The *supply chain* includes everyone involved in the fashion process, from supplier to manufacturer to wholesaler to retailer to consumer.

VICS has developed guidelines for **floor-ready merchandise**—garments that are ready for immediate sale when received by the retailer. "Floor ready" can mean on a hanger with price tags already attached so that the retailer can quickly move the garments to the right department or branch location. By using standards that are acceptable to retailers, floor-ready preparation becomes part of the production process rather than a time-consuming task of the retailer. Reducing time to move garments to the consumer means improved productivity and cost savings.

VICS has worked within the fashion industry to develop guidelines for apparel product identification using the Uniform Product Code (UPC), a protocol for electronic data interchange, to employ bar codes for shipping and raw materials identification. *Electronic data interchange (EDI)* is a standard for businesses to exchange information with other businesses, known as peer-to-peer communication. As early as 1987, EDI was used to exchange purchase orders between suppliers and retailers.

The *Uniform Code Council (UCC)* is a nonprofit organization that serves as the management and administrative arm of VICS. UCC manages UPC code numbers and is involved in the ongoing development of international standards for electronic business communication. The most recent standards to impact fashion marketing are the Collaborative Planning, Forecasting, and Replenishment® (CPFR) standards. CPFR is a well-documented, nine-step process developed and maintained by VICS to allow members of the supply chain to seamlessly interact.

**What is VICS and what does it do?**

# EMERGING TECHNOLOGY

Technology-based changes in fashion marketing are happening rapidly. The industry is constantly looking for ways to become more efficient. Mass producers are finding new ways to automate production, but a trend to watch is technology-based customization of products.

## SMART GARMENTS

Many designers and manufacturers are using technology to improve both products and profit margins by bringing new ideas to the marketplace. Motorola Inc. is developing garments that will "talk" to washing machines to provide instructions on how they should be washed. Levi Strauss and Dutch electronics firm Phillips NV have created a jacket that has an MP3 player, a cellular phone, a headset, and a remote control device all built into the garment. The water-resistant outdoor jacket is available for sale in Europe. DuPont Co. has developed fibers that are shaped to contract or expand depending on what the wearer desires. At Nano-Tex, a San Francisco company, researchers wear the same socks every day to play basketball. The socks have been engineered to absorb foot odor and release it only when washed. Sensatec Inc., a New York company, has made a "smart shirt" that looks and feels like a T-shirt, but can monitor heart rate and track body temperature. The information is transmitted and stored on a tiny computer the size of a credit card that is worn at the waist. Mass producing and marketing these smart garments may take even more innovation.

## E-COMMERCE

After the dot-com bombs of the early 2000s, the use of the Internet as a marketplace for fashion was slowed, but e-commerce has not gone away. It has changed and continues to grow in a more mature manner.

VICS developed voluntary standards for e-commerce exchanges and published them in 1998. VICS has since updated the standards as the Internet has become a more fundamental component of business.

## CYBER MARKETING

At **www.unitedvirtualities.com**, a unique online advertising technology is shown. It is being used to create ads for fashion marketers like Ann Taylor. The technology, called a *Shoshkele*™, is attracting some real attention. A Shoshkele is not irritating like a pop-up ad and does not require any action on the part of the viewer. In the Ann Taylor ad, clothing items float across the web page one piece at a time to dress a model shown in a rectangular ad that otherwise might go unnoticed. The viewer can then click on the items for more information, but the ad does not take over the page. A Shoshkele works automatically on almost all computer systems.

**THINK CRITICALLY**
Why would an amusing ad be more effective than a strobe-blinking, pop-up ad?

**DISTRIBUTION**

**Bargain Hunters** Some people would not think of eBay, the Internet auction site, as a fashion site, but eBay sold more than $500 million in apparel in the first year of the site's apparel division. About 50 percent of the apparel sold on eBay is new. The other half is gently used.

EBay advertises in *Women's Wear Daily* as an outlet for retailers' and manufacturers' excess or outdated inventory. The primary sellers on eBay are small- and medium-sized retailers, wholesalers, and liquidators. **Liquidators** are businesses that purchase closeouts of excess inventory.

Although eBay does not usually have a lot of articles on its web site, it has hired a stylist to write a column called "Fashion Trends." Highlighted words in the column are interactive links that take the customer to the live auction for related items. EBay is also simplifying shopping by classifying clothing into themes—Designer Boutique, Fashion Outlet Mall, Country and Western, and Everything Wedding. The Designer Boutique area lists garments by luxury fabrics and by high-end designers in alphabetical order. The Fashion Outlet Mall area has well-known brands divided into women's, men's, girls', boys', and infants' clothing. The web site is expected to become a major player in fashion distribution, with big-name players jumping into the business to gain access to the 46 million registered eBay users.

**Electronic Fashion Business** E-commerce has allowed fashion merchants to provide customers with access to items that would otherwise be unavailable to them. It has also created opportunities for individuals to start fashion businesses and have a customer base that far exceeds that available to a local store.

Finding and filling a niche for fashion distribution is one way to become successful using the Internet. At a web site that specializes in fine lingerie for voluptuous and plus-size women, company president Lisa Judson has found a definite niche in the fashion distribution chain. Working from her home with the inventory stacked in the living room, Judson operates **www.feelpretty.com**. She believes that plus-size women are embarrassed to go into a department store and ask for their size lingerie. If a store even carries the size range, it is usually not on

Wal-Mart® removed apparel from its Internet site in April 2001, even though it was one of the better-selling categories of online merchandise. Wal-Mart discontinued online clothing sales because the handling costs and low price lines of its apparel made each sale too expensive. Wal-Mart is looking for ways to sell clothing online at a reasonable profit margin.

display but is kept hidden in drawers. Online shoppers at feelpretty.com can shop in the privacy of their homes and find more than just a basic style of lingerie. Sleepwear and accessories are also offered. Yahoo!, the Internet portal site, rates feelpretty.com as a five-star merchant, the highest rating given based on quality of merchandise and service received.

# TRY IT ON

**Why would big names in fashion marketing consider working with eBay to sell fashion?**

_____

_____

_____

## TrendSetters

### ONLINE PERSONAL SHOPPERS

Careers that use technology to solve fashion marketing problems are growing. Robert LoCascio, founder and CEO of LivePerson, recognized the opportunity to provide a solution for e-commerce fashion sites where people were leaving without purchasing. LoCascio recognized that people needed answers they weren't getting. LivePerson allows the customer to communicate by phone, e-mail, or instant chat mode with a personal shopper at the e-commerce business.

LivePerson keeps count as customers visit such high-end retailers as NeimanMarcus.com. _USA Today_ quoted Neiman Marcus personal shopper David Isaacs as saying he has a customer to whom he sells at least $2,000 of merchandise every month. The customer's online purchases include a ball gown with matching shoes and handbag. The customer lives only ten minutes from a Neiman Marcus store, but chooses to shop online.

Tony Ruiz, a personal shopper for **www.Nordstrom.com**, told _USA Today_ that it makes her "feel really good at the end of an order when they take it all," after she has made suggestions for purchases. Online personal shoppers make shopping convenient and personal and answers readily available.

#### THINK CRITICALLY
**1.** Why are personal shoppers successful?
**2.** Discuss with a partner other ways to make online shopping more convenient for customers.

## UNDERSTAND MARKETING CONCEPTS
Circle the best answer for each of the following questions.

**1.** Standards for product classification are needed to
   **a.** identify products.
   **b.** move products to market more quickly.
   **c.** know where products originated.
   **d.** achieve all of these.

**2.** Companies that handle closeouts of excess fashion inventory are
   **a.** sales professionals.
   **b.** sources.
   **c.** liquidators.
   **d.** markers.

## THINK CRITICALLY
Answer the following questions as completely as possible. If necessary, use a separate sheet of paper.

**3. Social Studies**   Why does the U.S. Customs Service care about fashion products? Why are there tariffs on certain fashion products?

_____

_____

_____

_____

_____

**4. Communication**   Write a paragraph about how e-commerce is used to successfully sell fashions. Include some information about what fashion items might best be suited to e-commerce.

_____

_____

_____

_____

_____

_____

_____

# CHAPTER 7 REVIEW

## REVIEW MARKETING CONCEPTS

**Write the letter of the term that matches each definition. Some terms will not be used.**

_____ **1.** A person representative of the size of the target customer

_____ **2.** Inventory that arrives when needed

_____ **3.** Optically scanned lines that contain the garment's Uniform Product Code (UPC)

_____ **4.** Layering fabric on a table so that the marker can be placed on top for cutting

_____ **5.** The process of selling out old stock and bringing in new items

_____ **6.** The plan for the layout that shows how all the pattern pieces will be placed on the fabric for its most efficient use

_____ **7.** A listing of the component parts of a garment and their costs

_____ **8.** A system in which the manufacturer decides how much of a product the retailer needs based on POS data

_____ **9.** Businesses that purchase closeouts

**a.** bar codes
**b.** bill of materials
**c.** fit model
**d.** floor-ready merchandise
**e.** inventory turnover
**f.** just-in-time inventory
**g.** liquidators
**h.** markdown optimization
**i.** marker
**j.** production pattern
**k.** prototype
**l.** spreading
**m.** tariff
**n.** vendor-managed inventory

**Circle the best answer.**

**10.** The acronym that describes manufacturing controlled by computers is
    **a.** MAC.
    **b.** CAM.
    **c.** SAM.
    **d.** MAS.

**11.** People involved in the later steps of fashion production are
    **a.** in the creek.
    **b.** out of touch.
    **c.** downstream.
    **d.** on the move.

**12.** Floor-ready merchandise is prepared for the sales floor by
    **a.** sales professionals.
    **b.** retail buyers.
    **c.** receiving clerks.
    **d.** the manufacturer.

# THINK CRITICALLY

**13.** Work with a group and list the steps in garment production. Write a brief description of each step.

POINT YOUR BROWSER

fashion.swlearning.com

_____

_____

_____

_____

_____

**14.** Describe how technology has changed the production of clothing. How has this impacted the time it takes garments to arrive at a store?

_____

_____

_____

_____

**15.** Some fashion items never seem to be marked down for quick clearance. Work with a partner and make a list of the types of fashion items that might not ever be marked down, and explain why.

_____

_____

_____

_____

_____

**16.** Why is the timing of the arrival of fashion items so important to a retail store?

_____

_____

_____

_____

_____

**CHAPTER 7 REVIEW**

## MAKE CONNECTIONS

**17. Marketing Math**   You want to produce 100 dresses that require two yards of fabric each, and you are looking at domestic as well as foreign sources for assembly. It will cost $10.00 per dress to have them assembled in the United States and $150.00 to transport all of them to the retail store. It will cost $6.00 each to have the dresses assembled in another country. There is a $1.00-per-yard-of-fabric import tariff on goods assembled in that country, and transportation will cost $3.50 for every ten dresses. Which is the less expensive location for assembly?

_____

_____

_____

_____

_____

_____

_____

**18. Economics**   Why is the United States losing garment manufacturing to other countries? Are U.S. consumers willing to pay more for clothing to keep jobs in the United States? Why or why not?

_____

_____

_____

_____

_____

**19. Technology**   Why are standards for data exchange important to fashion marketers?

_____

_____

_____

_____

_____

# RETAIL MERCHANDISING ASSOCIATE LEVEL ROLE PLAY

You are a sales associate for a local clothing store located in a shopping mall that has two nationally recognized department stores as anchors. Large department stores, outlet malls, and first-quality discount stores have made it increasingly difficult for your store to survive.

Most of the national department stores have their own credit cards to offer customers. Credit card customers are in a database and receive early notice of sales, special discount coupons, and other privileges. Your store will not offer a credit card, but the computerized cash registers allow sales associates to accumulate information about customers (name, address, birthday, and so forth).

The clothing store must have unique customer incentives to attract business away from the large department stores. Your manager has asked you to work with another sales associate to create a customer rewards program to show appreciation for customer loyalty. Your manager definitely wants an idea that recognizes customer birthdays.

Work with a partner and devise a plan for recognizing customer birthdays and at least four other promotional strategies. You will have ten minutes to present your ideas, and the manager (represented by the class) will have five additional minutes to ask questions.

# PROJECT: The COLLECTION POINT

A technology company working with tennis star Serena Williams has developed and perfected a smart garment using cutting-edge technology. It is seeking to hire a group to help market the product. Develop a proposal for marketing the product, and present your proposal.

**Work with a group and complete the following activities.**

**1.** Brainstorm and choose a product to use for this project. Assume it works well.

**2.** Include information about the target customer.

**3.** Decide how the product should be distributed through existing channels of distribution.

**4.** Determine the types of promotion and media you would recommend for this type of product. Include at least one type of print media.

**5.** Develop a sample print media ad.

**6.** Assemble all of your material into a written plan.

**7.** Present the information to the class in a five-minute presentation, acting as if the class were the company considering hiring you.

CHAPTER 8

# MERCHAN-DISING AND BUYING

## LESSONS

### 8.1 SURROUNDING STYLE

### 8.2 DISPLAYING STYLE

### 8.3 BUYING STYLE

# WINNING STRATEGIES

## OFC

Retail stores want to look inviting to customers. Beautiful furnishings help them accomplish that purpose. *Fixtures* are the furniture and wall units used in stores to display and house merchandise. Upscale retailers have custom fixtures built specifically to achieve a unique look and feel for their stores, much like the interior of a luxurious home. "Dillard's is the envy of other department stores wishing to emulate a rich look," says Tim Griffin of the Oklahoma Fixture Company (OFC). Dillard's store fixtures are custom built by OFC. Headquartered in Tulsa, Oklahoma, OFC has ten divisions for custom furnishings, ranging from residential to hospitality.

OFC works with customers to create designs for store fixtures. Using state-of-the-art technology, each store's designs are followed to custom build beautiful wood, glass, metal, and solid-surface furnishings. Software programs are used to design the fixtures. The software automatically updates the materials list as changes are made in a design. For example, if a glass-front showcase is changed from a four-foot length to a five-foot length, the software automatically updates the amount of wood, metal, and glass on the plans. The changes are electronically communicated to all parties, from the designer to those on the shop floor where the items are to be built.

The National Association of Store Fixture Manufacturers has recognized OFC numerous times for excellence, including a Grand Prize Design Award in the Full Department Store category for Saks Fifth Avenue's fixtures. OFC has also been recognized for work in Bass Pro Shops Outdoor World.

### THINK CRITICALLY

1. Why would a store want custom-made fixtures?

2. Why are store fixtures important to the image of a store?

# CHAPTER 8
## Lesson 8.1

# SURROUNDING STYLE

**Describe** the basics of retail fashion mall and store layout.

**Discuss** why the customer is key to store planning.

## The Latest Style

**P**rada was described as the "wow" store when it opened in Manhattan's SoHo neighborhood. The 30,000-square-foot store cost about $40 million to build, or about $1,333 per square foot of construction.

In case the size and price are not "wow" enough, there is a wooden "wave" the entire length of the store from the entrance to the basement. One side of the wave is pale steps that are a giant shoe display/try-on area. The steps can be used as seating for hundreds to view the stage that unfolds from the smooth upside of the wave. The stage is used to host cultural events and in-house fashion shows. Plasma screen monitors are suspended among the hanging apparel displays. Steel cages, suspended from the ceiling, are also used to display clothing. The store's interior is reported to be a major tourist attraction.

Work with a group. Discuss why Prada would build such a unique store. Will the novelty of such a unique store become stale with customers? What should be the focus of a fashion store's design?

## MALL AND STORE DESIGN

**R**etail developers and fashion store designers have a strategy in mind when they design malls and fashion stores. The layout of a mall or store may be convenient or inconvenient to customers, depending on the goals of the developer.

### MALL LAYOUT

DISTRIBUTION

Malls were traditionally designed to be intentionally inconvenient for customers. Similar stores were spread as far apart as possible, and traffic was directed by plants, kiosks, and other barriers so that customers would have to walk past potential impulse-purchase points. Store directories in malls were made as confusing as possible, using colors and numbers instead of store names, and very few additional signs led the customer directly to a store.

Planned inconvenience is just that, inconvenient. The traditional design strategy was intended to keep shoppers in a mall as long as possible. Developers were envisioning a 1950s-era family where most women were not employed outside of the home and had time to stroll leisurely through the mall. Women were thought to be more likely to tolerate the inconvenience and more likely to be impulse shoppers.

In the late 1990s, shoppers were visiting malls less frequently and buying less. Frustrated, busy customers didn't want to bother with the inconvenience of the malls and were taking their business elsewhere. Consequently, the issue of customer convenience returned to focus. The convenience of Internet shopping may have helped focus the mall and store designers, since customers now have a convenient way to shop at upscale stores or mass markets from home. Today, very few customers have patience for an inconvenient shopping experience, as evidenced by a drop in the average number of mall visits per month since 1995.

A mall with a customer-convenient layout is a new approach to combat the decline in mall shoppers. Newer malls are trying to group similar stores so that children's clothing or shoe stores, for example, are clustered together. Some new mall designs locate the anchor stores close together so that the walking distance between them is reduced. Customers like being able to comparison shop and choose with whom they do business. However, this synergistic idea does not please some retailers who believe they should be located as far away as possible from their competitors.

## STORE STRATEGIES

Like malls, store designs are developed with customer convenience, or inconvenience, in mind. Big-name designers create flagship stores that project their personal image. The goal is to reinforce their brands and provide customers with a unique experience. Some retailers try to provide the customer with multiple reasons for visiting the store, including entertainment.

**Convenience** Kohl's®, usually a freestanding, mass-market store, has mastered the technique of making shopping a quick, convenient process. Kohl's maintains sales per square foot of about $279 compared to $220 at Target®. Kohl's stores average about 86,000 square feet in total size and use wide, circling aisles that divide the store into no more than five departments, all located on one floor. The track around the store is about one quarter of a mile, while most Dillard's® and JCPenney® stores are about one-half mile around. Kohl's philosophy is to help shoppers buy more in less time, and the strategy is

*GlobalShop* is an international conference on store design and fixtures. At **www.globalshop. org**, a feature called "eMatchMaking" allows people who will attend the conference to maximize the time they will spend there. Attendees can log into a section called "My Conference Planner," click on the eMatchMaking option, and enter their business objectives and the products or services of interest to them. The feature sorts through hundreds of exhibitors and instantly provides a list of those who carry products matching the attendees' interests, saving time and effort.

**THINK CRITICALLY**
Visit **www.globalshop. org** and make a list of other services provided to conference attendees.

paying off with continued growth. Kohl's opened over 50 new stores in 2001.

**Retail-tainment** The store as an entertainment destination is the focus for some store designs. Providing a café, beauty salon, lounge area, or event area within the store creates additional reasons for people to visit. Of course, the hope is that visitors will also make purchases while they are there. Audience seating and a stage in the Manhattan Prada store are examples of creating additional reasons for customers to visit the store.

Issey Miyake, an upscale designer, has his worldwide flagship store in the lower Manhattan neighborhood of TriBeCa. The space was designed to accommodate the designer's showroom, stockroom, corporate offices, and retail store, as well as serve as a cultural center for music and art.

**Designing the Stores** Computer-aided design (CAD) software is used to design the interior and exterior of a store. A store designer draws a virtual store layout with an overhead view of the floor plan. Virtual fixtures and furniture can be placed on the floor plan, and three-dimensional virtual tours can be taken of the store during the design process. The virtual tours allow fashion merchandisers to see what the customers will see as they walk through the store. Changes can be made easily at this design-planning stage before any funds are spent on construction or remodeling.

## TIME OUT

A major international conference called *GlobalShop* is held each spring in Chicago. The three-day event is the world's largest annual store design and in-store marketing show. More than 1,000 exhibitors are featured in five different pavilions. The featured areas include store fixturing, visual merchandising, retail operations and construction, in-store interactive ideas, and point-of-purchase marketing.

## TRY IT ON

**Name two strategies for mall and fashion store layout.**

_____

_____

_____

## WELCOME, CUSTOMER

MARKETING-INFORMATION MANAGEMENT

**K**nowing the customer is the key to effectively designing a store. Many retailers who design stores to please their stockholders by keeping costs down end up displeasing both customers and stockholders. Stockholders want to see costs reduced, but that should not mean limiting space and services. For example, wide aisles cost more to build than narrow aisles, but narrow aisles are not designed with the needs of the customer in mind, possibly resulting in lost sales. Being too conservative with the store design can cost more in lost sales than is saved in construction expenses.

## CONSUMERS' AGE

The population of the United States is aging. The number of people who are over age 50 will continue to increase through 2012, making this one of the largest U.S. age groups. Store designers who design with only young people in mind will miss a huge population with a large discretionary income to spend on clothing. Attracting the over-50 crowds will require stores to accommodate their interests and provide the services that will keep them coming back.

## OBSERVE THE CUSTOMER

If a retail store's goal is to avoid holding the lost, confused customer hostage in a maze, it may require the help of a research firm. Redesigning a store into one that welcomes the customer to a comfortable, convenient experience requires information on customer behavior. Consumer research firms are in the business of watching customers. Part of this research often involves videotaping customers as they walk through a store and watching where they go and how they interact with the environment of the store. One example of the results of such research has shown that right-handed people tend to turn right at the first opportunity and continue around the store in a counterclockwise direction. About 90 percent of the population is right-handed. Placement of high-volume items to the right will assure that most customers see them as they move through the store.

## MAINTAIN THE IMAGE

When economic times become difficult, stores often make the mistake of cutting back on the store's appearance and reducing the visual merchandising staff. This strategy only serves to drive more customers away. Even a "wow" store needs to maintain visual appeal to draw customers and maintain the bottom line.

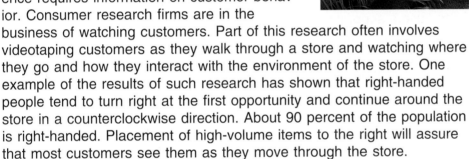

## TRY IT ON

**Why should stores be interested in attracting people over age 50?**

## UNDERSTAND MARKETING CONCEPTS
Circle the best answer for each of the following questions.

**1.** Inconvenient stores are designed to
   **a.** keep the customer shopping longer.
   **b.** irritate the customer.
   **c.** give experience to new architects.
   **d.** get ahead of the competition.

**2.** The key to effectively designing a store is
   **a.** holding down costs.
   **b.** knowing the customer.
   **c.** making the shopping experience inconvenient.
   **d.** limiting space and services.

## THINK CRITICALLY
Answer the following questions as completely as possible. If necessary, use a separate sheet of paper.

**3. Communication**   Discuss with a partner how a store might become an entertainment destination. Briefly describe additional services that might be offered to attract customers to a store.

_____

_____

_____

_____

_____

**4.** How would you improve mall directories? Design a directory that could be used for a mall near you, or design a directory for your school. Jot down ideas below, and use poster board for your final design.

_____

_____

_____

_____

_____

# DISPLAYING STYLE

## The Latest Style

Tourists in New York often plan to "do Fifth Avenue," meaning they start at one end and walk by all of the window displays of the major fashion retailers housed on Fifth Avenue. The windows are usually worth the effort of the walk.

Many of the visual merchandising staffs of major Fifth Avenue department stores or specialty stores include full-time electricians, painters, and carpenters who help construct the eye-catching displays. When centered on a specific fashion designer, the display concept is usually developed around the designer's image. If a lifestyle is part of the designer's advertising emphasis, then that concept is reflected in the window display as well.

Most stores on Fifth Avenue change window displays at least once every three weeks, and some of them change as often as once a week. Some stores are able to borrow props, such as antique chandeliers and chairs. Borrowing a painting from a museum and providing acknowledgment of the museum in the window can provide mutually beneficial publicity for the store and the museum.

Work with a group. Discuss why stores spend money creating window displays. How do window displays impact the image projected to potential customers who have never entered the store?

**GOALS**

**Explain** the steps of effective visual merchandising displays.

**Describe** the use of fixtures, signs, and lighting in fashion display.

## VISUAL MERCHANDISING

PROMOTION

The promotional presentation of fashion apparel and accessories is called **visual merchandising**. There are three purposes of visual merchandising—selling merchandise, projecting the image of the store, and educating customers. Visual merchandising helps create the image and ambiance of the store. Visual merchandising takes place both inside the store and in window displays viewed from the exterior of the store.

As with all components of fashion marketing, how to visually merchandise the garments is dependent on the target customer. Top-notch visual designers are artists who develop beautiful displays relevant to the customer and valuable for the retailer.

## CREATION

Visual merchandising includes the creation of displays in windows and showcases and throughout a store. The three-dimensional arrangement of apparel and accessories is a creative art. Quality displays require the application of the principles and elements of design.

Visual displays are designed around criteria developed to meet the purpose of the display—selling, projecting an image, and/or educating. To keep the customer interested, a standard for successful visual merchandising is *frequent revision* of the display, whether it is in an exterior window or inside the store. The use of *color* can attract consumers and *simplicity* can focus their attention. Allowing the viewer's eye to focus on a few objects, rather than many, helps achieve visual impact.

## THE STEPS

Three steps generally take place when creating a store window display—designing, building, and installing.

**Designing** Designing is the creative, conceptual, and planning stage of visual merchandising. Designing is often constrained by realities, such as the purpose for the display, the space to be used, the budget, and the materials available.

Professionals use design software to provide a "sketch" of how the completed display will look before work begins. A list of materials and costs is completed for the budget managers before the design is finalized.

Window displays, as well as displays within the store, will generally be tied together with a theme created by the visual merchandising department. The theme may be based on a season, a holiday, or an event that the store is promoting. In a large chain, the theme may first be tried as a concept in a few selected stores. For example, Christmas displays may be designed in September and test marketed. Customer comments are invited, and the concept is adjusted before being rolled out to the other branch stores.

**Building** Building the display includes gathering all materials and assembling props. Props used to show the merchandise to the best advantage usually include *mannequins*, the human body forms that wear the apparel merchandise. Preparation of the apparel and accessories includes steaming or pressing the items to make sure they look perfect.

Mannequins are frequently the focal point of a display and serve as a backdrop for garments. They come in endless sizes, colors, and poses,

Lightolier, a specialty lighting firm, offers on-line education in lighting at **www.lightolier.com**. The 21-part course is self-administered, beginning with lighting fundamentals and covering the lighting process. The course is provided free of charge to companies and professionals in the lighting business. It also qualifies for continuing education credit required to maintain certification by professional lighting associations.

**THINK CRITICALLY**
Why would a company provide a free, online course in professional lighting?

with or without heads, and can be representative of an ethnic group. Great-looking mannequins are expensive and fragile.

**Installing** Installing the display is the final step. Since changing displays can be disruptive to business, this step generally takes place after business hours. This is the time to make sure a display window is perfectly clean. Dust or streaks on the window glass can ruin the best design.

Dressing a mannequin requires knowledge and skill so that the expensive props are not damaged. Most garments have to be pinned to fit the mannequin properly. Tiny straight pins are used to pin the garment where customers will not notice. Mannequins used in an in-store display will usually end up with more wear from being bumped or having the garments changed more frequently than mannequins in a window display. Mannequins are sometimes attached directly to the floor in a window display to avoid using a stabilizing base that would detract from the visual effect.

Lighting is part of the design process and is finalized once the merchandise is in place. The lighting should focus the customer on the most important characteristic of the garment and help create the intended impact.

In the late 1930s, Bonwit Teller, a New York department store, hired surrealistic artist Salvador Dali to create a window display. Dali used a claw-footed bathtub lined in white lambskin and filled with murky water. Mannequin arms and hands reached eerily out of the water. Each hand held a mirror that reflected the face of the mannequin about to step into the tub. The mannequin was wearing only a few feathers and had waist-length blond hair filled with fake bugs. The weird display offended and shocked customers and store executives, who promptly had the display changed. When Dali saw the changes, he entered the window and pushed the tub through the glass onto Fifth Avenue. Some biographers say the tub went through the glass accidentally. Nevertheless, Dali was arrested for malicious mischief, but Bonwit Teller reportedly paid his fine.

**THINK CRITICALLY**
Discuss with a group why a store would want to avoid controversial displays.

# TRY IT ON

**Why should a display be kept simple?**

_____

_____

_____

# FIXTURES, SIGNS, AND LIGHTING

**PROMOTION**

Store fixtures, signs, and lighting are critical elements, the impact of which may dwell outside the direct consciousness of customers but weighs heavily in their decision to shop at a particular store. *Fixtures* are the furniture and wall units used in stores to display and house merchandise. *Signage* provides information or directions for customers. *Lighting* attracts attention and shows off the entire formation. There are endless choices of sizes, shapes, and colors for all three of these elements, and making the right combination of choices is of great importance.

## FIXTURES

Store fixtures, like the furniture in a home, are functional as well as helpful in creating the image of the store. A high-end luxury store will use fixtures that enhance the store's image and that highlight the apparel and accessories to the best advantage.

**Versatile fixtures** are store fixtures that are easily changed to meet a new need—a concept that appeals to both customers and retailers. Stores are using versatile fixtures that roll and change to keep a department looking new and fresh.

At Kohl's® department stores, racks of clothing are placed 30 to 36 inches apart to allow plenty of room for shoppers to maneuver carts.

**TIME OUT**

The National Association of Store Fixture Manufacturers (NASFM) and *VM+SD*, a visual merchandising and store design magazine, sponsor an annual national competition for store fixture design. Awards are given for the fixture of the year and in categories such as new full department store.

Because all product displays are at eye level, they do not block the view. Clothing racks are placed in a semicircle so that all merchandise can be seen. Where multiple tables are used, they graduate in height so that the lowest table is up front and the highest is in the back toward the wall. This leads the customer's eye toward the wall display.

With five or fewer racks in a department, Kohl's presents a clean look. Merchandise is displayed with light colors first, leading to darker colors. Research shows that this sequence of colors leads the eye of the shopper.

## PROVIDING INFORMATION

In addition to signs required by law, such as fire exit signs, the amount of signage used in a store depends upon the store's philosophy. If a store believes in inconveniencing customers to keep them in the store longer, then few signs are used. For customer convenience, signs can quickly lead customers to the departments they seek, can grab their attention, or can provide size and pricing information. The selection of sign size, lettering size, and colors should be based on how far away you want the customer to be able to read the sign.

Goody's Family Clothing, headquartered in Knoxville, Tennessee, wants to make shopping pleasant for customers and uses signage to enhance the experience. The large signs are about two feet by six feet, with a dark green background, white border, and large, readable white lettering. The signs are similar in appearance to freeway direction

signs, with simple wording and arrows pointing to the departments. The signs are suspended from the ceiling and are visible from a great distance.

## LIGHTING THE WAY

Lighting impacts the image of the entire store and is used to focus the customer. Planning the lighting within a department or for a specific display means making decisions about what to light, what to use to accomplish the lighting, and how much light is needed.

Lighting falls under three categories based on purpose—task lighting, accent lighting, and space lighting. *Task lighting* is used where a task or job must be done, such as the lighting over a cash register or checkout area of a store. *Accent lighting* is directed at a particular spot with the intent of focusing the customer on specific garments or accessories. *Space lighting* creates the ambiance of the store and provides lighting to

move through the store. Mass-merchandise stores are well lit with generally adequate space and task lighting. Accent lighting is used more often in high-end stores. Lights can also be controlled to create a different feeling for a space as the need changes.

Selecting the appropriate lighting device to meet the purpose involves knowledge of luminaires. A **luminaire** is the complete lamp, including parts used to focus the lamp, such as a swivel on a spotlight. The cost of the luminaire and its energy use are major criteria when choosing the kind of luminaire to use.

How much light to use means, once again, knowing your customer. At age 55, twice as much light is needed to see the merchandise as at age 20. When customers must ask if an item is navy blue or black, this generally means that lighting is inadequate for them to make a selection. Poor lighting does not provide convenience for the customer. If a man buys navy socks when he intends to buy black socks, he will associate the store with a disappointing experience.

Consideration must also be given to the natural light available. Windows in malls that face the interior halls have different lighting needs than windows that face the exterior. Exterior windows must show well in both bright sunlight and at night. The lighting can be set to automatically adjust to the exterior lighting conditions. Correct lighting takes knowledge and skill to perfect.

# TRY IT ON

**What are versatile fixtures?**

## UNDERSTAND MARKETING CONCEPTS

Circle the best answer for each of the following questions.

1. Two of the purposes for visual merchandising are
   a. providing jobs for people and covering the space.
   b. projecting an image and educating customers.
   c. providing customers with a place to go and a place to shop.
   d. using distribution and financing.

2. The three major steps of creating a display are
   a. identifying, budgeting, and creating.
   b. ordering, creating, and installing.
   c. designing, building, and installing.
   d. financing, distributing, and installing.

## THINK CRITICALLY

Answer the following questions as completely as possible. If necessary, use a separate sheet of paper.

3. Describe the role fixtures play in visual merchandising. How are they used throughout a fashion store?

_____

_____

_____

_____

4. Think about the color combinations used on roadway signs in the United States. Give an example of the color combinations you might use for the background and lettering of a sign in a fashion store. What is the purpose of the sign? Approximately what size would you make the sign, and why?

_____

_____

_____

_____

_____

# CHAPTER 8
## Lesson 8.3

# BUYING STYLE

**Explain** the role of the buyer in retailing.

**Describe** the process of selecting and merchandising apparel and accessories for retail.

## The Latest Style

**W**omen in Saudi Arabia like to own fashion businesses just like women in other parts of the world. To operate a fashion business, Saudi women must overcome a number of cultural and legal barriers. The barriers make staying in touch with fashion trends and buying fashions for resale difficult. Those barriers include limits on women working, limits on travel, and laws forbidding women to drive.

The Internet has opened the world of fashion, allowing Saudi women to view fashion shows from around the world and make virtual buying trips. Thanks to a web site that streams live runway shows at **www.virtualrunway.com**, women like Samira al-Hamad, who manages her own small business, can access couture fashion information or buy apparel online for their clients.

Janet Hobby and Grace Kim started Virtual Runway in 1999. Hobby, who had the idea for the online runway shows, has a bachelor's degree in finance, has worked as a model, and previously worked at the Dallas Apparel Mart for Esprit de Corps. Grace Kim has a master's degree in computer graphics and is involved in the technical end of the business. The site has streaming videos and slide shows from New York and European designers that are presented in an efficient and convenient format for fashion businesses.

Work with a group. Discuss other legal ways fashion buyers faced with governmental, religious, geographic, or physical limitations can gain access to fashions for their clients.

## SELECTING APPAREL AND ACCESSORIES

**B**uyer is one of the job titles in the fashion industry with which most people are familiar. Thought to be a glamour job, it is in reality a workhorse job. The job title *buyer* is used to describe positions that purchase for resale and for organization use. A fashion buyer purchases for resale to customers. An example of a buyer who purchases for organization use would be the buyer of store fixtures.

MARKETING-
INFORMATION
MANAGEMENT

### PLANNING

The buyer is the person responsible for actual selection of the merchandise from vendors. The buyer should also be called a planner because of the tremendous amount of planning that must take place before the buyer actually selects garments.

Once a buyer knows the target customer, the price points, what's selling, what's not selling, future trends, and how much is left in the open-to-buy budget, the buyer must go to market with a plan for the assortment of garments to be purchased. A **merchandise plan** is a list of current inventory, projected sales, the quantity already on order, and the quantity of garments still needed to cover projected sales. A subset of the merchandise plan is the **assortment plan**, which includes the quantity of each type of item, specific information about the style and fabric of each item, and the quantity of each size and color.

The following is a condensed example of a spreadsheet that could be used for planning a junior-sized top assortment plan.

| Junior Assortment Plan | | | | SIZE | | | | | | | |
| Item | Description | Quantity | Colors | 1 | 3 | 5 | 7 | 9 | 11 | 13 | TOTAL |
|---|---|---|---|---|---|---|---|---|---|---|---|
| Top | Short sleeve, velvet | 250 | White | 2 | 6 | 8 | 8 | 12 | 10 | 8 | |
| | | | Black | 6 | 8 | 10 | 10 | 18 | 12 | 12 | |
| | | | Navy | X | 4 | 6 | 8 | 8 | 8 | X | |
| | | | Green | X | 4 | 6 | 8 | 8 | 10 | X | |
| | | | Red | 4 | 6 | 6 | 8 | 10 | 10 | 6 | |
| | | | **TOTAL** | **12** | **28** | **36** | **42** | **56** | **50** | **26** | **250** |
| Top | Blouse, sequined detail | 50 | White | X | 1 | 2 | 4 | 4 | 2 | 1 | |
| | | | Black | X | 1 | 2 | 4 | 4 | 4 | 1 | |
| | | | Tan | X | X | 1 | 2 | 2 | 1 | X | |
| | | | Red | X | X | 2 | 4 | 4 | 2 | 2 | |
| | | | **TOTAL** | **0** | **2** | **7** | **14** | **14** | **9** | **4** | **50** |

The assortment plan is completed by the buyer based on previous sales data. The tops can be purchased from one or multiple vendors. The delivery dates can be spread over several months to make sure new items arrive continually to keep the merchandise mix fresh. The quantity of any one size of garment is based on information the buyer has about how well a size has sold. An assortment plan helps the buyer provide the exact merchandise mix needed in the department.

Buyers use spreadsheet software programs that maintain the merchandise plan with data about sales, inventory levels, and past performance of apparel items. Many of the programs use Excel® software to manage the data. Developing a spreadsheet for basic items that are always in stock, such as underwear, is much simpler than calculating the assortment plan for a junior department. Juniors is a fashion area with a very short life cycle, requiring that the plan be updated frequently.

## WORKING WITH VENDORS

Since thousands of vendors offer apparel and accessories at the manufacturer or wholesaler level and buyers have limited time to spend with vendors, buyers must know which vendors might fill their needs. In addition to offering the right styles at the right price points, the vendor must maintain a reputation for quality garments delivered as promised. A buyer is expected to negotiate with vendors on the costs of products as well as persuade the vendor to accept the return of goods that don't sell. The terms of payment for the products are also negotiable.

PRODUCT/
SERVICE
MANAGEMENT

Prêt-à-Porter, the organizer of the largest ready-to-wear shows in Paris, has worked to establish partnerships with U.S. retailers in order to increase interest in French fashions. It carefully organizes its shows to provide service and make it easier for U.S. buyers to find the right vendors.

**Terms of payment** include how many days after receipt of the merchandise the retailer has before payment is due, any discount for early payment, and who will pay for the shipping costs.

**Relationships** Relationships are developed between buyers and vendors based on trust and mutually beneficial business. A buyer must be able to count on the vendor to fulfill the order. Vendors of popular brand names can also select the retailers to whom they will sell based on a minimum quantity order. A small, one-store boutique might not be able to order a large enough quantity and thus could not carry particular brands. On the other hand, a small, exclusive brand might not be able to produce the quantity needed for a chain store with 500 locations.

**Differentiation** Differentiation of one store from another is very important, because customers quickly tire of seeing an item so frequently that it appears to be a school uniform. Vendors work with buyers to help make sure that competitors don't have the exact same styles in the same colors. Vendors know who is buying specific apparel. They can give **exclusive rights** to a store, meaning that they agree not to sell a particular style or color to any other store.

Fashion buyers must spend some of their time looking for new vendors. New vendors are one of the risks of the business, but they can offer opportunities for real growth and differentiation. If a buyer finds a new, young designer with great ideas, buying a few pieces from the designer may be well worth the risk and effort in order to establish a profitable relationship.

**Product Development** Product development is another way buyers can ensure that their merchandise mix is different from that of competitors. Buyers can work with manufacturers and designers directly to develop apparel that is sold only in their stores, either as an exclusive item or as a private label.

In Germany, there are multiple ready-to-wear shows held in various cities. Traditionally, Cologne was the home of the men's wear and the Inter-Jeans shows, and Düsseldorf was the capital of the women's wear show. There had always been cooperation on marketing and advertising between the Düsseldorf and Cologne shows, attracting buyers to both. In 2001, participation in the jeans show began to decline and the Düsseldorf show broadened to include men's wear, formerly Cologne's exclusive territory. The organizers of the two shows began to trade accusations and insults. Cooperation ended, and they started trying to outdo each other by upgrading the services provided for buyers. Consequently, the costs for both shows increased.

**THINK CRITICALLY**
**1.** Who benefited when the shows cooperated to attract buyers?
**2.** Who benefited when the shows competed against each other for buyers?

PRODUCT/
SERVICE
MANAGEMENT

# TRY IT ON

**Why must buyers be excellent planners?**

_____

_____

_____

_____

# MERCHANDISING THE GOODS

**S**election of apparel and accessories is only one part of a fashion buyer's job. The buyer is also the merchandiser. The buyer in a large store or chain generally reports to a *divisional merchandise manager (DMM)*, whose responsibility covers multiple buyers within a related group of departments, called a *division*. A division could be all of the women's fashion apparel and accessories departments. The DMM reports to a *general merchandise manager (GMM)* who is responsible for merchandising for all divisions.

## PRESENTATION OF FASHION

PROMOTION

The work of the fashion buyer, DMM, and GMM centers on merchandising. **Merchandising** is obtaining and presenting apparel and accessories for sale to customers. The buyer and most  people employed in the merchandising division are evaluated based on the results of merchandising, including meeting sales, profit margin, and inventory turnover goals.

## MARKETING AND MERCHANDISING

MARKETING-
INFORMATION
MANAGEMENT

Merchandising involves
- financial planning and analysis
- maintaining open-to-buy budgets
- forecasting
- reacting to sales and inventory levels
- assuring ad merchandise is in the store
- identifying and interpreting trends of the target customer
- transferring merchandise among stores
- presenting reports on strategies and results
- determining markdowns

While merchandising primarily focuses on looking at internal data, like sales and inventory, marketing information from outside sources reveals demographic or psychographic data about the customer. Merchandising data will indicate a need for 250 junior tops in each store, but marketing information will tell you that the colors of the school near branch store B are red and white, revealing a need for a different color assortment for that branch.

# TRY IT ON

**Why might different branches of the same store need a different merchandise mix?**

_____

_____

_____

## MINDY GREENBERG

The "M" in M Windows Visual + Display is Mindy Greenberg, an expert at visual merchandising. Greenberg is a New York City-based, freelance display professional who started in display at department stores after completing her degree in art at New York State University. Her next career move was to start her own business in what she refers to as "fun and work."

Greenberg teaches store staffs how to create award-winning visual presentations. Greenberg describes the job as very physical with lots of ladder climbing, prop lifting, and decoration hanging. She believes you can best learn the business by looking at what is being done in stores—observing how they are creating an image, looking at how items such as men's watches are displayed, and comparing one store's style to another.

According to Greenberg, department stores offer students a great place to start if they are interested in visual merchandising. She suggests that students bypass the Human Resource Department and talk directly with the display manager about their interest in working in visual merchandising. She offers a big hint—"visual merchandisers need a lot of help in September."

### THINK CRITICALLY
**1.** Why might visual merchandisers need more help in September than at other times of the year?
**2.** What characteristics are needed to be successful at visual merchandising?

## Final Fit

## UNDERSTAND MARKETING CONCEPTS
Circle the best answer for each of the following questions.

1. A list of current inventory, projections, sales, quantity on order, and quantity needed is contained in
   a. a product development plan.
   b. the open-to-buy budget.
   c. price points.
   d. a merchandise plan.

2. The agreement between the buyer and vendor on when payment is due and who pays shipping is
   a. part of pricing.
   b. the terms of payment.
   c. the merchandise plan.
   d. open-to-buy.

## THINK CRITICALLY
Answer the following questions as completely as possible. If necessary, use a separate sheet of paper.

3. Describe why it is important for a buyer to establish a relationship with vendors.

_____

_____

_____

4. **Marketing Math** You are helping Carlotta Williams, a buyer, complete an assortment plan. You know that 50 percent of her customers wear a size 10 dress, 25 percent wear size 8, 10 percent wear size 12, 10 percent wear size 6, and 5 percent wear size 14. She needs 300 black dresses and 200 green dresses. Using software, create a spreadsheet to show the distribution of the sizes and colors.

_____

_____

_____

_____

# REVIEW

## REVIEW MARKETING CONCEPTS

**Write the letter of the term that matches each definition. Some terms will not be used.**

_____ **1.** A list of current inventory, projected sales, the quantity already on order, and the quantity of garments needed to cover projected sales

_____ **2.** Store fixtures that are easily changed to meet a new need

_____ **3.** A complete lamp, including parts used to focus the lamp

_____ **4.** The promotional presentation of fashion apparel and accessories

_____ **5.** Include how many days after receipt of the merchandise the retailer has before payment is due, any discount for early payment, and who will pay for shipping

_____ **6.** An agreement that a vendor will only sell a particular style or color to one store

_____ **7.** A plan for buying specific quantities of styles, sizes, and colors of a type of garment

**a.** assortment plan
**b.** exclusive rights
**c.** luminaire
**d.** merchandise plan
**e.** merchandising
**f.** terms of payment
**g.** versatile fixtures
**h.** visual merchandising

**Circle the best answer.**

**8.** Which of the following is NOT a purpose of visual merchandising?
    **a.** producing merchandise
    **b.** educating customers
    **c.** projecting the image of the store
    **d.** selling merchandise

**9.** The three categories of lighting based on purpose are
    **a.** flood, general, and peak lighting.
    **b.** space, task, and accent lighting.
    **c.** space, reading, and sign lighting.
    **d.** table, overhead, and lamp lighting.

**10.** The population of the United States
    **a.** is about 90 percent right-handed.
    **b.** will have the over-50 crowd as one of its largest age groups in 2012.
    **c.** is both of these.
    **d.** is neither of these.

# THINK CRITICALLY

**11.** With a group, spend five minutes discussing the layout of a local department store. Is it set up to slow customers or to let them move quickly through on shopping trips? How could the store be changed to improve convenience for customers?

_____

_____

_____

_____

_____

_____

**12.** Describe the purposes of task, accent, and space lighting within a fashion store.

_____

_____

_____

**13.** List three or more of the activities for which a buyer is responsible.

_____

_____

_____

**14.** What role do fixtures, signs, and lighting play in fashion merchandising?

_____

_____

_____

_____

**CHAPTER 8 REVIEW**

## MAKE CONNECTIONS

**15. Marketing Math**   You are helping Claude Carter buy T-shirts to sell in his store. He has ordered 210 X-large T-shirts. His records show that he sells about one-third as many small shirts as X-large shirts and half as many large and medium shirts as X-large shirts. How many small, medium, and large T-shirts should he order?

_____

_____

_____

_____

_____

**16. Communication**   If a store wants to communicate an image of high fashion and excellent service to customers, how can it reflect that image in its displays? Write a paragraph to describe the characteristics you would use for the store's window displays.

_____

_____

_____

_____

_____

**17. Technology**   What kind of information does a buyer need prior to making buying decisions? How might the buyer use technology to obtain the needed information?

_____

_____

_____

_____

_____

_____

## MARKETING MANAGEMENT ROLE PLAY

www.deca.org
/publications/HS_
Guide/guidetoc.html

You are the Logistics Coordinator/Manager for a major department store. You are responsible for visual merchandising and the furnishings of the store.

Recently, another upscale department store has located in your mall as an anchor store. This competitor has high-volume sales per square foot of floor space. The competing department store frequently is cluttered with large quantities of merchandise necessary for a high volume of sales. The competition carries lines of merchandise similar to the merchandise your store sells.

You have the responsibility to make your store distinctive from the competition. You must describe the floor plan, displays, and array of merchandise that separates you from the competition. You will present your proposal to the general manager (represented by the class). You will have ten minutes to present your plan and five minutes to answer questions about the plan.

## PROJECT: The COLLECTION POINT

Ernest Garner is the owner of a women's wear boutique. He wants you to develop a plan for displaying the new spring designer apparel that will begin arriving in about a month. He has three large, floor-to-ceiling display windows in the front and side of his store, which is located on a corner. He also has tabletop displays inside his store.

**Work with a group and complete the following activities.**

1. Determine the information that you need to know about the store's target customer.

2. Sketch your ideas for each of the three window displays. Use software for this if possible.

3. Create another drawing of two table displays for inside the store.

4. Make a list of the materials you need to complete the displays both inside and outside the store.

5. Develop a five-minute presentation to present the ideas to the class as if they were Mr. Garner.

6. For extra credit, ask a local store that targets the teen customer if you can develop a display for it, either at the store or within the school. The display should project a positive image of both the store and the school.

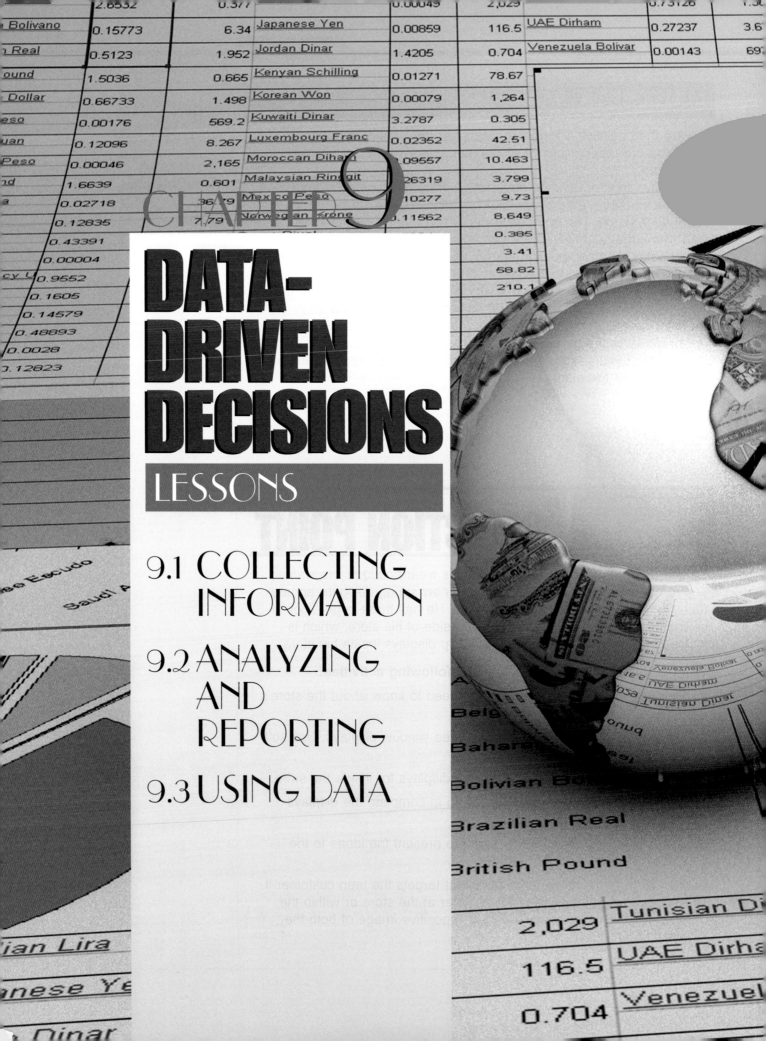

# CHAPTER 9

# DATA-DRIVEN DECISIONS

## LESSONS

9.1 COLLECTING INFORMATION

9.2 ANALYZING AND REPORTING

9.3 USING DATA

# WINNING STRATEGIES

## LIFESTYLE MONITOR™

Cotton Incorporated's Lifestyle Monitor™ records "America's attitudes and behaviors toward apparel," according to its web site at **www.cottoninc. com**. The research is published each Thursday in *Women's Wear Daily* and covers a specific topic as it relates to fashion and clothing.

Lifestyle Monitor™ has conducted research on cultural diversity in the United States and its impact on retail apparel sales. The U.S. census showed the growth of minorities to be 34 percent from 1990 to 2000, compared to 5.9 percent growth for Caucasians. The household income for minorities also grew at a much faster rate than for Caucasians. The growth, according to Lifestyle Monitor™, translates into buying power, particularly for apparel because "minority groups rate fashion as a high priority."

Lifestyle Monitor™ found that African-American and Hispanic shoppers rate store displays as very high in influencing their purchases. Additionally, they rate "family, sales associates, and celebrities" as major influences on what they choose to wear.

Fashion trends are often spotted "on the street" and spread from a specific culture or ethnic group to a wider population. The influence of a specific culture or ethnic group on fashion tends to cycle in and out. Some ethnic items become classics, such as the mandarin collar, which is based on a style attributed to the Mandarin region of China. Smart fashion marketers are aware of cultural influences on current fashion, as well as the needs and wants of the cultural diversity of customers in the United States.

### THINK CRITICALLY

1. What kinds of information do fashion marketers need to know to please culturally diverse shoppers?
2. How would a culturally diverse population impact the product mix offered by a store?

In US$

olivar    0.00143    697.7

# CHAPTER 9
## Lesson 9.1

# COLLECTING INFORMATION

## GOALS

**Explain** the characteristics of marketing-information systems.

**Explain** the benefits and limits of marketing research.

## The Latest Style

Knowing what teens want and providing it is the business of New York City-based Alloy. Alloy started out selling snowboarding gear and clothing for Generation X, people born between 1961 and 1981. It has evolved into a web site and catalog sales retailer for teens. As a reaction to marketing information, the company now provides a light mix of advice columns, movie information, celebrity profiles, and teen clothing for Generation Y, those born between 1982 and 1995.

The shift in the target customer was based on survey information from visitors to the web site. Separate surveys are provided for male and female visitors. Alloy continually uses surveys to gather visitors' opinions on fashion apparel. If the apparel is not popular with those surveyed, then it is not included in Alloy's catalog. The process results in what is called "user-generated content."

Work with a group. Why would Alloy let its web site visitors decide what goes in the Alloy catalog?

## THE SYSTEMS

**MARKETING-INFORMATION MANAGEMENT**

When the economy is thriving, fashion businesses focus on growth and expansion. When the economy is weak, they focus on efficiently operating the business and making a profit. Either focus requires information about past and current happenings. The information is used to make decisions about the future.

### PUTTING IT TOGETHER

A **marketing-information system (MktIS)** has the characteristics of a *system* in that it is a connected functional unit. The purpose of a MktIS is to manage information. An effective MktIS provides a way to track a rapidly changing product assortment, calls attention to data relationships, and provides information about the needs and wants of the customer. The system must be user-friendly and provide fast and reliable data on

demand. Marketing-information systems provide the capabilities of collecting, storing, reporting, analyzing, and using information.

## COLLECTING DATA

A fashion business can use technology to obtain details about what is selling and who is buying. Manufacturers collect information when retail buyers place orders. Retailers collect data as consumers make purchases. Software systems are used to automate the collection of details, such as style, color, size, and quantity sold. This information is collected as the price tag is scanned at the point of purchase or as store personnel scan box labels or clothing tags when transferring apparel to other branches of a store.

## STORING DATA

After the information is collected, it must be accumulated, sorted, and stored. Accumulating the information in an electronic format can be done quickly, efficiently, and in a compact manner. The amount of data generated from the sales of hundreds of styles of thousands of items would fill large file cabinets if stored on paper, but electronic storage on a computer's hard drive or CD is compact. Fashion marketers must remember that stored data is relevant for only a short period of time, as clothing trends change often.

### Fashion Flashback

In major department stores in the late 1960s, apparel was physically checked in at a central receiving department. Store personnel placed hang tags on each piece, hung the garments on hangers, placed the garments on rolling racks, moved them to the appropriate department, and placed them on display. When a different branch needed a specific garment for a customer, or if the style was selling really well at another branch store, the garments could be transferred. A transfer form was completed by hand in triplicate, and two copies were attached to the garment. The receiving store kept one copy and returned one copy to the sending store. The original copy and the returned copy were matched together and sent to the inventory control department where personnel manually made the change in the inventory control documents. The total time before the inventory records reflected the transfer was about two weeks.

**THINK CRITICALLY**
**1.** How has technology changed the inventory control process?
**2.** Why is speed important to the inventory control process?

## REPORTING DATA

Reporting is enhanced by the technology used in marketing-information systems. Software programs allow data to be sorted and reports configured to the specifications of the reader. If a buyer wants to know how many total garments in size 7 have sold during the month of October, the information can be compiled into a precise report. A second report could contain information about a specific brand or all apparel in a specific color.

Reports are frequently used to compare the past with the present. **Same-store sales reports** compare what is happening today to what happened on the same date in the previous year. Same-store sales reports can provide good information, but they can also be deceptive. If last year on this same date a hurricane hit the area and this year the weather is great, comparison of sales will be skewed. If an advertising campaign was recently launched, it will skew the report as well. Noting special circumstances is critical to the integrity of the data.

## ANALYZING DATA

Reports mean nothing unless they are properly analyzed and interpreted. A buyer, divisional merchandise manager, and general merchandise manager will spend a great deal of time reviewing reports and summaries of data collected from the sales floor, accounting department, and inventory records. The analysis puts the data into a context that shows relationships and helps lead to conclusions.

The data can show a relationship between price points and item sales or between two sizes of garments. The data analysis might reveal that, in Seeju Dupre's boutique, black slacks have sold well in all sizes, but blue slacks are selling out in the smallest sizes. A trend for the small sizes in the color blue is indicated. Catching a trend in time to react to it is an important purpose of data analysis.

## USING DATA

When a buyer has analyzed the data and has recognized its relationships, the buyer can formulate a plan of action. If the analysis showed that a vendor's line is not selling, the buyer can try to return the balance of the remaining line or exchange the colors or styles for something new. A buyer may be able to get a concession from the vendor if there is an established relationship. A **concession** is a yielding on the vendor's price or return policy. A buyer may also identify that it is time to mark down a specific style.

When a buyer identifies trends, the information may be used to update existing plans. Staying on top of the data when sales are slow is critical to remaining profitable. Retailers must be careful not to be overly cautious in limiting orders due to slow sales. For example, if orders are placed 45 to 60 days later than normal, this can pressure the manufacturer to produce and deliver in too tight of a time frame. Should sales suddenly pick up, the retailer may be caught with nothing to sell. If sales do not increase, conservative planning may reduce markdowns and closeouts that eat into profits. A buyer can effectively use a marketing-information system as a tool for improving profits.

# TRY IT ON

**What is the purpose of a marketing-information system (MktIS)?**

_____

_____

_____

# MARKETING RESEARCH

**MARKETING-INFORMATION MANAGEMENT**

Inputting only the data collected from within a fashion store does not fully utilize the capabilities of a marketing-information system. Marketing-research data is also needed for the buyer or merchandise manager to make sound decisions. **Marketing research** is the process of gathering information about current and potential customers. The research results are reported based on groups of people with similarities, such as females age 15 to 19.

## MARKET SEGMENTS

Fashion apparel is most successfully marketed to small, focused groups. Markets can be divided into **marketing segments** or subgroups based on demographics (age, gender, ethnic group, nationality, education, and income) or psychographics (ideology, values, attitudes, and interests) that the group members have in common. Age groups and gender groups are frequently used to subdivide the market. A disadvantage of segmenting people into such groups is the tendency to assume that everyone in the group has the same tastes and spending habits.

According to Betty Cortina, editorial director of *Latina Magazine,* and research conducted by Cotton Incorporated's Lifestyle Monitor™, about 65 percent of Hispanic women enjoy shopping for apparel, while only 40 percent of Caucasian women feel the same. Hispanic household income has risen over the past decade by more than 24 percent, and the Hispanic population in the United States is one of the fastest-growing segments. Fashion marketers who are aware of these three pieces of information are making extra efforts to learn what Hispanic women want to wear and to make the fashions available to them.

Generation Y refers to the 62 to 80 million people born in the United States between 1979 and 1995. This group is the second largest population group by age, topped only by its parents' age group, the Baby Boomers born between 1946 and 1964. In 2001, Generation Y spent an estimated $155 billion, making it a highly sought market segment.

## MASS VERSUS TARGET MARKETS

The **mass market** refers to a large number of potential customers with no specific similarities. An advantage of targeting the mass market is the large number of potential customers, but the disadvantage is that in trying to please all of them, you may please none of them. Retailers that cater to the mass market include JCPenney®, Kohl's®, and Target®. Each of these stores offers a wide range of merchandise, with some designed to target specific groups that are considered profitable, such as teen girls.

Rather than trying to please everyone, fashion marketers may target one market segment. This allows fashion marketers to fully focus and thoroughly get to know the target customer. They can anticipate how the customer will react to certain apparel, colors, price points, and brands.

Some target groups may have more market potential than others, while some very small groups may have special needs that are being overlooked. Matching the right target customer with the business can make the difference between failure and success. While Generation Y is

Anne Zehren, publisher of *Teen People* magazine, stays in touch with about 8,000 teens. She calls the group *trendspotters*, and they help her understand what's going on inside teens' minds. Today's teens are an empowered group using technology at an unprecedented level. Fashion advertisers are looking for new ways to connect with this group via the technology it is using.

a free-spending group, women aged 45 to 54 are the highest per-person spenders on fashion apparel. Members of this age group are more likely to be established and advanced in their chosen careers, with a higher income that allows them to spend more on clothing. On the other hand, if there are already many competitors targeting a group in the same area, then perhaps targeting a smaller group that is being overlooked by the competition will give the business an edge. Some specialty stores cater only to big and tall men, for example.

## RESEARCH

PRICING

Once the target market is established, data regarding those consumers' preferences should be added to the marketing-information system. The data should be based on research. Research can provide the fashion marketer with data needed to decide where to locate the store, how to lay out the store, where to place the merchandise in the store, and price elasticity. **Price elasticity** is the range between the lowest price a retailer can afford to charge and the top price a customer is willing to pay. If convenience is more important than price, then the top estimates of elasticity are higher and margins can be higher, providing more opportunity for profit. While marketing research provides the kind of beneficial data needed for decision making, its value is limited by the knowledge and skill of the individual who is analyzing and using the data.

## CYBER MARKETING

Online information about fashion manufacturers can be found at **www.hoovers.com**. Hoover's Online is an excellent source of free business information and also provides additional specific information for a subscription price. Hoover's provides the kind of information that a vendor and retailer might need about each other to determine if a working relationship would be profitable. Information about the top ten apparel manufacturers in the United States ranked by sales volume is included in the available information.

**THINK CRITICALLY**
**1.** What would a retailer want to know about a potential vendor?
**2.** What would a manufacturer want to know about a retailer?

# TRY IT ON

**What is a market segment?**

## UNDERSTAND MARKETING CONCEPTS

Circle the best answer for each of the following questions.

1. A comparison of today's store sales with last year's sales figures on the same date is
   a. distribution and demand.
   b. a same-store sales report.
   c. market total.
   d. retail sales.

2. A yielding by a vendor on its price or return policy is called
   a. a concession.
   b. wholesaling.
   c. a stockout.
   d. supply and demand.

## THINK CRITICALLY

Answer the following questions as completely as possible. If necessary, use a separate sheet of paper.

3. What are the five elements of a marketing-information system (MktIS)?

_____

_____

_____

_____

4. **Economics**  Discuss with a group the advantages and disadvantages of targeting market segments versus targeting mass markets. What is the difference between the two groups?

_____

_____

_____

_____

_____

_____

# ANALYZING AND REPORTING

## GOALS

**Explain** the use of inventory control information.

**Discuss** the use of inventory in financial reporting.

## The Latest Style

**F**ashion marketers are often operating on narrow profit margins with no room for mistakes. Finding ways to increase the margin without sacrificing the volume of sales or price image is a goal of all retailers. KhiMetrics Inc., a Scottsdale, Arizona company, has developed application software that uses customer demand to develop pricing strategies and improve financial performance for retailers.

KhiMetrics uses a retail revenue management (rrm) methodology based on a technology proven in other industries but adapted for retail. Using scientific modeling process software to carefully audit data collected and check for special events like advertised sales, the rrm provides data that is reliable and adjusted for any unusual events. The data can be used to optimize the price and promotion of the merchandise by category and by store. Pricing and promotion strategies may differ for each store based on the data on each store's customers. The result is that customers are pleased and sales and margin goals of the business are reached.

Work with a group. List and discuss reasons why a multi-store fashion business might charge different prices at different stores.

## INVENTORY CONTROL

**MARKETING-INFORMATION MANAGEMENT**

**T**he process used to track the quantities, wholesale value, and retail value of garments received and sold in a fashion store is called **inventory control**. It is a part of the marketing-information system. In all but the smallest of stores, the system is automated and information is scanned into a computer system that maintains the data. Accurate accounting of the inventory is critical for a number of reasons.

### ACCURACY COUNTS

For the marketing-information system to provide valid, usable data, accurate information must be entered into the system. An item may be entered into the system at the point at which it is placed on order with a vendor. Its status will change to "on-hand" when it is physically received into the store. Inventory control data is recorded on a departmental basis. Specific information about every apparel item in a store will include quantity received, quantity sold, quantity returned by customers, transfers to branch stores, and quantity removed from inventory due to age, theft, or damage.

## INVENTORY TURNOVER

The rate at which merchandise is sold and new merchandise brought in during a time period is called the **inventory turnover**. Turnover is considered one measure of efficiency of the business. Inventory is a major investment of money for a fashion business. A low turnover rate means sales are slow and there is excess inventory. Most department stores get about four turns of merchandise per year. Wal-Mart's accessories and intimate apparel can get 12 turns per year. The speed at which the turns are made allows Wal-Mart to earn more sales dollars per square foot of space and keep prices low.

**Excess Inventory**   The turnover rate also provides an indication of how much inventory needs to be on hand. Since fashion has such a short life cycle, inventory that does not turn over quickly becomes out of season, begins to look *shop worn* or dirty from being handled, takes up space, and ties up money needed for new products. When apparel is sitting in the store, it is not providing a return on investment (ROI). A **return on investment (ROI)** is the increased money received above an initial investment. The percentage amount of return on investment is an important financial reporting indicator of success.

The landlord for a Saks Fifth Avenue store in Los Angeles filed a lawsuit for breach of contract against Saks for allegedly failing to provide the landlord with documentation needed to audit sales figures. Under terms of the lease agreement, Saks was to pay a base rent and an additional amount based on a percentage of sales that exceeded a threshold of $20 million. Saks reported that it did not exceed the $20 million sales threshold between 1997 and 1999. The suit alleged that Saks misstated employee discounts, reduced sales based on returns for catalog sales items, and failed to retain cash register receipts that should have been kept for three years under terms of the lease. Complicating the issue, the store was split between two locations across the street from each other. One location was owned by Saks, and the other location was owned by the landlord. The landlord also accused Saks of placing the expensive and high-volume items at the site Saks owned to avoid achieving the threshold of sales in the rented space. Saks told *Women's Wear Daily* that the lawsuit was without merit.

**THINK CRITICALLY**

**1.** Does a company have an obligation to be honest in financial reporting?

**2.** Who can be harmed if companies create inaccurate financial reports?

**Fast Turns**   At Bonner's Boutique, apparel in the junior department turns over about eight times per year. Since teens frequently change their minds about what they want to buy, the fast turns help keep new merchandise coming in.

Bonner's usually figures turnover monthly and yearly. The following formula is one way to calculate inventory turnover, with the total sales at retail price for the period of time divided by the average retail dollar value of the inventory.

$$\frac{\text{Sales \$}}{\text{Average Inventory at Retail \$}} = \text{Turnover}$$

| Month | Average Inventory | Sales |
|---|---|---|
| January | $109,523.50 | $81,252.00 |
| February | $125,422.00 | $91,225.00 |
| March | $130,771.50 | $85,954.00 |
| April | $150,767.50 | $86,210.00 |
| May | $148,609.50 | $98,956.00 |
| June | $128,032.50 | $70,261.00 |
| July | $140,030.50 | $94,512.00 |
| August | $144,618.50 | $99,562.00 |
| September | $139,278.50 | $81,254.00 |
| October | $134,465.50 | $95,628.00 |
| November | $145,054.00 | $106,985.00 |
| December | $144,321.50 | $115,246.00 |
| Totals | $1,640,895.00 | **$1,107,045.00** |
| Total of averages/12 **= Yearly average inventory** | **$136,741.25** | |

An example of Bonner's average inventory and sales is shown in the chart to the left. To calculate a monthly average inventory, the value of the inventory at the retail price is determined at the first of the month and again at the end of the month and divided by 2. For example, to calculate the January average inventory, the inventory on January 1, $103,425, is added to the inventory on January 31, $115,622, and divided by 2 to arrive at the average of $109,523.50. The yearly average inventory is the total of the 12 monthly averages divided by 12 (for the 12 months of the year). The turnover for the year is calculated below.

$$\frac{\$1,107,045.00 \text{ Total sales for the year}}{\$136,741.25 \text{ Yearly average inventory}} = 8.10 \text{ Turns per year}$$

# TRY IT ON

**What is the purpose of an inventory control system?**

_____

_____

_____

# ANALYZE THIS

By comparing inventory levels to past sales, a pattern may emerge. By making inventory comparisons with other factors, a great deal of information can be obtained, including the extent and value of lost merchandise, the vendors most popular with customers, and relationships between categories of apparel such as sales of tops and slacks.

## OPTIMIZATION

SELLING

If inventory on hand can be minimized while keeping sales constant or growing, then profits can be improved. Reaching and maintaining this perfect level of inventory is called **inventory optimization**. In optimizing inventory, priority must be given to items that are selling quickly and in large volume. The **Pareto Principle** is a theory that a small number of causes is responsible for most of the results. The Pareto Principle applies to inventory analysis in that typically 20 percent of products sold in a store will account for 80 percent of the turnover. A smart buyer will make sure the "20-percent items" are always in stock.

## PRODUCT AVAILABILITY

**MARKETING-INFORMATION MANAGEMENT**

If a specific vendor's apparel is selling well, then a fashion retailer should work with that vendor to keep a constant supply flowing into the store. A "just-in-time" inventory system can be arranged with the vendor so that merchandise arrives as it is needed in the store. By using information from the MktIS about when merchandise was ordered and when it was received, the reliability and performance of a vendor can be analyzed. This information lets a buyer know how much lead time to provide a vendor to make sure stock arrives on schedule. *Lead time* is the time between placing an order and having the apparel available for sale.

## RISK MANAGEMENT

The chance that manufacturers may not perform as needed is called **upstream risk**. Upstream risk can cause a retailer to purchase too much inventory as a precaution against running out of stock. Risk management involves finding the right balance between precaution and using just-in-time inventory practices. It also means using only vendors with reliable track records for on-time delivery whenever possible.

## OUT OF SITE

The cost of apparel and accessories that are lost, stolen, or damaged must be covered by the profits from the sale of other items. One way to help prevent theft is to use an accurate inventory system. Missing merchandise not showing up in the system as sold will wave a red flag at those familiar with the inventory.

## FINANCIAL REPORTS

Since inventory represents a large expense and is the record of what a fashion store has to offer customers, it is a critical piece of data. Inventory data is used in the preparation of financial reports that show the health of the company. The inventory value is an asset and the cost of inventory owed to vendors is a liability on the balance sheet.

According to the U.S. Chamber of Commerce, employees steal $20 billion to $40 billion from their employers each year. Every person in the United States is paying on average an extra $400 each year for merchandise because of markup to cover theft. An employee is 15 times more likely than a nonemployee to steal from an employer. Employees with a theft record find future employment difficult or impossible to find.

## TRY IT ON

**Why is vendor reliability important to inventory control?**

_____

_____

_____

## UNDERSTAND MARKETING CONCEPTS
Circle the best answer for each of the following questions.

**1.** From a retailer's standpoint, upstream risk is based on the reliability of
   **a.** manufacturers.
   **b.** customers.
   **c.** employees.
   **d.** all of the above.

**2.** The time between ordering apparel and receiving it in the store is called
   **a.** down time.
   **b.** lead time.
   **c.** out of time.
   **d.** just in time.

## THINK CRITICALLY
Answer the following questions as completely as possible. If necessary, use a separate sheet of paper.

**3. Research**  Discuss with a group the number of times a store in your area has been out of the size of a garment you wanted to buy. Have others had similar problems? Is the same store involved? Share the discussion with the class. Reach a conclusion about the store(s) discussed.

_____

_____

_____

**4. Marketing Math**  Virginia Brown has an average inventory of $203,564 in her children's clothing store during the year and has annual sales of $1,453,567. What is her average yearly turnover of inventory?

_____

_____

_____

# USING DATA

## The Latest Style

**W**al-Mart® partnered with Sara Lee Branded Apparel to pilot a collaborative model for forecasting sales and replenishing stock. The model was created as a result of work by a Voluntary Interindustry Commerce Standards (VICS) committee. The model is called Collaborative Planning, Forecasting, and Replenishment (CPFR). The pilot was intended to validate the CPFR model and develop a system for execution of the model.

The CPFR model called for Wal-Mart to communicate standard pertinent information about sales and forecasts to Sara Lee. The pilot focused on 23 women's underwear items that are distributed to over 2,400 Wal-Mart stores. After 24 weeks, the results of the pilot at Wal-Mart showed an improvement by 2 percent of in-stock items, a 14-percent reduction in inventory level, a 32-percent increase in sales, and a 17-percent increase in turnover for the pilot items.

Work with a group. Discuss why improved communication with a vendor might result in faster inventory turnover. Why might the changes result in increased sales?

Explain the use of data in forecasting.

Explain the use of data for buying decisions.

# PREDICTING THE FUTURE

**F**or a fashion store to have the right quantity of apparel at the right time and at the right price takes planning. The planning must take place far enough in advance of the need at the store to allow the fabric to be woven, the garment to be designed, the buyer to select and order it, the manufacturer to produce and ship it, and the retailer to receive it. A planning step the retailer must take well in advance of this process is projecting sales and orders. A plan that estimates the dollar volume of sales ahead of time is called a **sales forecast**.

## SALES FORECASTS

**MARKETING-INFORMATION MANAGEMENT**

The buyer and merchandise managers need sales forecasts to estimate how much merchandise will sell in a given period of time. The information from the sales forecast must be available before the open-to-buy budget can be set for a buyer. Without the sales forecast, a new junior department buyer may not adjust the quantity of apparel needed to cover the increase in sales during back-to-school time, which is generally a high-volume sales period.

Just as in predicting the weather, developing the sales forecast requires analysis of available data and reliance on what has happened in the past. Some of the data that is used to develop a sales forecast includes point-of-sale data, special events, marketing research, incidental information, and the overall plan for the business.

## DATA INPUT

The point-of-sale data generated at the cash registers of checkout centers and service centers must include sales, returned items, and any price reductions. Special events that impact sales forecasts might include storewide promotions and sales, new store openings, holidays, and community events such as a rodeo or a fair drawing visitors into the area. Marketing research can provide data about customers' preferences that will influence their purchases. Incidental information that should be considered might include a predicted reduction in the cost of an item or a new line of apparel being designed. Communication with vendors to determine incidental information that may impact the forecast can vastly improve its validity. The vendor may have information that is not otherwise available to the fashion retailer, such as product availability and lead time. The overall business plan includes information about the target customers, price points, and margins. All of this data will impact a sales forecast.

**CYBER MARKETING**

Web sites that sell apparel are ranked by Nielsen//Netratings based on the number of unique visitors to the sites. Walmart.com often led the list when it sold clothing online. The monthly ratings are sometimes included in "Press Releases" at **www. nielsen-netratings. com.**

**THINK CRITICALLY**
**1.** What might impact which store is at the top of the ratings?
**2.** Visit the site and see what store is at the top of the latest ranking. Why do you think it is on top?

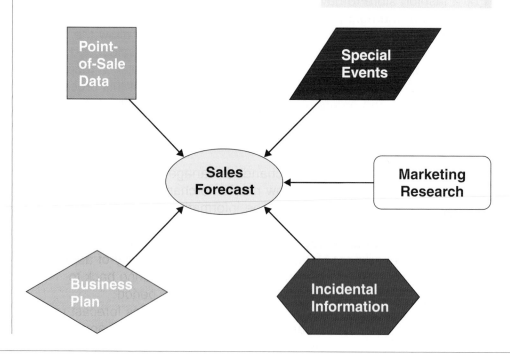

# TRY IT ON

## Why do fashion stores need an estimate of sales?

_____

_____

_____

# DATA-DRIVEN BUYS

**B**uyers can use inventory records to view the total dollar value of the current inventory and the level of units on hand. A low level of units is an indication to buy more, but it is not adequate information to use before committing an order.

## ORDER FORECASTS

**MARKETING-INFORMATION MANAGEMENT**

An **order forecast** is an estimate of the number and size of orders that need to be placed to cover the sales that have been forecast. The sales forecast will show sales over a period of time, gradually reducing the existing inventory to a point where stockouts will occur if the stock is not replenished. An order forecast takes into consideration the sales forecast, inventory, season of the year, special events, and information from the manufacturer.

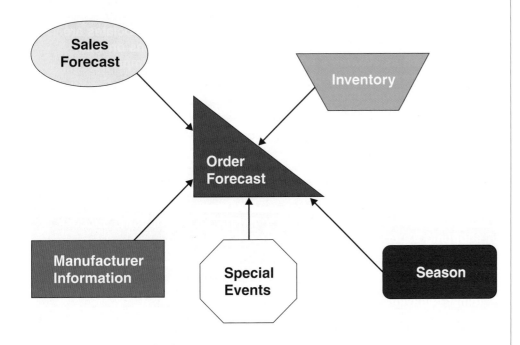

## PLANNING TO BUY

When developing the order forecast, the current inventory on hand as well as items on order or in transit will impact future buying. The time of the year will influence ordering for seasonal apparel, such as swimsuits, shorts, or heavy jackets. Smart planners communicate with manufacturers about the order forecast to assure that they can complete the orders to arrive when needed. Order forecasting helps fashion marketers please customers by having the ordered apparel they want when they want it and controlling inventory costs to keep prices down. At the same time, proper order forecasting improves profits for the store.

# TRY IT ON

**Why do fashion marketers need order forecasting?**

_____

_____

_____

## TrendSetters

### PACO UNDERHILL

**P**aco Underhill is frequently quoted in fashion trade publications such as _Women's Wear Daily_ as an expert on people's interaction with products and spaces. He is founder of Envirosell, Inc., a research and consulting agency for retailers and manufacturers. He is the author of an international best-selling book, _Why We Buy: The Science of Shopping._

His system maps customers' shopping experiences by using traditional marketing research and anthropological observation. Small video cameras record customer behavior. Exit interviews are conducted with customers who are offered a gift for answering survey questions. Additionally, store sales associates are asked their opinions on what could be done to improve the stores.

Underhill worked as a staff member of Project for Public Spaces in land use planning and taught courses in environmental psychology at New York City University. He began to apply research to retail when he formed Envirosell, Inc., a company that is now an international success.

### THINK CRITICALLY

**1.** Why would stores want to know the behavior patterns of shoppers?

**2.** What does anthropology have to do with fashion customers?

Final Fit

## UNDERSTAND MARKETING CONCEPTS
Circle the best answer for each of the following questions.

**1.** The sales data generated at the cash register is called
  **a.** wholesale data.
  **b.** punch card data.
  **c.** point-of-sale data.
  **d.** last year's data.

**2.** An estimate of the number and size of orders that need to be placed to cover projected sales is called
  **a.** a sales forecast.
  **b.** an order forecast.
  **c.** a weather forecast.
  **d.** a venture forecast.

## THINK CRITICALLY
Answer the following questions as completely as possible. If necessary, use a separate sheet of paper.

**3.** List the types of data that are used in sales forecasting. Provide an example of each type of data.

_____

_____

_____

_____

**4.** Explain how a buyer uses data to plan. Discuss the types of data that are used by buyers in planning.

_____

_____

_____

_____

_____

_____

# REVIEW

## REVIEW MARKETING CONCEPTS

**Write the letter of the term that matches each definition. Some terms will not be used.**

_____ **1.** Compares what is happening today to what happened on the same date in the previous year

_____ **2.** The process of gathering information about current and potential customers

_____ **3.** A yielding on the vendor's price or return policy

_____ **4.** The increased money received above an initial investment

_____ **5.** The chance that manufacturers may not perform as needed

_____ **6.** The process used to track the quantities, wholesale value, and retail value of garments received and sold

_____ **7.** The range between the lowest price a retailer can afford to charge and the top price a customer is willing to pay

_____ **8.** Theory that a small number of causes is responsible for most of the results

**a.** concession
**b.** inventory control
**c.** inventory optimization
**d.** inventory turnover
**e.** marketing research
**f.** marketing segments
**g.** marketing-information system (MktIS)
**h.** mass market
**i.** order forecast
**j.** Pareto Principle
**k.** price elasticity
**l.** return on investment (ROI)
**m.** sales forecast
**n.** same-store sales report
**o.** upstream risk

**Circle the best answer.**

**9.** Which of the following will impact a sales forecast?
  **a.** point-of-sale data and marketing research
  **b.** special events and incidental information
  **c.** both of these
  **d.** neither of these

**10.** Typically ____ percent of the products sold in a store will account for ____ percent of the turnover.
  **a.** 10, 80
  **b.** 15, 90
  **c.** 20, 80
  **d.** 50, 50

# THINK CRITICALLY

**11.** How does a store automatically collect data about what is selling? How is this information used?

_____

_____

_____

_____

_____

**12.** Why is it important to avoid being out of stock on an apparel item? How does being out of stock impact the image of the store?

_____

_____

_____

_____

_____

**13.** What is meant by upstream risk for a retailer? What can a fashion retailer do to manage this risk?

_____

_____

_____

_____

_____

**14.** Make a list of three special events that could impact a fashion store's inventory. Indicate whether each of the events would require an increase or decrease in the inventory on hand.

_____

_____

_____

_____

_____

## MAKE CONNECTIONS

**15. Marketing Math**  Grace Chang has a men's and women's designer fashion boutique. She wants to calculate her inventory turnover for the past year. Her inventory on January 1 was valued at $324,665. She sold $59,698 in January and did not receive any additional items. Total sales for the year were $1,985,746, and the yearly average inventory was $406,354.

**a.** What was the average dollar value of the inventory for January?

**b.** What is Ms. Chang's turnover for the year?

**c.** How does the rate of turnover compare to the average department store?

_____

_____

_____

_____

_____

_____

**16. Economics**  Why is inventory control so important to the financial health of fashion stores?

_____

_____

_____

_____

**17. Accounting**  What accounting statement does inventory impact? Does inventory add to or subtract from the financial value of the business?

_____

_____

_____

_____

_____

# RETAIL MARKETING RESEARCH EVENT

www.deca.org
/publications/HS_
Guide/guidetoc.html

You have been hired to conduct marketing research for a specialty clothing store that also carries jewelry. The store has been successful in the community for 85 years but now feels competitive pressure from major department stores and other chain retailers. You want to survey the current base of customers to find out what the store can do to maintain and increase customer loyalty. In addition, you want to find out where others shop for clothes and jewelry, what prices they are willing to pay, and what services they expect to receive.

Work with a group. Find a similar store in your community on which to base your research. You should survey an appropriate number of people to make up a relevant sampling. You will then make conclusions and propose a strategic plan of action. This project will consist of a 30-page written document and an oral presentation.

Your document should include a Summary Memorandum (one-page description of the project), Introduction (description of the business and community), Research Methods Used (description of your survey and how you conducted it), Findings and Conclusions of the Study (description of customers, buying behavior, measurement of existing customer satisfaction, and conclusion), Proposed Strategic Plan (goals and rationale, proposed activities with timelines, proposed budget, and a plan to evaluate effectiveness), Bibliography, and Appendix.

For the oral presentation, your group will have ten minutes to present and five minutes to answer questions. The written document will account for 70 points, and the oral presentation will account for 30 points.

# PROJECT: The COLLECTION POINT

Apparel manufacturer Anita Hinojosa has hired you to conduct marketing research. She designs junior-sized shorts and sells them to small retail stores. She needs information about the trends that will impact the styles and fabrics in demand next spring. She needs to know what to offer to retailers at the upcoming fashion market week in January. She is concerned about the length of shorts and the fit—relaxed, baggy, or tight. She also wonders if denim will be popular.

## Work with a group and complete the following activities.

**1.** Make a list of information you need to respond to Anita's concerns. From the list, develop a few questions for a survey.

**2.** Interview at least 10 girls in your school to collect the needed data.

**3.** If possible, contact a buyer at a store near your school that sells junior-sized shorts and share the data you've collected. Do your findings agree with the buyer's forecast?

**4.** Present a summary of your findings to the class. Include why you selected the particular students and store buyer to interview.

CHAPTER 10

# CREATING A FASHION BUSINESS

## LESSONS

10.1 A BUSINESS PLAN

10.2 RISK MANAGEMENT

10.3 LEADERSHIP

# WINNING STRATEGIES

## EVERARD'S CLOTHING

**L**ouis Everard, president of Everard's Clothing, is a man of style and substance who knew for many years that he would someday run his own clothing business. Everard's Clothing is a designer and specialty clothier located in the upscale Georgetown area of Washington, D.C. Everard's is a classy, vibrant store for discerning buyers who appreciate quality apparel with a superb fit. Everard's offers luxury apparel for both men and women.

Louis Everard grew up in Jamaica and learned how to perfectly fit tailored clothing in his parent's tailoring business. Later, Everard gained fashion business experience at Bloomingdale's, working in men's wear. The combination created a business magnet for repeat customers—the key to success. Customers come back when they like the service and the apparel.

Everard's Clothing is located in a city full of important people. The atmosphere of the store welcomes every visitor as if he or she were the most important person to walk through the door. Everard has focused his business on service.

Everard's business plan was developed three years before he found the space for the store. "The main component of the plan was to give us the edge over the competition through service, quality, and the human touch," states Everard. In addition to luxury Italian clothing and unique accessories, Everard's offers custom-designed and made-to-measure garments. Everard's maintains a full-time tailor on site whenever the store is open. Everard's is a premier clothing business based on a solid foundation of planning, business experience, and a passion for serving clients.

### THINK CRITICALLY

1. List at least three elements that make Everard's Clothing successful.
2. Why would Louis Everard base his business plan around his customers?

# CHAPTER 10
## Lesson 10.1

# A BUSINESS PLAN

**Define** legal structures for fashion businesses.

**Describe** a business plan.

## The Latest Style

After selling Banana Republic to Gap in 1983, Mel and Patricia Ziegler devoted the next ten years to raising their children before starting ZoZa, a new venture. ZoZa was a fashion business of couture-inspired apparel they dubbed "urban performance clothing." Their marketing strategy was to create great-looking apparel that did not require dry cleaning. Described in *USA Today* as having the look and feel of $1,400 designer blazers, ZoZa blazers cost $250 and were washable.

The Ziegler's business plan was designed around meeting the needs of fast, overscheduled lives. The business plan called for selling online and through physical sites they called "walk-in web sites," where people tried on clothing and placed orders. There were once plans for 50 such sites. After burning through $12 million in venture capital and $5 million in loans, ZoZa closed due to lack of money. The Zieglers still believe in their idea, but wish they had started on a much smaller scale, using business principles they knew instead of a grand, multimillion-dollar business launch.

Work with a group. Discuss some reasons ZoZa was unsuccessful. What could have been done differently?

## DEVELOPING A BUSINESS PLAN

Just as a buyer must spend a great deal of time planning, a business owner's first step is to develop a clear picture of all aspects of the potential new fashion business. Many businesses fail due to poor planning and inadequate financial management. A careful review of both business and personal goals early in the planning stage is a must. Some of the important issues that must be considered include

- reasons for wanting to start the business
- the personal knowledge and skill level needed to operate the business
- the niche the business will fill
- the outline of the legal business structure, operations, management, financing, and location

Many people want to be their own boss, but they frequently do not think through the complexity of being a business owner. The Small Business Administration (SBA), a federal government service organization, provides a wealth of information for people starting a business on its web site at **www.sba.gov**.

## SELECTING THE STRUCTURE

Potential owners should look at themselves and their interests in relation to a fashion business. Next they should complete research on the target customer—why a customer will buy from them instead of the competition. Then it is time to think about the legal structure of the business. The legal structure can be a sole proprietorship, a partnership, a "C" corporation, a subchapter S corporation, or a limited-liability company. Each structure has advantages and disadvantages.

**Sole Proprietorship** A **sole proprietorship** is a business owned and operated by one person. It is the simplest form of business to start, but creditors can take the private assets of the owner if the business fails while in debt.

**Partnership** A **partnership** is an agreement between two or more people to share in the ownership of a business. The decisions, responsibilities, profits, and losses are shared among the partners as described in an agreement signed by all.

Proprietorships and partnerships are easy to set up and are used by many individuals who are starting their first business. As a business grows, many business owners realize that they are putting their personal assets, including their savings accounts and homes, in jeopardy. Their assets could be lost if the business fails. Sometimes, it is a smart move to choose one of the other options as the legal structure for a business.

**"C" Corporation** A **"C" corporation** is set up as a legal entity that operates the business. The corporation has the legal rights and responsibilities for the business and is held liable rather than the individual owners. Personal and business assets are clearly distinguished, and only the business assets are at risk. A corporation must issue shares of stock. A **share of stock** is a unit of ownership issued to stockholders who control the company. Corporations pay taxes on profits at the corporate rate, and then stockholders pay personal income tax on dividends distributed from the profits. A

## CYBER MARKETING

DS Retail Technologies, Inc. was created from the ruins of a dot-com bomb. The online business was developed as a scaled-down, revised version of DailyShopper Network, Inc., which folded after trying to grow too big too quickly. DS Retail Technologies, like Daily-Shopper, uses a ZIP-code-driven search engine to find sales at stores near online visitors. Unlike DailyShopper, DS does not have its own web site to support. Instead, DS piggybacks on other well-known web sites. Corporations that have multiple chain stores spread across many states pay DS to provide promotional information to customers by ZIP code. If customers from a certain ZIP code visit the web site for The Bon Marché, a Federated store, they will see a localized version of a promotion called a *Net-Circular*. Visitors in a different ZIP code will see a different version.

THINK CRITICALLY
**1.** Why would stores want multiple versions of promotions?
**2.** Why would DS not want to have its own web site?

corporation is complex to set up and usually requires an attorney to file the forms needed by a state. When ZoZa went out of business, the personal assets of the Zieglers were not at risk because ZoZa was set up as a corporation.

**Subchapter S Corporation**  The **subchapter S corporation** combines some advantages of a "C" corporation and a partnership but retains the filing and stockholder complexity of a corporation. Personal assets are protected from creditors as in a "C" corporation. Just as in a partnership, income is only taxed as the personal income of the stockholders and not double taxed as in a "C" corporation. The requirements for incorporation apply. However, an S corporation must be an independent group not affiliated with any other corporation, so a major existing corporation cannot have a division that is an S corporation.

**Limited-Liability Company**  A **limited-liability company (LLC)** has the management and tax advantages of a partnership. It is not double taxed like a "C" corporation. The business does not pay taxes, but the owners pay personal income tax on the profits. It is similar in some ways to a corporation in that it protects the personal assets of the owner from the business's liabilities and is created by filing with the state. It is different from a corporation in that it does not issue stock or have stockholders. If a business intends to issue stock to raise funds, then the business cannot be an LLC. Everard's is an example of an LLC.

The SBA recommends obtaining legal advice from an attorney for help in deciding which legal structure of business is best for personal and business benefits.

## SELECTING THE SETTING

Choosing the location for a business is critical to its success, and the site selection should be made based on the target customers and their convenience. The general area and the building itself portray the image of the store to the customers. Customers need to feel secure when visiting. Knowing the demographics of the area and looking closely at other businesses in the area will help target the right space. Other factors to consider when choosing a location are the costs, size of the space needed, parking, and other transportation factors. Deciding if the store or business should be free-standing away from competition or part of a shopping

Several hundred residents of the Oak Lawn neighborhood in Dallas indicated their displeasure with a proposed Wal-Mart® Supercenter planned for their area. The residents believed that the 220,000-square-foot store jammed into a space half the size of typical supercenters would cause traffic jams and auto accidents. Traffic would be pushed into residential areas and increase crime. The store was estimated to bring 11,000 to 18,000 additional vehicle trips into the area each day. The Dallas City Planning Commission flatly turned down the proposal from Wal-Mart to create the radically different two-story, urban store. Wal-Mart traditionally builds in the suburbs and was "very disappointed" by the decision that kept it from entering the near-downtown market area.

**THINK CRITICALLY**
**1.** Should the residents of an area have control over what stores open there? Why or why not?
**2.** What do you think Wal-Mart should have done next?

center or mall for synergistic relationships will also influence the choice of space.

## OPENING SHOP

In both the United States and many other countries, people who have an interest in fashion and find a niche to fill can start a small fashion business. Some small businesses grow into huge corporations, while some intentionally remain small. Maro Lavis lives in Glyfada, Greece, a suburb of Athens. She is good at spotting American fashion trends that appeal to Greek women and

their daughters. Lavis used a connection with a Chicago fashion firm, I.B. Diffusion, and her talent to start a small business as a sole proprietorship. She makes three to four trips each year to the Chicago Apparel Mart and, with the able assistance of her U.S. friend Kathy Olsen, selects clothing to offer in Greece. Lavis personally delivers the apparel to her clients, and Lavis's husband assists her by keeping track of import taxes and other financial records. Her business thrives by providing unique clothing that cannot be found in U.S. stores located in Greece.

# TRY IT ON

**Describe two types of legal business structures.**

_____

_____

_____

# THE PLAN

**A** **business plan** is a guide used to help the owner make decisions. The plan is also used to "sell" the business idea to bankers or other investors as well as to vendors and potential landlords. The business plan represents the business until it physically exists.

## PUTTING IT TOGETHER

The SBA offers assistance in setting up a business as early as the planning stage. It divides the body of a business plan into four sections—the business description, the promotional plan, the financial plan, and the management plan.

The *business description* includes the type of business, its products and services, its location, its hours of operation, and an explanation of why the owner is starting the business. The goals and objectives of the business and information about the owner and his or her background are a part of the description. This is where fashion business experts, like Louis Everard, would show passion for the business. The description should be written with a tone that says the owner wants the reader to find the business intriguing. The words and phrases should create images for the reader of the dynamic, successful business the owner imagines.

The *promotional plan* includes all four of the components of promotion—advertising, public relations, publicity, and personal selling. Determining the right mix of the components is based on the details of the business description and the targeted customers.

The *financial plan* includes financial statements and budgets, such as start-up budgets, balance sheets, income projections, and cash flow statements. Other related documents that would be placed in this section of the plan are loan applications, personal financial statements, tax returns, resumes, lease or purchase agreements for building space, and required licenses. Letters of intent from vendors stating that they are agreeing to provide credit and ship goods to the business should also be included. The letters show that the business will have the fixtures and merchandise needed to operate.

The *management plan* details who will be on the management team, each manager's duties, what other personnel are needed to operate the business, and how the personnel will be trained. Managing people is a leadership skill that takes knowledge and practice.

Putting all of the pieces of a well-thought-out plan together requires time and effort. Once the plan is together, it should be shown to friends, other business people, and members of SCORE. The **Service Corps of Retired Executives (SCORE)** is a nonprofit association made up of retired executives and former business owners who are dedicated to helping small businesses start up and succeed. SCORE is a resource partner with the U.S. Small Business Administration. It has 10,500 volunteer members and 389 chapters throughout the United States and its territories. SCORE provides free business counseling and low-cost workshops for up-and-coming entrepreneurs.

People who really know that they want to operate their own business get excited when developing the business plan, and the plan will show their high level of initiative and interest.

**TIME OUT**

Enyce (pronounced en-ee-chay) started as a brand of unique men's hip-hop and urban-style apparel. The name Enyce is from the initials for New York City. The brand was started as a small business by three designers—Lando Felix, Tony Shellman, and Evan Davis. The brand grew to include women's apparel and is now a wholly owned subsidiary of Fila Sportswear.

## TRY IT ON

**How is a business plan used?**

## UNDERSTAND MARKETING CONCEPTS
Circle the best answer for each of the following questions.

1. A legal structure for business that is simple to set up and is controlled by an individual is a
   a. sole proprietorship.
   b. partnership.
   c. subchapter S corporation.
   d. limited-liability company.

2. A legal structure that protects the owners' assets but does not double tax the business income or have stockholders is a
   a. sole proprietorship.
   b. partnership.
   c. "C" corporation.
   d. limited-liability company.

## THINK CRITICALLY
Answer the following questions as completely as possible. If necessary, use a separate sheet of paper.

3. List and discuss three issues that should be considered before starting a fashion business.

_____

_____

_____

_____

4. **Economics** Describe two of the legal structures for a business that protect the owners' assets.

_____

_____

_____

_____

_____

_____

# CHAPTER 10
## Lesson 10.2

# RISK MANAGEMENT

# GOALS

**Identify** business risks.

**Explain** methods to control risks.

## The Latest Style

The Sue Wong Collection is one of three labels designed by Sue Wong. She was born in China and grew up primarily in California. After designing junior dresses for Arpeja, she started her own business focused on sportswear. Management decisions to shift the focus to dresses, hire a new sales manager, and move manufacturing out of the United States are credited with turning Wong's business from lackluster to blazing.

The new sales manager, Joanie Graham-Pepper, succeeded in selling Sue Wong Nocturne, an evening line, to five large specialty chain stores, including Neiman Marcus. The line is carried in all 33 Neiman Marcus stores. Sending all manufacturing to China, where the magnificent handwork is completed on each garment, has kept production costs low. The combination of decisions led to significant improvements in profits.

Work with a group. Discuss the changes that Wong made to improve her business. What kinds of risk were involved in making such drastic changes?

# BUSINESS RISKS

Opening a fashion business has risks. **Risks** are hazards or exposures to loss or injury. The risks could include failure of the business or losses from a disaster such as a fire. Identifying and addressing potential risks can lessen the negative impact they may impose.

## CATEGORIZING RISKS

Fashion business risks can be categorized based on the results of the risk, the controllability of the risks, and the insurability of the risks.

**Risk Results** Certain kinds of risk can result in loss. If a fire burns down the building where a fashion business is housed, it results in a loss of the building and the apparel and equipment inside. It could also result in workers or customers being injured, which is a very serious loss. This kind of risk is called **pure risk** because there is no chance to gain from the event. Another type of risk offers the possibility of gain or loss,

such as investment in a fashion business. The risk result could be a gain or loss of money. Risk where gains or losses are possible is called **speculative risk**.

**Risk Control**   **Controllable risks** are those that can be prevented or those in which the frequency of occurrence at least can be reduced. If a merchandise display includes a mannequin, the mannequin can be secured to prevent it from toppling over if bumped by a customer. This is preventable and, thus, is a controllable risk. A risk of windows being broken by a sudden hailstorm is an example of an uncontrollable risk. With an **uncontrollable risk**, the fashion business cannot take any action to prevent the event from occurring.

**Risk Insurance**   Insurance companies will provide risk coverage and payment for losses caused by insurable risks. **Insurable risks** are pure rather than speculative risks that possibly could happen to a large number of businesses. They include risks where the chances and amount of the loss can be predicted. Glass breakage and fire damage are insurable risks. When the chances of a risk occurring cannot be predicted or the amount of loss cannot be estimated, the risk is an **uninsurable risk**. Investing in a fashion business is a speculative risk and an uninsurable risk because no one can predict the success or failure of the business.

## MARKETING RISKS

Within a fashion business, the marketing risks generally fall into two categories—environmental risks and business management risks. Occasionally the two types overlap.

**Environmental Risks**   Risks that relate to safe conditions within the business are **environmental risks**. They are usually pure risks that are preventable, predictable, and generally insurable. The Occupational Safety and Health Administration (OSHA) is a federal agency that develops safety regulations and enforces the law covering working conditions. OSHA regulations govern the ways in which a business must act to provide safe conditions for workers and customers.

**Business Management Risks**   Risks that relate to decisions such as the customer segment to target or the price points of merchandise to offer are **business management risks**. They are uninsurable, speculative risks because the results are not predictable. If a new, small business carefully selects a target market segment that is underserved at a specific price point, the business has reduced the risk of failure but is not assured success.

Small business owners find the 24/7 business world of today to be tiring and stressful. Businesses that are located in malls or near other fashion businesses feel pressured to stay open seven days a week to successfully compete. Some small businesses have risked closing one day a week because of religious beliefs or to allow the owners and employees to spend time with their families.

## TRY IT ON

**Investing in a fashion business involves what kinds of risk?**

_____

_____

_____

# CONTROLLING RISK

Loss happens on occasion even when every precaution has been taken. Smart business owners and managers develop written procedures that help prevent incidents from occurring and help employees know what to do when incidents happen. Written procedures help reduce the risk of business decisions and protect the health and safety of customers and employees.

## MINIMIZING ENVIRONMENTAL RISKS

A business has a legal responsibility to maintain a safe place for employees and customers. Businesses are *liable,* or responsible under the law, for accidents caused by negligence and failure to eliminate known hazards. Meeting governmental health and safety codes is a first step toward accident prevention, but businesses should go beyond the minimum. Smart businesses have written safety procedures that call for routine safety checks, training for every employee regarding the procedures, and rigorous enforcement of safety rules.

Just as fire drills are important in schools, plans for evacuating a building must be made before an actual disaster occurs. Employees can help customers evacuate only if they have rehearsed themselves. When an accident occurs, employees need to know the exact steps for reporting the incident. A reporting procedure should be known and followed by every employee. Generally, an incident report form is completed once people are out of immediate danger. The report form has prompts for all needed information, such as the names of the people involved. The information from the report is used to evaluate the need for any further safety measures that could prevent future occurrences. Further, the documented information may prove useful for insurance claim purposes and possible legal action.

## MINIMIZING BUSINESS MANAGEMENT RISKS

Business owners and managers who follow sound business practices and understand and apply the seven functions of marketing have taken a major step toward reducing the risk of poor decisions. Using the data available through marketing-information management and marketing research can assure that the decisions are based on a solid foundation. Potential business owners can gain experience by working for other successful businesses and joining professional organizations where knowledge is shared. There are no guarantees, but the results of owning a fashion business can be worth the risks.

# TRY IT ON

**Why are procedures for accident reporting needed?**

_____

_____

_____

_____

## UNDERSTAND MARKETING CONCEPTS

Circle the best answer for each of the following questions.

**1.** When there is no chance to gain from an event, it is characterized as
   **a.** high risk.
   **b.** pure risk.
   **c.** speculative risk.
   **d.** dangerous risk.

**2.** When the risk can result in gains or losses, it is called
   **a.** high risk.
   **b.** pure risk.
   **c.** speculative risk.
   **d.** dangerous risk.

## THINK CRITICALLY

Answer the following questions as completely as possible. If necessary, use a separate sheet of paper.

**3. Research** Visit **www.osha.gov/SLTC/firesafety/index.html**. On this fire safety page, scroll to "Control" and look at the document titled "How to Prepare for Workplace Emergencies." Find safety issues mentioned in this article and select two to discuss below.

_____

_____

_____

_____

_____

**4.** Why do employees need to know safety procedures?

_____

_____

_____

_____

_____

# CHAPTER
# 10
## Lesson 10.3

# LEADERSHIP

# GOALS

**List** and **explain** the characteristics of a good leader.

**Explain** the role of student and professional organizations in fashion marketing.

## The Latest Style

**C**arl Williams, a.k.a. (also known as) Karl Kani, grew up in Brooklyn, New York. He began making apparel for himself and others when he could not afford to buy what he wanted. He dreamed of starting his own fashion business and moved to Los Angeles to work for Cross Colour, a clothing manufacturer. Williams designed his own line while at Cross Colour and later bought the Karl Kani label from the company.

In 1993, Williams opened Karl Kani-Infinity. In the first year of business, over $34 million in sales were generated. Eight years later, the company had 42 employees and $76.9 million in sales. The company is still a privately held corporation, and Williams serves as the president and CEO. His corporation has been recognized by *Black Enterprise Magazine* as one of the most successful African-American-owned firms in the world.

Work with a group. What characteristics might Williams have that are needed to become a successful business owner?

# BECOMING A LEADER

**T**o succeed as a fashion business owner or as a manager of a business owned by others requires leadership skills. **Leadership** includes the ability to influence the behavior of others. To be a great leader means to be willing to accept great responsibility. A person must be willing to learn what it takes to be a good leader and should continually update his or her leadership skills.

## THE CHARACTERISTICS

Developing and applying leadership skills requires knowledge and practice. There are many opinions on the exact characteristics of an effective leader, but the list usually includes effective skills in communications, problem solving, team membership, resource management, knowledge acquisition, and ethical behavior.

**Communications** An effective leader must be able to express himself or herself clearly in both written and verbal communications. A leader must communicate the vision of the business to investors, partners, and employees. Most employees want to

do a good job, but they have to understand what is expected of them.

**Problem Solving** When faced with monumental barriers to the success of a fashion business, a strong leader can step back, listen to the ideas of others, consider all of the alternatives, visualize the results of each alternative action, and decide which strategies are best for the company. A leader does not have all the answers, but a leader knows where to find the answers and how to ask others to help.

When Anita Hinojosa's apparel manufacturing company was faced with low sales, she knew she had to make some choices to stay in business. She had to cut expenses. She had an extremely loyal and well-paid staff to whom she presented the entire financial picture. She asked them for alternatives. They volunteered to take a pay cut until sales improved, and she agreed to pay them a bonus when the margin allowed. The company survived difficult times because Hinojosa was an effective communicator and problem solver who rallied her employees together as a unified team.

**Team Membership** An effective leader must have good *interpersonal skills* that show appreciation and respect toward all team members and customers in a way that develops loyalty and trust. The team must know they can depend on the leader to keep his or her word. Leaders are accountable for their own personal actions as well as those of the employees.

**Resource Management** Resource management is more than just balancing the financial records. Managing resources includes considering data when making decisions and directing people so that they are working at the most important tasks.

**CYBER MARKETING**

Fashion companies that use the Internet to conduct business, whether for buying, selling, or learning, can belong to an arm of the National Retail Federation (NRF) called Shop.org. With more than 400 members, this organization provides store-based, Internet-based, and catalog-based retailers and manufacturers with a professional forum to meet their needs. Conferences are held both online and at conference centers where members can attend sessions focused on best practices in online merchandising. The organization's web site address is **www.shop.org/**.

**THINK CRITICALLY**
**Why would the NRF offer a division that works with online retailers?**

In addition to solving the immediate problem through pay cuts, the sales staff of Hinojosa's company agreed to research what their most successful competitors were doing right and to seek new clients to expand sales. They used the Internet to find retail stores and the names of buyers at those stores from whom they could solicit new business. Instead of waiting until market week, they took samples to the buyers. They offered to help with promotions, such as trunk shows, to increase interest in their brand. Hinojosa is a leader of a team that pulls together.

**Knowledge Acquisition** Education does not stop at the school exit. Learning must become a lifelong habit. If leaders are not learning on the job, then they are falling behind. Fashion business leaders are avid readers. They read about the economy, what their competition is doing, what is new in technology, and most of all what their customers are saying. Fashion business leaders also make sure their employees are continually learning by providing opportunities for them to take college courses, attend seminars, and learn new skills.

**Ethical Behavior**   Ethical behavior does not make the front page of the newspaper. Unethical behavior does make the news and tends to make some people think that everyone is unethical. Strong leaders behave ethically even when no one is watching. Leaders want their employees and customers to know that they can be trusted to follow through and honestly and consistently mean what they say.

Anita Hinojosa took advantage of the slow production time to encourage employees to attend seminars that would allow them to learn about new ideas and processes. She also spent time looking for new vendors. She met with a findings vendor who told her that there were zippers available that cost about one-fourth the usual price. When Hinojosa questioned the reasons, the vendor admitted that they were defective. The zippers would work through the first two or three washings but then would begin to disintegrate. Risking the trust of customers by producing low-quality garments was not even an option for Hinojosa. The offer also made her question the integrity of the vendor offering the zippers, and she declined further business with the vendor.

## DEVELOPING CONFIDENCE

Do you aspire to own or manage a successful fashion business? Take time to understand and develop the characteristics of a good leader. Take advantage of opportunities to participate in professional organizations and gain work-based experience in fashion businesses. These experiences will help you develop the skills and confidence you need.

The Fashion Business Incubator is an organization whose mission is to help and support small to mid-size apparel manufacturers in Los Angeles. The organization offers new members training and networking opportunities with established professionals experienced in the business.

## TRY IT ON

**List six characteristics of an effective leader.**

_____

_____

_____

_____

# PROFESSIONAL ORGANIZATIONS

An interesting way to continue to acquire knowledge as a fashion leader is to belong to student and professional organizations. **Professional organizations** are organized around a purpose by groups of career-minded individuals with common interests. Some of the student and professional organizations in fashion are DECA, Delta Epsilon Chi, National Retail Federation, and Fashion Group International, Inc.

## DECA

The purpose of the Distributive Education Clubs of America (DECA), an association of marketing students, is to develop future leaders in marketing, management, and entrepreneurship through leadership and career-development activities. DECA starts at the local level with the organization of a high school chapter that meets on a regular basis. A DECA chapter can be a starting point in which to safely practice leadership skills at local, state, and international levels. Competitive events related to marketing occupations allow students a chance to compare themselves to marketing students around the world. The winners receive recognition, trophies, scholarships, cash, and travel opportunities.

## DELTA EPSILON CHI

While in college, students can participate in Delta Epsilon Chi, a national association that is the collegiate division of DECA. College students majoring in marketing, management, and entrepreneurship will find opportunities to grow professionally with this organization. As part of DECA, Delta Epsilon Chi shares a National Advisory Board (NAB). Major companies and other professional organizations serve as NAB members and provide marketing-related opportunities for students.

## NATIONAL RETAIL FEDERATION

The National Retail Federation (NRF) is the world's largest retail trade organization. The mission of NRF, as expressed on its web site at **www.nrf.com**, is "to conduct programs and services in research, education, training, information technology, and government affairs that protect and advance the interests of the retail industry." This professional organization has an affiliated nonprofit foundation that gathers information and provides it to members. NRF supports knowledge acquisition on the part of its members through publications, a major annual convention with outstanding presenters, and specialized conferences throughout the year that focus on topics such as loss prevention and effective advertising.

## FASHION GROUP INTERNATIONAL, INC.

The Fashion Group International, Inc. (FGI) is a professional association of fashion and interior design executives. Part of the organization's mission is to advance professionalism in fashion and

In 1928, Edna Woolman Chase, the Editor-in-Chief of *Vogue* magazine, invited 17 women to lunch in New York City. Most of the invitees held jobs in high-level positions in the fashion industry. They were all mutually respected, and they all believed that fashion needed a support system that allowed for the exchange of ideas and resources. Elizabeth Arden, Edith Head, and Eleanor Roosevelt were among the lunch group. That meeting marked the beginning of the professional organization known today as The Fashion Group International, Inc. (FGI). FGI was formalized as an organization two years later in 1930.

**THINK CRITICALLY**
**1.** Why would professionals want to share ideas with competitors?
**2.** How might professional organizations help individuals?

to encourage men and women to seek career opportunities in fashion through scholarships, internships, and career counseling. FGI offers members an opportunity to interact with other members throughout the world.

# TRY IT ON

**What are the purposes of professional fashion-related organizations?**

_____

_____

_____

## TrendSetters

### LINDA KUYKENDALL

Linda Kuykendall is a fashion executive who has dedicated her life to serving her family, her community, and the fashion industry. She is the Director of Special Events and Fashion Events for Foley's, a division of the May Department Stores Company. She is also a member of Fashion Group International, Inc. and served as the Houston Regional Director of FGI for two years. Under her leadership, FGI increased membership by 20 percent and provided support for up-and-coming fashion students. "I truly believe in mentoring those who are coming after, and in FGI, I have that opportunity," states Kuykendall.

Kuykendall started her career at Northern Natural Gas Company in Omaha, Nebraska, where part of her job was to organize special events for the company. Later in Houston, she served as a volunteer developing special events for charities. She found her real passion when she put together a fashion show for the March of Dimes. From there, she developed a freelance special-events business. Due to her success and reputation for excellence, she was offered the job as Manager of Fashion Events by Foley's and eventually became Director of Special Events and Fashion Events for all 67 Foley's stores in five states.

The Federation of Houston Professional Women honored Kuykendall as a "Woman of Excellence." The recognition was based on her service to FGI and the thousand of hours of her time given to helping many community charities raise funds through special events.

### THINK CRITICALLY

**1.** Why would Linda Kuykendall think FGI is important?

**2.** What might Kuykendall have gained by belonging to professional organizations?

## UNDERSTAND MARKETING CONCEPTS
Circle the best answer for each of the following questions.

1. Leadership characteristics include
   a. team membership and ethical behavior.
   b. effective communication and problem solving.
   c. knowledge acquisition and resource management.
   d. all of these.

2. An organized group of career-minded individuals with common interests is a
   a. leadership group.
   b. team membership.
   c. professional organization.
   d. venture capitalist.

## THINK CRITICALLY
Answer the following questions as completely as possible. If necessary, use a separate sheet of paper.

3. Why is continued learning so critical to an effective leader? What are ways a professional fashion leader can continue to learn?

_____

_____

_____

_____

_____

4. What is meant by ethical behavior? When do leaders need to behave ethically?

_____

_____

_____

_____

_____

_____

_____

# CHAPTER 10 REVIEW

## REVIEW MARKETING CONCEPTS

Write the letter of the term that matches each definition. Some terms will not be used.

_____ **1.** A guide used to help the potential business owner make decisions, sell the business idea, and represent the business until it physically exists

_____ **2.** Unit of ownership issued to stockholders

_____ **3.** Type of risk that can be prevented or in which the frequency of occurrence at least can be reduced

_____ **4.** A nonprofit association made up of retired executives and former business owners who are dedicated to helping small businesses start up and succeed

_____ **5.** A legal entity that operates a business and must issue stock

_____ **6.** Type of risk where there is no chance to gain from an event

**a.** business management risks
**b.** business plan
**c.** "C" corporation
**d.** controllable risk
**e.** environmental risks
**f.** insurable risk
**g.** leadership
**h.** limited-liability company (LLC)
**i.** partnership
**j.** professional organizations
**k.** pure risk
**l.** risk
**m.** SCORE
**n.** share of stock
**o.** sole proprietorship
**p.** speculative risk
**q.** subchapter S corporation
**r.** uncontrollable risk
**s.** uninsurable risk

**Circle the best answer.**

**7.** Business structures that put owners' personal assets at risk are
   **a.** sole proprietorships and partnerships.
   **b.** partnerships and subchapter S corporations.
   **c.** subchapter S corporations and "C" corporations.
   **d.** "C" corporations and limited-liability companies.

**8.** Business structures that are taxed at both the business and personal levels are
   **a.** sole proprietorships and partnerships.
   **b.** subchapter S corporations and limited-liability companies.
   **c.** "C" corporations.
   **d.** both a and b.

# THINK CRITICALLY

**9.** Briefly describe the parts of a business plan. How is the business plan used and who might see the plan?

fashion.swlearning.com

_____

_____

_____

_____

_____

**10.** Discuss why planning before opening a fashion business is so important.

_____

_____

_____

_____

_____

**11.** Why might a fashion business be liable for loss due to injury of a customer in the store?

_____

_____

_____

_____

**12.** What can a business do to reduce health and safety risks? What part do employees play in safety at work?

_____

_____

_____

_____

_____

## MAKE CONNECTIONS

**13. Language Arts**  Write a narrative about what might have been the consequences if Anita Hinojosa had bought the defective zippers as described in Lesson 10.3 instead of turning them down. What possible reaction might she have received from the retail buyers who were her customers? Would the decision to buy the zippers have impacted the opinion of her employees about her leadership characteristics? Include two sentences about how you feel about Hinojosa's decision not to buy the zippers.

_____

_____

_____

_____

_____

_____

_____

**14. Economics**  Why is investing in a fashion business a type of risk? What type of risk is it?

_____

_____

_____

_____

_____

**15. Business**  What is the purpose of belonging to a professional organization? How can membership benefit the career of a fashion marketer?

_____

_____

_____

_____

_____

_____

## ENTREPRENEURSHIP PARTICIPATING EVENT

www.deca.org
/publications/HS_
Guide/guidetoc.html

You have decided to open a clothing store in your community. Determine what type of store meets the needs of your target market. What type of business structure will work best for your business?

Work with a group. Prepare a business plan for your store that will help you make decisions and sell the business idea. This project will consist of a 10-page written document and a 20-minute oral presentation (15 minutes to present and 5 minutes to answer questions). Since this project is rather lengthy, you will complete it in segments to be combined for the final project. The parts of your business plan will include

- Summary Memorandum
- Description and Analysis of the Business Situation
  - Rationale and marketing research
  - Introduction (type of business and brief description of product(s)/service(s) involved)
  - Self-analysis
  - Analysis of the trading area, customers, and location
  - Proposed organization
- Proposed Marketing/Promotion Plan
  - Proposed product or service
  - Proposed pricing policy
  - Personal promotion
  - Nonpersonal promotion
  - Place
- Proposed Financing Plan
  - Projected income/cash flow statement (projected budget describing income and expenditures for the first year)
  - Projected three-year plan
  - Capital and repayment plan

# PROJECT: The COLLECTION POINT

You have been hired to develop a procedure for reporting risk or safety hazard incidents. Search the Internet for tips on managing business risk and minimizing loss.

**Work with a group and complete the following activities.**

**1.** Develop a computer presentation with tips on business risk management.

**2.** Write a one-page procedure for reporting risk incidents.

**3.** Using a word-processing program, develop an incident report form to collect data.

**4.** Present your findings, and review the incident report procedure and form with the class.

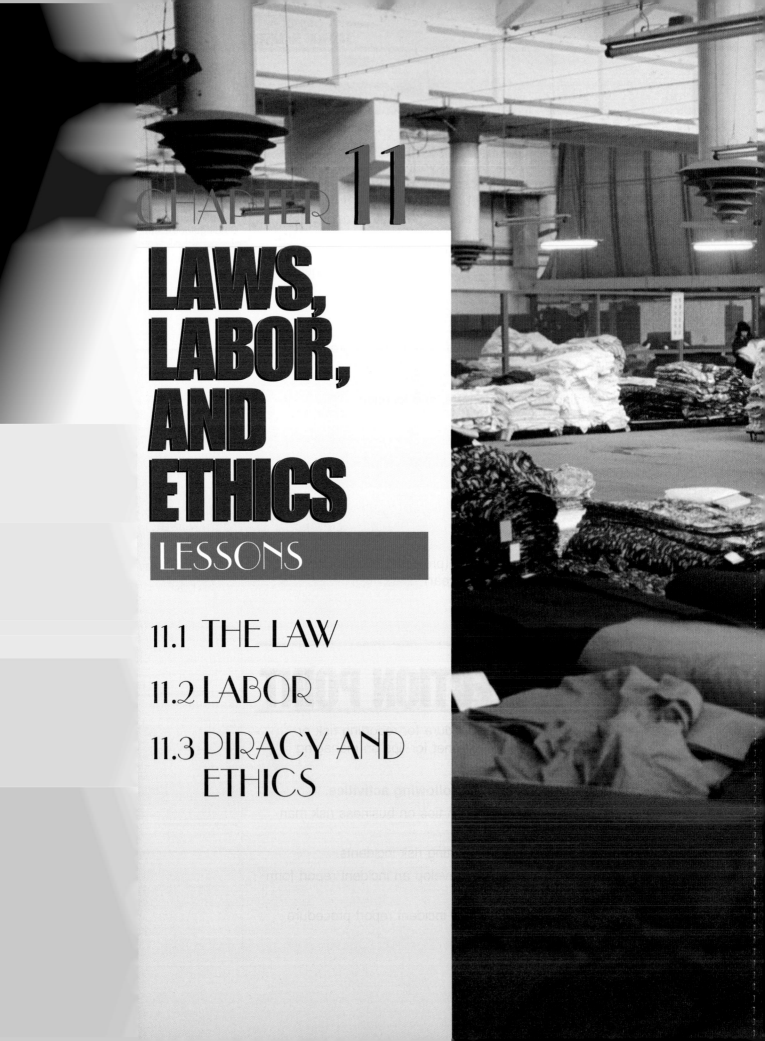

# LAWS, LABOR, AND ETHICS

## LESSONS

11.1 THE LAW

11.2 LABOR

11.3 PIRACY AND
      ETHICS

# WINNING STRATEGIES

## AMERICAN APPAREL

The trend to send apparel manufacturing out of the United States to countries where wages and living standards are very low was growing when Los Angeles-based American Apparel opened for business in 1995. At the same time, other U.S. apparel manufacturers were cutting back or filing for bankruptcy. Company founder and CEO Dov Charney is a bit of a rebel and runs a business that is intriguingly out of step with the industry as a whole.

American Apparel manufactures knit T-shirts, underwear, and innerwear from 100 percent, U.S.-grown cotton. It is a lean operation with approximately 1,000 employees and only Charney serving as designer, but it sold more than 5.5 million T-shirts in its sixth year of business. The apparel is sold through distributors such as All American Tees in Lubbock, Texas and TSC Apparel in Cincinnati, Ohio.

Charney emphasizes in his advertising that American Apparel garments are high quality and made in a "sweatshop-free environment." The company's web site at **www.americanapparel.net** emphasizes its excellent working conditions and "better workplace ethics" as compared to those of foreign manufacturers. The issues of high-tech equipment, heating, ventilation, lighting, childcare, transportation, parking, immigration assistance, above-average wages, benefits, and on-site training for workers are addressed. American Apparel provides consumers and retailers with an alternative to exploitative garment production. It is a model for an industry in need of direction.

### THINK CRITICALLY

1. Should consumers and retailers be concerned about the conditions under which the garments they buy are produced? Elaborate on your answer.

2. What does American Apparel mean by "better workplace ethics"?

# THE LAW

**GOALS**

**Explain** legislation that impacts the fashion industry.

**List** requirements of laws governing apparel labeling.

## The Latest Style

Garment manufacturers outside of the United States sometimes ship goods to another country, and from there, the goods are forwarded to the United States. This action, called *transshipment*, is taken in an attempt to circumvent quotas on the amount of goods each country can send into the United States. The quotas are set to protect U.S. companies from being overwhelmed by inexpensive garments from low-wage, low-standard-of-living countries. By shipping through another country, the garments can be mislabeled so they deceive U.S. Customs' officials about their true origin.

Enforcement of the quotas is the responsibility of the U.S. Department of Commerce (DOC). This department is charged with formulating international economic policies, promoting international trade, enforcing trade agreements, and improving access to overseas markets for U.S. industries. A cabinet-level secretary heads this federal department.

The U.S. Department of Commerce is focused on opening foreign markets to U.S. textile exports, but it faces the reality of negotiating in a politically charged atmosphere. The interests of the garment industry frequently lose out to other causes, such as gaining cooperation from a country on ending terrorism or nuclear proliferation.

Work with a partner. Discuss how international policy impacts the fashion industry in the United States.

## LEGISLATION

In the late 1990s and early 2000s, the U.S. Congress passed a series of trade bills covering sub-Saharan African nations, the Caribbean Basin, and the Andean nations of Peru, Colombia, Ecuador, and Bolivia. The bills renewed and expanded trade preferences for the regions, opening up U.S. markets to import goods from these nations.

### BOTH SIDES

Many retailers who believe that easing import tariffs would provide new sources of apparel production and keep costs low for consumers praised the free-trade agreements. The bills were cited as providing ways for countries like Colombia to end dependence on illegal drug trade as a mainstay of their economy. The bills would build prosperity, end poverty, and strengthen democracy in the developing nations.

However, there was opposition from labor activists and some U.S. apparel and textile manufacturers who viewed the passage of the trade bills as another erosion of manufacturing in the United States. They also believed that employers in the countries benefiting from the trade bills would disregard workers' rights, seize the proceeds from the increased trade, and continue drug trade as usual, with no gain for the United States.

There are multiple arguments to the debate regarding protection for U.S. companies in labor-intensive businesses. U.S. companies face competitors that have low production costs because their workers are paid substandard wages, have terrible working conditions, or both. Additionally, some countries have laws that set up burdensome restrictions that hinder the importing and selling of U.S. garments and textiles.

In 2001, 124 textile plants in the United States were either closed or downsized. During 2000 and 2001, 50,000 textile workers were laid off, leaving about 448,000 textile workers in the United States. This number is far fewer than the number of textile workers in the United States in 1939, the first year the number was recorded. About half of the remaining textile jobs are expected to be lost in the future.

It costs more to produce goods in clean, well-lit, air-conditioned spaces with workers who are well paid and provided with benefits such as health insurance. The costs must be passed on to consumers. When consumers choose lower-priced garments, they are influencing the decision about where garment manufacturing takes place.

## INTERNATIONAL IMPACTS

Decisions made about opening or closing trade in other industries can heavily impact the fashion industry. Tariffs passed by the United States in an attempt to protect an unrelated industry can sometimes cause a backlash that affects all exports, including those of the fashion industry.

## Fashion Flashback

Antitrust laws prohibit price fixing in the apparel industry. These laws are enforced by the Federal Trade Commission (FTC). In 1995, the FTC reached an agreement with the Council of Fashion Designers of America (CFDA) regarding price-fixing charges. The agreement prohibited the CFDA and 7th on Sixth, Inc. from collectively negotiating prices paid to runway models. The consent agreement prohibited the CFDA from setting one price to be paid to all models during the fashion shows produced for CFDA members by 7th on Sixth. The FTC requires each CFDA member to negotiate with models and modeling agencies rather than fixing a set price.

### THINK CRITICALLY
**1.** Who would benefit from the prohibition of price fixing the wages of models?
**2.** Why would the CFDA have wanted to collectively negotiate the models' wages?

Converse Inc., the U.S. athletic shoe company, is the owner of the All Star canvas sneaker with the trademark star logo. Millions of cheap knockoff pairs of All Star sneakers have been sold in Brazil by a Brazilian company that registered the All Star brand in Brazil. Converse was successful in Brazilian courts in winning the right to stop the illegal use of the logo.

**Retaliation**   The United States imposed heavy import tariffs on steel after some countries illegally sold large quantities at prices below the cost of production. The high tariffs were meant to protect the U.S. steel industry. Consequently, the European Union (EU) threatened to impose retaliatory tariffs of as much as 100 percent on U.S. apparel products to be imported into EU countries. Because the United States and the EU are members of the World Trade Organization (WTO), both are subject to WTO processes to stop the retaliatory action. Such trade retaliation can hinder exporting opportunities for the U.S. apparel market. According to the U.S. Department of Commerce, the United States exported $255.8 million worth of apparel and $1.03 billion worth of textiles to the EU in 2001.

**Cooperation**   In the United States, brand names and trademarks can be registered and protected from use by others. For specific product designs, creators may obtain a **patent,** which protects the design from being copied. International agreements also protect the trademarks and designs from being copied in other countries.

The enforcement of copyright laws is dependent upon trade agreements and other alliances between the nations involved. Even when nations have enacted copyright laws, they do not always properly enforce them. One of the purposes of the WTO is to help negotiate the enforcement of copyright laws among member nations.

# TRY IT ON

**Why might tariffs in another industry hurt the apparel industry?**

# LABELS

PRODUCT/
SERVICE
MANAGEMENT

The Textile Act and the Wool Act govern labeling of apparel in the United States. Proper labeling of apparel provides protection to consumers and assists in the enforcement of regulations covering imports and safety laws.

## LABEL REQUIREMENTS

Apparel labels are required by law to have four pieces of information—the fiber content, the country of origin, care instructions, and an indication of a business name.

**Fiber Content** The generic names and the percentage of content of the fibers used in a garment are listed in descending order on its label. When a fiber makes up less than five percent of a garment, it may be listed as "other fiber." The exception is wool, which, if present, must be listed on the label no matter what percentage makes up the garment.

**Country of Origin** "Made in the USA" can be listed on the label only if the apparel is both made in the United States and made of material from the United States. A garment that is partially produced in the United States can be labeled as "Made in Mexico (or another country), finished in the U.S." or "Made in the USA of imported fabric." The country of origin must be on the front of the label that is sewn inside the neck or center back of the garment. This placement of the label makes it easy for customs officials to check the country of origin.

**Care Instructions** Manufacturers are required to provide instructions for care of apparel. The care instructions include directions for washing the garment or indicate the need for dry cleaning. A care label must be permanently attached and made to endure the useful life of the garment. Research shows that four out of five consumers read the care label before purchasing a garment and then follow the care instructions after purchasing.

**Business Name** Garment labels must include the name of the manufacturer, importer, or seller of the garment. The business may be represented by a registration number issued by the Federal Trade Commission (FTC), which oversees apparel labeling.

**CYBER MARKETING**

Apparel manufacturers may use standard symbols on care labels to represent the care options. The symbols are intended to help non-English readers interpret the instructions as well as to save space on the labels. A list of common care symbols are found at **www.textileaffairs. com/lguide.htm**. Textile Industry Affairs is a unit of the Clorox Company. At the web site, Textile Industry Affairs lists its mission as "to assist apparel/textile professionals in understanding and implementing the FTC Care Label Rule."

**THINK CRITICALLY**
Why would a bleach company want to assist apparel professionals with care label rules?

## TRY IT ON

**Name four pieces of information required on apparel labels.**

_____

_____

_____

_____

## UNDERSTAND MARKETING CONCEPTS

Circle the best answer for each of the following questions.

**1.** Patents protect designs from
   **a.** designer fees.
   **b.** being copied.
   **c.** tariffs.
   **d.** fading.

**2.** The federal agency that oversees apparel labeling is the
   **a.** FTC.
   **b.** DOC.
   **c.** WTO.
   **d.** DES.

## THINK CRITICALLY

Answer the following questions as completely as possible. If necessary, use a separate sheet of paper.

**3.** What are the advantages and disadvantages of trade bills that open U.S. markets to low-priced apparel from foreign sources?

_____

_____

_____

_____

**4.** What is the significance of each of the four items that must be included on apparel labels? Can you think of other information that would be helpful to include on labels?

_____

_____

_____

_____

_____

_____

# LABOR

## The Latest Style

**S**weatshop Watch is a coalition of labor groups whose goal is the protection of workers. Sweatshop Watch helps workers file lawsuits against *sweatshops*, or companies that allegedly mistreat workers.

Nineteen workers filed a lawsuit against retailer Forever 21 for unpaid wages and poor working conditions at its manufacturing shops. The claims were mostly dismissed by a federal judge, but Sweatshop Watch continued a boycott campaign against the retailer for more than a year. Sweatshop Watch posted a 45-foot billboard across from Forever 21's flagship store in Los Angeles and carried signs around the area stating "Boycott Forever 21." The billboard was up for about a month and was included in a lawsuit that Forever 21 filed against Sweatshop Watch and the 19 workers for defamation.

Work with a group. Discuss Forever 21's responsibility to the workers who manufacture the clothing it sells. Do workers have the right to disrupt a retailer's business because of poor working conditions at a manufacturer when claims have been dismissed by a judge?

## GOALS

**Identify** areas of garment labor abuse.

**Explain** the role of labor unions in the fashion industry.

# WORKERS' RIGHTS

**U**nions have formed over the past 125 years to protect workers from abuse, inhumane working conditions, and substandard pay. Unions apply the advantage of many workers collaborating to effect change. In the United States, laws are in place to protect workers, but violations of the law continue to occur.

## THE TRIANGLE FIRE

Protection of U.S. workers under the law and their right to organize into unions shield them from exploitation, but that has not always been the case. Garment worker abuse has a long history. One of the most horrific incidents happened in New York City on March 25, 1911. On that date, a fire broke out in the ten-story building that housed the Triangle Shirtwaist Company. Of the approximately 500 people in the building at the time, 145 died. Those who died were primarily young women, some as young as 14. Investigation of the fire and survivor testimony showed that some of the exit doors in the building were locked because the owners wanted to prevent thefts by the workers. Additionally, inadequate fire escapes and ladders too short to assist those on the top floors contributed to the deaths.

## THE ABUSE CONTINUES

The Triangle fire serves as a tragic example of worker abuse in the United States, when greed overcomes a company's sense of ethics and humanity. The young women who died in the fire were primarily recent immigrants who were vulnerable to the company's abuse and greed. The vulnerability of immigrant workers continues today in the United States. There are estimated to be as many as 2,000 illegally operating sweatshops in the United States. An example is the 1995 case of 72 immigrants from Thailand who were discovered in captivity in El Monte, California. They were forced to produce garments under inhumane conditions. The Thais worked 18 hours per day and slept in tiny, rat-infested rooms of a building surrounded by barbed wire and armed guards who forced them to meet production quotas. A sister sweatshop in Los Angeles exploited Latino workers.

Five major retail companies that bought apparel from the sweatshops paid $2 million in damages to the slave laborers. The retailers were held responsible for the conditions under which their clothing was produced. The operators of the El Monte sweatshop were convicted of civil rights violations and were sentenced to seven years in prison. The Thai and Latino workers were rescued and eventually were able to find homes and other jobs.

## U.S. WORKERS

Most U.S. citizens know that they are protected by law against work abuse. Sometimes, however, they are hesitant to complain about mistreatment due to fear of losing their jobs. Recent immigrants will frequently not complain about work abuse because they fear retaliation from their employers or an authority such as the police.

Two groups in the United States have formed to help oversee workers' rights in apparel plants. The Worker Rights Consortium (WRC) began as a militant college student group that organized to address concerns of worker abuse in the production of apparel with college logos. WRC is made up of students from approximately 70 universities who have joined together to investigate the working conditions of the

Information about the tragic Triangle fire is available on the web site of Cornell University at **www.ilr.cornell. edu/trianglefire/**. The site features articles and research about the tragedy. The story of the fire and its major impact on the garment industry and workers' rights are told in detail.

**THINK CRITICALLY**
**1.** After visiting the web site, what impression do you have about the Triangle fire?
**2.** What is the historical significance of the fire to the apparel industry?

college apparel producers. *The Wall Street Journal* reported that Nike Inc. CEO Phil Knight withdrew a promised $30 million gift when he learned that his alma mater, the University of Oregon, had joined the WRC. The University of Oregon has since withdrawn its membership from the WRC and has instead joined the Fair Labor Association (FLA). Approximately 170 universities are represented by the less radical FLA. The FLA also has corporate members such as Nike and Reebok. There is concern among critics that the manufacturers' support of FLA will taint the credibility of its reports.

## GLOBAL WORKERS

Workers' rights throughout the world are a continuing concern. There are no worldwide laws that protect labor, and in some countries workers are afraid to stand up for their rights. U.S. unions have watched in dismay as clothing manufacturers have moved production from the United States to countries where labor laws are not enforced or are nonexistent.

## CHILD LABOR

The International Labour Organization (ILO) has reported that more than 246 million children are engaged in child labor in both poor and rich industrial countries. Spain is estimated to have about 200,000 children under age 14 working in the footwear industry. Underdeveloped countries like Bangladesh are estimated to have as many as 6.3 million working children. The ILO is a specialized agency that is part of the United Nations. On the ILO web site at **www.ilo.org**, the agency sets "minimum standards of basic labor rights—freedom of association, the right to organize, collective bargaining, abolition of forced labor, equality of opportunity and treatment, and other standards regulating conditions across the entire spectrum of work-related issues." There are 175 member countries that belong to the ILO.

In July 2002, the U.S. Department of Labor released a report required under the Trade and Development Act of 2000. The report identified nine countries that are known to have child labor in textile, apparel, and footwear production. The countries were Bangladesh, Egypt, India, Indonesia, Kenya, Lebanon, Pakistan, Turkey, and Venezuela. The Department of Labor was working with the ILO to provide funding for programs in these countries to keep children in school and their parents at work.

# TRY IT ON

**Why does the United States report on child labor in other countries?**

_____

_____

_____

# UNICONS

A **union** is a legal organization of workers that obtains a majority consent to represent them to the management of a business. A unionized business is often called a **closed shop** because the management can employ only union members and can negotiate only with the union regarding wages and benefits. By joining the union, workers give up their right to independently bargain with the company. When the union negotiates with the business on behalf of all members, it is called **collective bargaining**. When agreements cannot be reached regarding wages, benefits, and working conditions, union members may go on strike, essentially shutting down the business until an agreement is reached.

## UNITE

In 1995, the Union of Needletrades, Industrial and Textile Employees (UNITE) was formed when the International Ladies Garment Workers Union and the Amalgamated Clothing and Textile Workers Union joined together. The combined unions had over 250,000 members across the United States, Canada, and Puerto Rico. Dating back to the early 1880s, garment workers have banded together to protest inhumane conditions and substandard wages. That beginning has led to today's union strength.

UNITE is famous for its successful anti-sweatshop movement that has pressured U.S. manufacturers and retailers to take a hard look at the conditions under which their apparel is being produced. UNITE demands that production shops have no child or prison laborers, pay minimum wages and overtime pay, do not force overtime on unwilling workers, and allow the workers to organize. UNITE has repeatedly embarrassed retailers and brand-name companies by drawing attention to their use of sweatshops. UNITE's efforts motivated the U.S. Labor Department to list the names of fashion businesses that do not use sweatshops.

The apparel business faces a never-ending conflict between the pressure to keep production costs low and the rights of workers to have a safe, clean workplace and adequate wages. Unions add weight to the workers' side of the conflict through the strength of numbers and by calling attention to workplace abuses through the news media. Apparel manufacturers and retailers try to balance their concern for workers with their concern for the price points that target customers are willing to pay. Ultimately, consumers decide by buying or not buying apparel that is made in sweatshops.

## TRY IT ON

**How do unions impact working conditions?**

_____

_____

_____

_____

## UNDERSTAND MARKETING CONCEPTS
Circle the best answer for each of the following questions.

1. An organization that collectively bargains for workers' rights is called a
   a. sweatshop.
   b. closed shop.
   c. union.
   d. professional organization.

2. The Triangle Shirtwaist Company was an example of a
   a. sweatshop.
   b. closed shop.
   c. union.
   d. professional organization.

## THINK CRITICALLY
Answer the following questions as completely as possible. If necessary, use a separate sheet of paper.

3. **Research** Visit **www.ilo.org** and obtain information on current child labor concerns. Write a paragraph about the issue.

_____

_____

_____

_____

_____

4. Discuss what gives unions power to negotiate with management.

_____

_____

_____

_____

_____

_____

# PIRACY AND ETHICS

**Identify** fashion counterfeiting and piracy issues.

**Explain** ethical issues pertaining to business conduct in the fashion industry.

## The Latest Style

The International AntiCounterfeiting Coalition (IACC) is the largest organization in the world focused on fighting counterfeiting and piracy. The IACC initiates action and supports the action of governments throughout the world to stop counterfeiting. The group provides information and training to member businesses and law enforcement agencies.

The IACC holds conferences at which international piracy issues are addressed. Some of these issues include enforcement of standards and laws in the United States and abroad and the role of trade associations in the protection of copyrights for the apparel industry.

The IACC believes that there is a direct connection between organized crime, terrorism, drug smuggling, and counterfeit merchandise. In New Jersey, drug dogs found heroin inside fake Chanel and Louis Vuitton handbags. The handbags were identical to the ones sold at flea markets and out of car trunks.

Work with a group. Discuss why counterfeiting is an international problem. Why would a fashion retailer buy counterfeit goods to sell? Who do counterfeit goods harm?

## PIRACY

The price of brand-name apparel that is legally produced includes the costs of the original design, materials, production, and marketing. The marketing costs accumulate through years of advertising and the creation of consumer demand. When a brand has been advertised for a number of years, the difference between the actual costs of production and the market price can be significant. **Piracy** is the creation of illegal copies of apparel that are sold at a lower price. The illegal copies dilute the demand for the brand name by making it widely available.

### COUNTERFEIT APPAREL

When garments are the exact copies of items that are registered with the U.S. Patent and Trademark Office, the items are **counterfeit**. Counterfeit apparel is an international problem. One snowboarding boot manufacturer reported losing over $1 million in annual sales to counterfeit boots manufactured in Korea and South America. The cost in U.S. jobs due to counterfeiting is estimated to be hundreds of thousands of dollars, and the loss of taxes that support local infrastructure, such as roads, is estimated to be in the billions. Some studies have shown that counterfeiting costs brand-name companies as much as 22 percent of sales.

## CONSUMER ATTITUDES

The attitude of consumers about purchasing counterfeit goods is sometimes very relaxed. A large number of people do not understand the economic consequences of purchasing illegal copies of brand-name products. Globally, counterfeiting is a major problem that takes international cooperation to address.

## INTERNATIONAL ENFORCEMENT

Countries that join the World Trade Organization must pass laws prohibiting counterfeiting of apparel as part of the membership requirements. Enforcement of the laws is a different story, however. The current penalties for counterfeiting are very low. The lack of enforcement of related laws increases the impact of the problem. Counterfeiting is extremely profitable for criminals because they benefit from the marketing paid for by the legitimate sellers to create demand for the product. The profits from counterfeit products may be used to finance illegal activities such as terrorism and drug smuggling.

Counterfeiting takes place on many levels and with varying degrees of sophistication. People who copy the logos of sports teams onto T-shirts using equipment set up in their garages are counterfeiters. In poor nations, these cottage industries are politically difficult to stop. If a government prevents impoverished families from earning enough money to feed their children, it can be portrayed as being at the command of a multibillion-dollar corporation. In reality, enforcement protects legitimate jobs of other workers employed in legal manufacturing businesses.

Harley Lewin is a legal expert on counterfeit apparel. In an interview published on **www.just-style.com**, Lewin stated that every brand that is being advertised or marketed is also being counterfeited. Mr. Lewin indicated that blue jeans and athletic shoes are the most frequently counterfeited apparel items. He estimates that 20 percent of the gross domestic product of China comes from counterfeiting.

A large percentage of counterfeit goods comes from manufacturers who are hired by a company to produce its brand of product. In addition

Products with the official 2000 Summer Olympics' logo were worth over $500 million. The products were primarily apparel items displaying the Olympic logo to commemorate the games held in Sydney, Australia. To combat counterfeiting, the products were printed with ink that included DNA from an anonymous athlete. Officials then could determine the authenticity of the garments by examining the ink, using a process similar to one that is used in modern crime investigation.

to producing what the brand holder orders, the manufacturer produces additional runs of the apparel and sells them with no proceeds going to the brand holder. The goods may be identical to those that are legal, but sell for much less. If a manufacturer is producing a line for a brand owner and shipping it to stores in the United States, it may also produce more of the same garments illegally and ship them to stores in Asia. This action steals the profit from the rightful owner and dilutes the brand name.

# TRY IT ON

**Why do consumers buy counterfeit apparel?**

_____

_____

_____

# FASHION ETHICS

**P**eople in the fashion industry, as in all businesses, face ethical dilemmas. **Ethics** is a system of deciding what is right or wrong in a reasoned and impartial manner. Ethical people can be trusted to make the right decisions, even when the decisions are not to their benefit.

## DEVELOPING MORALS

Ethical behavior is based on solid moral principles and high standards in both business and personal life. Morality is developed as people mature from children into adults. Children learn that bad behavior results in punishment. Mature adults have grown to understand that they should act based on moral principles and high standards, even if no one knows the basis of their actions.

Since bad actions make the news more often than good behavior, this leads some people to believe that everyone behaves unethically. People begin to think that unethical behavior

In 2002, London Fashion Week organizers agreed to change the date of their show to accommodate planned commemoration of the September 11, 2001 terrorist attacks in New York. When a group of designers decided to show their lines in New York on the last day of London Fashion Week in spite of the agreement, the British Fashion Council was insulted and incensed. The overlapping dates caused journalists and buyers to miss some designers' shows. The failure of the cooperative agreement was a disappointment, and the designers' behavior was considered unethical.

**THINK CRITICALLY**
**1.** Should all designers have agreed to honor the agreement with Britain? Why or why not?
**2.** Why shouldn't the show dates for London and New York overlap?

is appropriate because everyone is doing it. This is simply not true, and those who behave unethically risk their reputations, careers, and the businesses they operate. Unethical behavior is not something that stays hidden. Customers and employees become aware of unethical behavior, and they quickly lose trust and respect for those who act in an unethical manner.

## MAKING CHOICES

All businesses face the choices involved with accurately tracking and reporting their financial situation. The consequences of not using ethical accounting practices are known to eventually destroy a business. Management that places value only on maximizing investors' earnings and managers' incomes does so at the risk of jail time and damaged reputation. Some of the ethical issues in the fashion industry go beyond those of other businesses. Besides accounting practices, fashion industry executives face issues of providing appropriate working conditions, using practices that are environmentally friendly, and avoiding unethical bribes to retailers and journalists.

## ETHICS COUNT

A question that is frequently asked in a serious discussion of ethics is "Whose ethics are to be taught?" Almost all societies can agree on some moral principles such as "do not commit murder" or "do not steal," but other issues are more difficult. The use of animal fur in fashions is an example of a controversial topic that splits groups. Stella McCartney is one fashion designer who has taken a strong stand against the use of fur in fashions.

No fashion business publicly supports sweatshop practices, but many have chosen to ignore the issue in favor of obtaining a great price on apparel construction. Some companies have paid little attention to the

issue until unions or other groups have made the public aware of the horrendous conditions suffered by workers. Some countries sign agreements to put an end to sweatshops but do not enforce the agreements. Ethics must be demonstrated with proper actions, not just by saying what is "politically correct" in public.

# TRY IT ON

## What is meant by ethical behavior?

_____

_____

_____

### HARLEY I. LEWIN

**W**hen the Los Angeles County Sheriff's Department raided three El Monte, California-area shoe importers and distributors, more than 50,000 pairs of counterfeit Vans shoes were seized and the owners were arrested. Attorney Harley Lewin led the investigation. The illegal shoes were being imported and distributed in Southern California, Mexico, and Latin America and were worth more than $2.35 million.

When 3,700 pairs of illegal shoes with the New Balance-registered 'N' Saddle design were seized in Highland Park, New Jersey, Harley Lewin was again leading the effort. More than 160,000 pairs of counterfeit New Balance shoes were seized in Indonesia as a result of work done by Lewin.

Lewin is an attorney at Greenberg Traurig, a national law firm. He specializes in intellectual property rights, trademark, and copyright enforcement. Lewin completed his undergraduate work and his law degree at the University of Wisconsin. He is conversational in Spanish, French, and Italian. Lewin is a frequent speaker to groups such as the International AntiCounterfeiting Coalition (IACC).

**THINK CRITICALLY**
**1.** Why would apparel manufacturers need to hire an attorney to fight counterfeiting?
**2.** List three ideas for educating consumers about the harms caused by counterfeiting.

## UNDERSTAND MARKETING CONCEPTS

Circle the best answer for each of the following questions.

**1.** Illegal copies of apparel are
 **a.** foreign made.
 **b.** hard to find.
 **c.** sold in stores.
 **d.** counterfeit.

**2.** A system for deciding what is right or wrong is called
 **a.** a political system.
 **b.** a production system.
 **c.** ethics.
 **d.** all of these.

## THINK CRITICALLY

Answer the following questions as completely as possible. If necessary, use a separate sheet of paper.

**3.** Whose job is it to make sure that sweatshops are not used to manufacture apparel?

_____

_____

_____

_____

_____

**4.** Discuss who is hurt by counterfeit apparel.

_____

_____

_____

_____

_____

_____

# CHAPTER 11 REVIEW

## REVIEW MARKETING CONCEPTS

Write the letter of the term that matches each definition. Some terms will not be used.

_____ **1.** When a union negotiates with a business on behalf of all members

_____ **2.** A business that can employ only union members and can negotiate only with the union regarding wages and benefits

_____ **3.** The creation of illegal copies of apparel that are sold at a lower price

_____ **4.** Exact copies of items that are registered with the U.S. Patent and Trademark Office

_____ **5.** A legal organization of workers that obtains a majority consent to represent them to the management of a business

_____ **6.** A system of deciding what is right or wrong in a reasoned and impartial manner

**a.** closed shop
**b.** collective bargaining
**c.** counterfeit
**d.** ethics
**e.** patent
**f.** piracy
**g.** union

**Circle the best answer.**

**7.** Information that must be on apparel labels includes
 **a.** fiber content, country of origin, and business name.
 **b.** designer, care instructions, and source.
 **c.** city name, union, and washing instructions.
 **d.** all of these.

**8.** Counterfeiting apparel does harm to
 **a.** legal workers.
 **b.** tax payers.
 **c.** legitimate manufacturers.
 **d.** all of these.

**9.** UNITE wants apparel production shops to
 **a.** have no child or prison workers.
 **b.** pay minimum wages and overtime.
 **c.** not force overtime.
 **d.** do all of these.

# THINK CRITICALLY

**10.** How might trade in an unrelated industry impact the apparel industry?

_____

_____

_____

_____

_____

_____

**11.** Could an event like the Triangle fire happen today in the United States? Why or why not? What safeguards should be in place to prevent similar tragedies?

_____

_____

_____

_____

_____

_____

**12.** Discuss competing forces that define the conflict between workers' rights and management decisions.

_____

_____

_____

_____

_____

**13.** Discuss ethical issues facing fashion industry executives. How do the issues compare to issues facing other industries?

_____

_____

_____

_____

_____

_____

## MAKE CONNECTIONS

**14. Marketing Math** You have been hired to help determine how much wage increase can be given to the 100 workers at an apparel plant that currently pays $6.00 per hour. Each employee works 170 hours per month. The plant makes and sells 10,000 blouses per month at $32.00 each and has contracts for the next year to continue to sell this quantity. Management wishes to keep $30,000 each month in reserve for emergencies. Using the figures in the chart below, determine the maximum amount the company can offer each of the 100 employees as an hourly raise.

| Current Operating Expenses | Monthly |
|---|---|
| Electricity and other utilities | $ 4,200 |
| Building loan | 13,900 |
| Insurance | 1,300 |
| Transportation | 5,000 |
| Materials to produce 10,000 blouses | 150,000 |
| Wages for 100 people @ $6 per hour for 170 hours per month | 102,000 |
| Sales, management, and clerical salaries | 6,000 |
| Total | $282,400 |

_____

_____

_____

_____

_____

_____

**15. Geography** Locate Bangladesh on a map. List nearby countries. Use the Internet to obtain information about the current economic and political conditions in Bangladesh. Write a brief description of happenings that might impact efforts to improve working conditions in apparel manufacturing in Bangladesh.

_____

_____

_____

_____

_____

_____

## MARKETING MANAGEMENT SERIES ROLE PLAY

You work at an upscale clothing store that specializes in designer clothing. Customers pay high prices for big-name brands. Recently you have realized that your store is selling imitation designer clothes. Many of the clothes sold in your store are illegal imitations of designer brands. The imitation merchandise carried by your store earns a larger profit margin while customers think they are buying actual top-designer names.

You realize the danger of carrying counterfeit merchandise. You must try to persuade the store manager to stop carrying the fake brands. Your argument should also include an alternate strategy for earning good profits.

You have ten minutes to develop your strategy, ten minutes to present the information to the store manager, and five minutes to answer any additional questions from the manager. The manager will be represented by the class.

**www.deca.org /publications/HS_ Guide/guidetoc.html**

# PROJECT: The COLLECTION POINT

You have been hired to assist Gary Olsen, director of an apparel manufacturers' association, in development of a code of ethics for his group. He likes the codes used by the Better Business Bureau and the American Advertising Federation and believes they can be adapted. Further, he believes there are additional issues not covered by the two codes that need to be addressed for his organization.

**Work with a group and complete the following activities.**

1. Visit **www.iit.edu/departments/csep/PublicWWW/codes/** for information about business codes of ethics.

2. Read the codes of ethics for the Better Business Bureau and the American Advertising Federation.

3. Make a list of the best points from the two codes, adapting them to apparel manufacturing.

4. Add to the list any points that are not included that would be needed for apparel manufacturers.

5. Use presentation software to develop a two-minute presentation that you could use to present your points to the apparel manufacturers' association.

6. Present your findings to the class as if they were a group of apparel manufacturers.

CHAPTER 12

# FASHION MARKETING CAREERS

## LESSONS

12.1 FASHION BUSINESSES

12.2 FASHION CAREERS

12.3 FINDING AND KEEPING A FASHION CAREER

# WINNING STRATEGIES

## MOJA DESIGN

**A**dam Wolman and Jamil Myrie met in high school and maintained a strong friendship throughout graduate school. Wolman's family owned a lenscrafting business, and he recognized that there were no companies that designed eyewear for the younger market. Wolman and Myrie thus began plans for Moja Design, which would create trendy eyewear under licensing agreements with existing fashion businesses.

Wolman serves as Moja Design's CEO and director of product development, and Myrie is director of sales. The company is headquartered in Manhattan and develops eyewear with iCB clothing, a Tokyo bridge label, and with designer Maurice Malone.

To obtain Malone's business, Wolman and Myrie literally crashed a party Malone was giving and approached him with the idea for designing eyewear. The joint venture has been a success, making Malone the first African-American fashion eyewear designer in the United States. Malone eyewear typically retails for $150 to $240.

The Moja Design team also partners with *Ocean Drive*, a Miami-based fashion magazine, to design an eyewear line. This line is more moderately priced, selling from $65 to $90.

Wolman and Myrie continue to add new ventures with other fashion-forward lines. In its fourth year of business, Moja Design earned $10 million in net revenue. Moja Design has combined marketing to an underserved niche with a lean business structure to create an "out of sight" business success.

### THINK CRITICALLY
1. What are some reasons Moja Design is successful?
2. Discuss another fashion niche that is underserved and might have business potential.

# FASHION BUSINESSES

**GOALS**

**Describe** businesses related to the fashion industry.

**Describe** the role of fashion retailers and the variety of careers in retail.

## The Latest Style

The success of some fashion-related businesses is based on the failure of others. DJM Asset Management is a firm that helps sell off the assets of bankrupt retailers. The firm's web site at **www.djmasset.com** contains copies of news articles written about the business. Headlines include "Going Out of Business? They Can Help," from *New York Times,* December 2001, and "Repo Men of Retailing" from *The Wall Street Journal,* November 2001.

DJM Managing Director Thomas Laczay spends a great deal of time looking at dark, empty stores. Laczay auctions bankrupt retailers' assets. His job requires a combined knowledge of bankruptcy law and retail real estate. When a major chain such as Kmart declares bankruptcy, it may close hundreds of stores. The auctions can result in hundreds of leases changing hands in a matter of hours. DJM provides an invaluable service to fashion retailers in trouble and earns four- to seven-percent commission on the resulting cash.

Work with a group. Discuss other fashion-related businesses that exist because of the mistakes of others. Can companies learn from studying the mistakes of failed businesses? Why or why not?

# PRODUCTION AND PUBLICATIONS

There are hundreds of businesses related to the fashion industry. Although many of the businesses have a major presence in New York or Los Angeles, they are actually headquartered throughout the United States.

## TREND FORECASTERS

**MARKETING-INFORMATION MANAGEMENT**

Companies that create trend forecasts provide valuable information and serve as the research arm for retailers and other businesses in the fashion industry. The companies offer information and services that would otherwise be too expensive for clients to acquire on their own through in-house divisions.

Trend spotting can be a tricky business. If the customer segment is a large group of people in the mainstream, their tastes will have a broad appeal. Forecasting trends of a small group of on-the-edge fashion consumers may not be commercially viable for a retailer who needs a large volume of customers to make a profit.

The Doneger Group is a service-oriented corporation that started as a buying office for U.S. women's specialty retailers. A **buying office** is located in a market center, like New York, and buys for multiple retailers from a large base of vendors. Founded in 1946, The Doneger Group has expanded by adding a forecasting and trends division, which is led by creative director David Wolfe. Wolfe is considered one of the world's most quoted fashion forecasters. The forecasting and trends division is called Doneger Creative Services. It provides information to retailers, manufacturers, magazines, and other fashion industry segments. In addition to color forecasts, Doneger prepares custom color and trend research, lifestyle analysis, and assistance with product line development.

## FASHION PRODUCERS

**PRODUCT/ SERVICE MANAGEMENT**

Companies that produce fashions include manufacturers of textiles and findings, designers, pattern makers, and more.

Kellwood is a manufacturer of fashion apparel headquartered in St. Louis, Missouri. Kellwood products are marketed under 14 different brand names, including

Sag Harbor, David Dart, and Koret. The brands are sold at major department stores and specialty stores, as well as online and through catalogs. Kellwood also manufactures private labels for certain stores. In 2000, Kellwood used more than 240 domestic and 470 international subcontractors. Kellwood understands that marketing is essential to distinguishing the brands and keeping retailers interested in selling Kellwood fashions. Kellwood has a division president devoted specifically to marketing.

Stephen Ruzow is the president of Kellwood's women's wear division headquartered in New York. Ruzow's job is to work with the women's wear managers to develop marketing, licensing, and brand-name products. Ruzow came to Kellwood with 30 years of fashion experience, which includes founding Pegasus Apparel Group, Inc. and serving as a division president of Warnaco.

## FASHION PUBLISHERS

PROMOTION

Fashion magazines are popular throughout the world. In the United States, the top ten fashion magazines are all headquartered in New York and have an audience of over 30 million readers. In developing nations, the number of readers is increasing along with the income of the people. The content of fashion magazines in China would be considered boring in the United States but of great interest to shoppers just learning to make fashion choices. Fashion magazines are extremely influential in marketing fashions and helping consumers decide what to buy and where to buy.

Fashion magazines earn the majority of their revenues from advertisements rather than from subscriptions. Beauty products contribute a large amount of the ad pages in fashion magazines. Sales of most beauty products are sensitive to economic slowdowns. Thus, when the economy is down and fashion sales are slow, magazines suffer.

Condé Nast Publications is a major publisher of magazines. The Condé Nast titles include *Glamour, Vanity Fair, GQ,* and *Vogue.* Condé Nast was scheduled to launch *Teen Vogue* in 2003. Company president Steven T. Florio made the announcement along with the news that

*Details* is a fashion magazine for men ages 25 to 35. *Details* covers men's fashion trends and claims to speak to this generation of men from an insider's point of view. *Women's Wear Daily* ran a feature pointing out that *Details* had published a major blunder in its August 2002 edition. A feature article titled "Dudes Who Dish" was credited to Kurt Andersen, an author and cultural radio talk show host on National Public Radio. There was also an editorial by *Details'* editor Daniel Peres discussing the article and a small photo and contributor blurb about Andersen. The problem with the article was that the alleged author, Kurt Andersen, denied having any knowledge of it. He was quoted in *Women's Wear Daily* as saying, "I did not write this article and had no role in its creation." Peres issued a statement that *Details'* apology would be published in its October 2002 issue.

**THINK CRITICALLY**

**1.** Do fashion magazines have an obligation to check the accuracy of published information? Why or why not?

**2.** Why might someone have deceived the magazine with a fake article?

the magazine would be produced in the new Euro magazine size (6 3/4" by 9"), which is smaller than most U.S. magazines. Steven Florio's brother, Tom Florio, is a vice president and publisher of *Vogue*, one of the best-selling fashion magazines.

*Nylon* is a fashion magazine that focuses on women ages 21 to 34. The magazine showcases designer, alternative, and streetwear fashions. The target reader has a household income of $64,500, is very active, and is interested in fashion. *Nylon* claims a circulation of 250,000. Entrepreneur Marvin Jarrett and his wife Jaclynn founded the magazine as a voice for urban fashion.

# TRY IT ON

## Why are fashion magazines popular with consumers?

# RETAIL AND DISTRIBUTION

**DISTRIBUTION**

Fashion retailers provide the latest styles and serve as intermediaries, moving the apparel from the manufacturer to the consumer. The variety of careers in retailing include buyer, salesperson, divisional merchandise manager, and general merchandise manager. The types of careers and the responsibilities of the positions vary greatly depending on the size of the business. In a small business, employees may wear several hats, while in a large business, positions may be very specialized.

Juliana Collezione is a fashion company that sells high-quality women's apparel in a unique and personal way. Sales consultants are hired and trained through Home Marketing Associates (HMA), Inc. The sales consultants present the season's collection four times per year to clients, one person at a time, in pleasant surroundings where they can try on the clothing.

Jeanette Coon owns an image consulting business and shows the Juliana line in her home, scheduling her clients for about 90 minutes each. Her Juliana business has grown to

the point that customers book their dates and times months in advance to be one of the first to see a new line.

Juliana Collezione implements its distribution plan because it believes there is a niche to be filled with quality design, value, and personalized service. The niche was vacated when fashion moved from an art to a convenient, profit-driven commodity.

The Juliana designer, Julijana Kos, was born in Europe, studied in the United States, and was a sportswear designer for eight years before founding Juliana. Kos and a work associate, Irvin Spitalnick, formed Juliana Collezione together. Spitalnick has served as the president of HMA since it was formed in 1994. The companies have found a way to provide extraordinary service to a discriminating customer.

Wal-Mart® is the largest retailer in the world and a major apparel retailer. Wal-Mart has had its share of accusations about poor treatment of employees and the use of sweatshop suppliers, but in general Wal-Mart is seen as a company with integrity that cares about customers. Wal-Mart pushes suppliers and landlords for the lowest prices, but in turn passes the savings on to the consumer.

Wal-Mart CEO H. Lee Scott is quoted by the International Council of Shopping Centers at **www.icsc.org** as saying, "What is meaningful is three basic building blocks—service to the customer, respect for the individual, and striving for excellence." These three principles have paid off with over $218 billion in sales in over 4,000 Wal-Mart stores.

**CYBER MARKETING**

Moja Design's web site at **www.mojadesign. com** offers eyecare professionals an opportunity to buy directly from the company with an account that can be set up online. Once retailers' accounts are established, they can view Moja Design's entire line, check availability and pricing, and order online. Consumers are also welcomed to the site and can locate a Moja Design retailer near them by entering their area code.

**THINK CRITICALLY**
**1.** How could Moja Design persuade eyecare professionals to visit its web site?
**2.** How would consumers know about the web site?

# TRY IT ON

**Describe the difference in sales positions between Juliana Collezione and Wal-Mart®.**

# Final Fit

## UNDERSTAND MARKETING CONCEPTS
Circle the best answer for each of the following questions.

**1.** Fashion magazines receive the majority of their revenues from
- **a.** purchasing and distributing fashions.
- **b.** subscriptions.
- **c.** advertising.
- **d.** newsstand sales.

**2.** A buying office
- **a.** is usually located in a market center.
- **b.** buys for multiple retailers.
- **c.** buys from a large base of vendors.
- **d.** is characterized by all of these.

## THINK CRITICALLY
Answer the following questions as completely as possible. If necessary, use a separate sheet of paper.

**3. Communication** Reread the quote from Wal-Mart® CEO H. Lee Scott on page 266. Write a paragraph about the attitude conveyed by the basic building blocks of Wal-Mart.

_____

_____

_____

_____

**4.** Describe businesses other than retailers that play a role in the fashion industry.

_____

_____

_____

_____

_____

_____

# FASHION CAREERS

**Describe** careers in fashion marketing.

**Describe** behind-the-scenes careers that support the fashion industry.

## The Latest Style

**D**avid Yurman was a sculptor, and his wife Sybil was a painter. They opened their jewelry business in 1979. Together, they have combined art and design to create luxurious jewelry, the first brand of its kind in the United States. The Yurman brand of luxury jewelry is one of the most recognized in the world and provides about $500 million in annual retail sales.

The Yurmans have slowly grown the business and added new lines as the business was ready for them. Watches and children's jewelry are two of the product lines that have helped double sales in five years. There are more than 425 stores and 30 in-store shops that sell the Yurman brand. There are also two David Yurman stores, one on Madison Avenue in New York and one in Costa Mesa, California.

David Yurman is the CEO and main designer while Sybil Yurman is the president and chief marketing officer. The Yurmans' web site at **www.davidyurman.com** refers to the brand as representing "authentic American glamour." The Yurmans love their business, and it shows in their success.

Work with a partner. Discuss why the Yurmans' business is so successful. What characteristics might the Yurmans possess that have helped their business succeed?

## MARKETING CAREERS

**T**here is a multitude of careers related to fashion marketing. Careers within each of the seven marketing functions require a wide range of education and experience. Apparel and accessories designing and supermodeling are two well-known fashion careers that are difficult to achieve, but Nima New York's Jewelry and model Tyson Beckford are examples of how it can be done.

### NEW DESIGNERS

Successful designers break into designing in many different ways but share a common creativity, imagination, understanding of the seven marketing functions, and desire to succeed.

Two young women with a love of fashion and a sense of style have propelled a hobby into a successful business. Niria Portella and Marilyn Lopez had made their own jewelry for years. They received so many compliments and questions about where it could be purchased that opening a business seemed like a natural next step. They joined the first two letters of their first names and created Nima New York's Jewelry.

Portella and Lopez studied advertising and public relations in college and were both working full-time jobs when they started their business. Portella was a fashion editor for *Twist* magazine, and Lopez was handling publicity for Jive Records.

Portella and Lopez use their marketing backgrounds to help promote their jewelry line. The jewelry follows high-quality, classical, vintage styles, but is moderately priced. Nima has three distribution routes—retailers, direct sales to customers, and on-line sales at **www. nimanewyork.com**. The business is set for continued growth with a solid marketing plan as the foundation.

## MODELS

Fashions are made to be worn and are best shown on live models. Models are professionals who represent the body size and shape of the typical target cus-

Designer Ann Lowe left a legacy of fashion style and grace for wealthy and powerful families in the United States. One of her most famous designs was for Jacqueline Bouvier's marriage to John F. Kennedy in 1953. The wedding dress was made of 50 yards of ivory silk taffeta and took two months to make. It featured a portrait neckline and bouffant skirt decorated with interwoven bands of tucking and tiny wax flowers. Lowe also designed the pink silk gowns and matching tudor caps worn by the bridal attendants. Lowe, the granddaughter of a former slave, was born in Clayton, Alabama in 1898 and overcame great barriers to become an amazing designer of elegant and classical apparel. Her work is featured in an exhibit, "A Stitch In Time: 1800 to 2000," that has toured the United States highlighting the contributions of African-American fashion designers. The tour was organized by the Black Fashion Museum of Washington, D.C.

**THINK CRITICALLY**
**1.** Why do you think Ann Lowe's work was so well received?
**2.** What obstacles make it difficult for any new designer to succeed?

tomer. Some models are fit models, whose job is to work with designers to assure the fit of garments. Other models are well-known for appearing in runway shows, print, and other media presentations of fashions.

Tyson Beckford's discovery and his jump from street thug to supermodel is a "Cinderfella" kind of story. Beckford admits he was headed toward a life of crime when he was "discovered" by an editor of a hip-hop magazine and introduced to fashion photographers. Beckford's photographers introduced him to Ralph Lauren, who immediately hired him in 1993 to represent Polo with an exclusive contract. Beckford, born in Rochester, New York, has all-American good looks that are a combination of his Jamaican, Panamanian, and Chinese heritages. Beckford has graced the cover of most major fashion publications.

# TRY IT ON

**Why do designers and models often have other full-time jobs at the beginning of their careers?**

_____

_____

_____

## SUPPORTING FASHION

**B**ehind the scenes of the fashion industry are people in careers that make the public show appear exciting and relevant. Two of those careers are fashion educator and trade show organizer.

### FASHION EDUCATOR

Everyday in high schools and colleges throughout the world, educators are helping students learn about fashion careers. Those who are teaching courses in fashion marketing speak from experience in the business, and those who administer the programs help make it all possible.

Joyce F. Brown is president of the Fashion Institute of Technology (FIT) located on Seventh Avenue in New York City. FIT is a college that offers associate's, bachelor's, and master's degrees in fashion design, interior design, advertising, and marketing communications, among others. Brown moved into her leadership role after working in several positions at City University of New York (CUNY). As president of FIT, a college that serves more than 12,000 students, Brown's typical day is spent working on strategic planning and fundraising for the college. Her responsibilities include acting as chief administrator and educational officer of the college.

Paul Campbell serves Polo as vice president of human resources. Human resources is the department that handles personnel issues. Campbell started a "fair employment program" aimed at ensuring that there were no discrimination issues at Polo.

## TRADE SHOW ORGANIZER

Trade shows bring together business people who want to learn something new and make connections with other people in the same industry. Attending functions that allow you to meet and connect with other people interested in doing business is called **networking**. Networking with all of the key players in a fast-moving industry is to everyone's advantage. Most fashion trade shows include exhibit areas as well as special sessions held on topics of interest to the target audience. A trade show requires a tremendous amount of planning and organization. The right people must learn about the show, understand how it will benefit them, be willing and able to commit the funds and time it takes to attend, and find everything ready at their arrival. Pleasing several thousand people at a trade show is a major feat.

Deborah Baum is in charge of pleasing about 10,000 people five times a year. As the general manager of the East Coast Fashion Group of Advanstar Communications, Baum leads the production of *femme*, the largest international accessories and apparel trade show in New York. *femme* takes place three times a year. Additionally, Baum manages *I-TexStyle*, an international textiles show that takes place twice a year.

Planning and executing a trade show requires outstanding organizational and interpersonal skills. Baum oversees the scheduling of all events that run during the trade shows. Her staff arranges for the hundreds of vendors who will set up their exhibit spaces and registers the thousands of visitors who will attend the shows.

# TRY IT ON

**What are some common characteristics and skills of successful people in the various behind-the-scenes fashion careers?**

_____

_____

_____

## UNDERSTAND MARKETING CONCEPTS

Circle the best answer for each of the following questions.

1. Successful designers share a common
   a. creativity.
   b. imagination.
   c. desire to succeed.
   d. all of these.

2. Meeting and connecting with people for business purposes is called
   a. sponsoring.
   b. hiring.
   c. networking.
   d. selling.

## THINK CRITICALLY

Answer the following questions as completely as possible. If necessary, use a separate sheet of paper.

3. Why is it important to network with people when starting a fashion marketing career?

   _____

   _____

   _____

   _____

   _____

4. **Communication**   Write a paragraph about the role of trade shows in the fashion industry. Why are the shows important?

   _____

   _____

   _____

   _____

   _____

   _____

# FINDING AND KEEPING A FASHION CAREER

## The Latest Style

For aspiring fashion designers, Gen Art offers an opportunity to meet, work with, and be recognized by people in the business. Gen Art is an organization that promotes arts, entertainment, fashion design, filmmaking, and musicians. Founded in San Francisco in 1993, the organization has grown to include offices in five cities.

Gen Art provides a high-profile audience of industry executives, media representatives, and celebrities to view the work of up-and-coming fashion designers. The designers submit digital photographs of their work for review, and five finalists are selected to display their designs at a New York show. Details regarding how to enter the competition may be found at **www.genart.com**. Entries are accepted in the categories of eveningwear, ready-to-wear, accessories, men's wear, and avant garde. Avant garde category winners have included Jorge Luis Salinas from Lima, Peru. His designs were based on the Inca culture in a cosmopolitan world.

Work with a group. Discuss why it is important for the fashion industry to assist new designers. How can people who want to learn about fashion careers gain experience in the industry?

**GOALS**

**Explain** how to prepare for a career in the fashion industry.

**Describe** ways to find and keep a fashion career.

# PREPARE FOR THE JOB

If students in high school or college find excitement at the prospect of working in the fashion industry, then they may have found the area in which to focus their career goals. The next steps are to research, explore the possibilities, and prepare for the future.

## RESEARCHING

The first step toward a career in the fashion industry is taking the time to think about interests and goals. Like all other careers, fashion careers require planning and preparation.

**Who Are You?** Every individual in the world is unique and has special talents and interests. By the time individuals are in their teens, they know that some activities are more interesting to them than others. For example, one person may be able to draw very well while another has a talent for math. Both may have an interest in a fashion marketing career, and there is probably a place for each of them. They need to think about their own talents and interests and relate them to specific careers within the industry.

**What's Out There?**  The Internet makes finding information about the fashion industry easy. There are hundreds of web sites with useful content and search engines that can help you find them. Some of the sites that offer valuable information are

- **www.fashioncenter.com/ResourCen. html**
- **www.fashioncareercenter.com**
- **www.fashion.about.com/cs/cooljobs/**

Each of these sites provides information that can be used to narrow the research and match available jobs to interests, skills, talents, education, and experience.

## EDUCATION AND EXPERIENCE

The educational requirements and pay for fashion industry positions vary, but these two essentials generally parallel each other—the more education, the more pay. There are exceptions with the more creative fashion jobs, but a college degree is a requirement for most high-paying positions, and experience is a must.

**High School**  High school courses, like Marketing Education, help prepare students for a fashion career. Marketing Education courses offer opportunities for work-based experiences. The core courses like English, algebra, sciences, social studies, computer skills, and a foreign language are a must for all fashion careers. Additional course work can specifically focus on the career area of interest. For example, a future fashion designer might want to explore additional courses in clothing construction or textiles.

In most high schools, there are ways to earn college credits for elective or advanced courses taken in high school. A Marketing Education teacher or a counselor can provide information about how to earn the college credits. Earning college credits while in high school is a smart way to get a head start and save money, because credits earned in high school are usually less expensive and sometimes even free.

Worth Global Style Network (WGSN) offers college students special online access to information, provided the college or university has registered with WGSN. For example, fashion majors may have access to insider information on trends and can see delayed versions of collection shows from around the world.

**THINK CRITICALLY**
Why would WGSN want to cater to college students with fashion-related majors?

**Colleges and Universities** Colleges and universities offer fashion-related majors. State-operated colleges offer degree and certificate programs that are generallly less expensive than those of private career schools. State colleges are always *accredited* or recognized as meeting specific standards. Some of the best programs are at local community colleges that offer associate's degrees related to the fashion industry. For example, Houston Community College offers Associate in Applied Science degrees in Fashion Design, Fashion Merchandising, and Interior Design. The **associate's degree** generally takes a full-time student from four to five semesters of college work to complete. An associate's degree is also called a two-year degree.

Certificate programs are offered at many community colleges. Certificates that may be obtained include an Image Consultant certificate and a Visual Merchandising certificate. A **certificate** requires about three semesters of coursework and is recognized by some professional associations and employers as adding value to a person's experience and education. A quick check with potential employers can confirm if they value the certificate when they are hiring.

All college work is important, but completion of a bachelor's degree usually qualifies people for higher-paying positions. A **bachelor's degree** takes about four years as a full-time student and is referred to as a four-year degree. A list of colleges and universities that offer degrees related to fashion marketing can be found at **http://www. fashioncareercenter.com/fashion_colleges.html.**

**Experience** "Experience is the best teacher" is an old saying, but it is very true in the case of preparing for a career in the fashion industry. Trying out the industry while in high school and college has a number of advantages, including

- People exploring the fashion industry can see if they like the business before making a total commitment or completing a related degree.
- Employers value work experience because it allows them to see a potential employee in the work setting.
- Employers also value the opinion of other companies about the quality of work a person has done. This information is often exchanged as part of the hiring process.

Preparing for a career means researching, taking educational courses, and gaining work experience, but even these preparations do not guarantee a job. Finding and keeping a job requires additional skills.

Many high schools and colleges provide opportunities for students to visit major fashion industry centers. A visit to the New York fashion center is offered through the National DECA Inc. New York Experience Conference. Marketing students are accompanied by their teachers as they visit with designers and manufacturers and attend fashion seminars.

# TRY IT ON

**Why should a high school student look at requirements for jobs they might want five years from now?**

# FIND AND KEEP THAT JOB

The perfect career is usually not something that is found after just one try. Careers evolve and change throughout a person's work life. Careers are developed much like a beautiful oak tree that starts with a small acorn and grows and strengthens over many years. You can prepare the soil for that seed now with the right research and education. Next, you must provide the potential employer with the reasons to hire the right person, you!

## JOB OPENINGS

Applicants are made aware of fashion job openings through trade publications, on the Internet at company web sites, at job search sites such as **www.monster.com**, and by word of mouth. When people in the industry have a chance to get to know each other, they network and share information about job openings. Additionally, some companies will create jobs for people they believe will add great value to their company.

## RESUMES, APPLICATIONS, AND INTERVIEWS

Once a target job has been selected, a resume, application, and cover letter should be developed for the specific job. These three important documents may be transmitted electronically, mailed, or hand delivered to the potential employer.

**Resume**  A **resume** is a summary of information about the job applicant. A resume for a high school or college student should be only one page long and should include name, mailing address, e-mail address, phone number, education, work experience, hobbies, and interests. The appearance of the resume is critical. A resume should be completed using a word-processing program to achieve a professional look. There may be hundreds or even thousands of resumes submitted for one job opening. Most employers decide within three to five seconds whether to give further consideration to an applicant based on the resume. A resume should be tailored to the specific job opening and should highlight skills and experience sought by the employer. Some employers also request that a list of references accompany a resume. A work **reference** is information provided by a former employer about a person's job qualifications and personal qualities.

**Cover Letters**  Cover letters are sent with the resume to the potential employer. The **cover letter** should be a one-page formal letter telling the employer of the applicant's interest in the specific position for which the applicant is applying, briefly describing why the applicant is qualified, and referring the employer to the enclosed resume. Additionally, the cover letter should request an interview if one has not already been established.

**Applications**  Applications are forms provided by the potential employer and completed by the applicant. Many employers require a filled-in application in addition to a resume. Applications usually ask for the same information as is included on a resume. This ensures consistent information and format that makes it easier for employers to review and compare candidates quickly. Falsifying information on a resume or application is a reason for immediate dismissal from a job, ruins the chances of getting a good reference from the employer, and could result in criminal charges.

Sometimes an application is mailed to an applicant to complete and return, but many times the applicant completes the form at the job location. When completing an application at the job location, the applicant must be prepared with the information that may be requested. It helps to bring along the following items.

- A copy of your resume
- Names, addresses, and phone numbers of references
- Social security number
- Previous work history dates and employer addresses
- A good pen

Having these items handy makes completion of the application fast and effective. Neatness, grammar, and spelling count on job applications. Applications and resumes are used to screen the applicants and to select those to be considered for interviews.

**Interviews**   Interviews are usually arranged only when the potential employer has narrowed the search to a few top applicants. An interview should be treated as extremely important, with time and effort spent in preparing for it. Doing research about the company from its web site or brochures can provide valuable insight into what the company expects of future employees. Role-playing and rehearsing answers can help the applicant to feel more at ease. Keeping answers short and to the point holds the interest of the listener. When offered the opportunity during the interview, an applicant should be prepared to ask a few questions about the position and the company.

**Thank-You Letters**   A follow-up thank-you letter is a must after an interview. It should be written using a word processor and mailed the same day as the interview, if possible. The short message should confirm the applicant's interest in the position and in working for the company. The letter should also express pleasure in having had the opportunity to meet and talk with interviewers and should offer to provide any additional information needed.

## MOVING UP

Although the first few jobs taken in the fashion industry may not be the ones a person wants for the rest of his or her life, they are critical steps toward a career goal. Even the least significant first job should be treated as if it is extremely important and should be performed with the utmost of care. People in the fashion industry know each other and exchange information often. Information about someone who does an excellent job will spread quickly. Information about someone who does a poor or sloppy job will also circulate and will be difficult to overcome.

Most people change jobs five or more times during their work life. Opportunities for advancement to the next level of responsibility may open within the same company and may come with a larger salary. The time to prepare for the next job is the first day of the current job. Besides the ability to accomplish specific job tasks, getting along with people and being a team player are the most important skills needed. People—whether customers, suppliers, fellow employees, or supervisors—are important to present and future careers. Being a trustworthy, caring person can hasten the steps to becoming a fashion industry leader. Individuals hold all of the keys to their own futures and can use them to plan, prepare, and reach their goals.

# TRY IT ON

**Why is it important in a career to work well with others?**

_____

_____

_____

## TERI AGINS

Teri Agins credits her ninth-grade journalism teacher for sparking her interest in becoming a journalist. Agins is a columnist for _The Wall Street Journal_ who covers the fashion beat from the industry standpoint. The journal is not dependent on the fashion industry for advertising and presents a picture of the industry that is not distracted by the need to attract fashion advertising revenue.

One aspect that makes working for _The Wall Street Journal_ so unique is that reporters, rather than story editors, generate the feature ideas. Agins creates an idea for a feature and submits it as a proposal to her editor who "shops the idea around to other editors." If an editor likes the story, then Agins begins writing. She may work on several feature stories at once, spending much time making calls and researching the companies or stores about which she writes. She gets some of her best leads from the competitors of a focus company. Agins stops several times during the day to write up current news about the fashion industry that will appear in the next day's paper.

Agins attends fashion shows to talk with people rather than to write about the shows. She talks to salespeople, shoppers, and fashion-industry experts. "You can't be shy. If you are curious and listen, people will talk with you," says Agins. Agins is also the author of _The End of Fashion_, a book that chronicles fashion's move from an art to a commodity. Agins suggests that students who are interested in fashion journalism learn journalism first, then concentrate on fashion.

### THINK CRITICALLY
**1.** How is _The Wall Street Journal_'s perspective on fashion different from the typical fashion magazine's view?
**2.** What personal characteristics have made Agins successful?

## UNDERSTAND MARKETING CONCEPTS
Circle the best answer for each of the following questions.

**1.** A four-year college degree is called a(n)
   **a.** bachelor's degree.
   **b.** associate's degree.
   **c.** master's degree.
   **d.** full degree.

**2.** A written summary of information about a job applicant is called a(n)
   **a.** cover letter.
   **b.** application.
   **c.** resume.
   **d.** certificate.

## THINK CRITICALLY
Answer the following questions as completely as possible. If necessary, use a separate sheet of paper.

**3. Research**   In groups, determine if employers value the certificate and degree programs offered at local colleges. Look online at the certificate programs related to fashion that are offered near you. Contact the human resources department of two retail stores or other fashion industry businesses. Ask if any preference or additional salary is given to people with one or more of the fashion-related certificates. Ask what college degree programs are valued by the business. Ask if there are higher starting salaries for people with the preferred degrees. Write a paragraph about the information you obtain and share it with the class.

_____

_____

_____

**4. Communication**   Make a list of information about yourself, including name, address, phone number, e-mail address, education, work experience, and hobbies. Use a word processor and format the information into a resume.

_____

_____

_____

# CHAPTER 12

# REVIEW

## REVIEW MARKETING CONCEPTS

Write the letter of the term that matches each definition. Some terms will not be used.

_____ **1.** A business located in a market center, like New York, that buys for multiple retailers from a large base of vendors

_____ **2.** Attending functions that allow you to meet and connect with other people interested in doing business

_____ **3.** A degree earned with about four years of college

_____ **4.** A one-page formal letter telling the employer of the applicant's interest in the specific position for which the applicant is applying, briefly describing why the applicant is qualified, and referring the employer to the enclosed resume

_____ **5.** Information provided by a former employer about a person's job qualifications and personal qualities

_____ **6.** A summary of information about the job applicant

**a.** associate's degree
**b.** bachelor's degree
**c.** buying office
**d.** certificate
**e.** cover letter
**f.** networking
**g.** reference
**h.** resume

**Circle the best answer.**

**7.** Magazines generally receive most of their revenues from
    **a.** subscribers.
    **b.** newsstands.
    **c.** advertisers.
    **d.** none of these.

**8.** Trend forecasting is used by
    **a.** retailers.
    **b.** fashion magazines.
    **c.** manufacturers.
    **d.** all of these.

**9.** Fashions are best shown on
    **a.** live models.
    **b.** hangers.
    **c.** mannequins.
    **d.** clothes racks.

# THINK CRITICALLY

**10.** In pairs, discuss why a manufacturer like Kellwood would market 14 different brand names. How can a manufacturer that uses 240 domestic and 470 international subcontractors ensure that it is not using sweatshops?

POINT YOUR BROWSER

fashion.swlearning.com

_____

_____

_____

_____

_____

**11.** In pairs, discuss the purpose of fashion magazines. Do they provide useful information or just fluff? Are they one big ad for the fashion industry?

_____

_____

_____

_____

_____

**12.** What role do high school and college programs play in the fashion industry?

_____

_____

_____

_____

**13.** What topics might retail buyers like to see discussed at trade show seminars? List at least three ideas.

_____

_____

_____

_____

_____

**CHAPTER 11 REVIEW**

## MAKE CONNECTIONS

**14. Marketing Math** You have an opportunity to work full-time upon graduation from high school making $20,000 per year for nine years. You also have an offer to work part-time making $6,000 per year while you go to college for four years and then move into a full-time position earning $35,000 per year for five years. Which offer will net the larger amount in nine years?

_____

_____

_____

_____

_____

**15. Communication** Write a sample cover letter that would accompany a resume to be sent in application for a job of your choice at a fashion retailer.

_____

_____

_____

_____

_____

**16. Technology** Use the Internet to research the social responsibility statements made by a fashion-industry business. Do the statements address sweatshops? Does the business employ people of all ethnic heritages?

_____

_____

_____

_____

_____

_____

## RETAIL MERCHANDISE MANAGEMENT

www.deca.org
/publications/HS_
Guide/guidetoc.html

You have been the top sales associate at Jones Fine Clothing Store for the past five years because you give customers superior service. Business has been good, and the owner/general manager has decided to create an assistant manager position that will pay almost $5,000 more per year than your current position as sales associate. The assistant manager will be responsible for creating new customer-relation strategies and for motivating associates to sell more merchandise.

You must convince the general manager that you are the best candidate for assistant manager. You must also explain some of your creative ideas for the position.

You have ten minutes to develop your strategy, ten minutes to present the information to the store manager, and five minutes to answer any questions. The manager will be represented by your class.

## PROJECT: The COLLECTION POINT

Plan a fashion career. Write a description of the place you will live, the car you will drive, and the type of work you will be doing in ten years. Then start the research on how to get there. The research results need to be realistic about the salary that it will take to support the lifestyle you are choosing and the number of years it will take to reach that salary.

**Work individually and complete the following activities.**

**1.** Describe the place that you will live in ten years. Find the expected monthly rent or mortgage payment by calling a real estate agent or looking at advertisements in the newspaper or online. Determine the cost of the car you want using the same research methods.

**2.** Research other monthly costs of living or use these figures: $100 insurance, $300 food, $150 clothing, $50 gasoline, $30 repairs and cleaning, $200 utilities, $500 savings for unexpected events, and $100 taxes. Add all the monthly expenses together.

**3.** Select a position in the fashion industry that you might like. Research the minimum education and experience requirements for the position.

**4.** Check with a human resources department or research salary information online to determine the average salary of your position.

**5.** Compare the monthly salary to your expected monthly expenses.

**6.** Write a paragraph about what you will need to do to reach your goal. How long will it take? What education do you need? Where are the job openings? What job or intern experiences will help?

# GLOSSARY

## A

**advertising allowance** A percentage paid to retailers by vendors for cooperative advertising.

**associate's degree** A college education program that takes a full-time student from four to five semesters to complete.

**assortment plan** A subset of the merchandise plan which includes the quantity of each type of item, information about the style and fabric of each item, and the quantity of each size and color.

## B

**bachelor's degree** A college education program that takes about four years to complete as a full-time student.

**balance sheet** Financial record that reports the amount of assets, liabilities, and capital of a business as of a given time.

**bar codes** Optically scanned lines that contain the garment's Uniform Product Code (UPC).

**better** Garments defined by middle-to-high prices and generally sold in specialty shops or department stores.

**bill of materials** A listing of the component parts of a garment and their costs.

**brand building** Establishing an identity or image for a line of apparel.

**brand names** Designations that identify the product for consumers.

**bridge** The low-price end of a designer line of fashions.

**budget** Those garments sold at below-average prices; also, a plan that helps a business determine what revenues and expenses to expect.

**business management risks** Risks that relate to decisions such as the customer segment to target or the price points of merchandise to offer; they are uninsurable, speculative risks because the results are not predictable.

**business plan** A guide used to help the owner make decisions.

**buying office** An office located in a market center that buys for multiple retailers from a large base of vendors.

## C

**"C" corporation** Legal entity that operates as a business and must issue stock.

**capital expense** A new building or major new equipment.

**cellulose fibers** Fibers produced using plants combined with chemical processes.

**certificate** A college education program that requires about three semesters of coursework and is recognized by some professional associations and employers as adding value to experience and education.

**channels of distribution** The paths and businesses involved in moving a product from the idea stage to the consumer.

**classic** Traditional style with a long product life cycle that appeals to many people in a wide age group and various sizes.

**closed shop** A business that employs only union members and negotiates only with the union regarding wages and benefits.

**collection opening** The first opportunity for buyers to view new fashions.

**collective bargaining** When a union negotiates with a business on behalf on all members.

**commission** The pay a salesperson receives based on a percentage of what he or she sells.

**concession** A yielding on the vendor's price or return policy.

**controllable risks** Risks that can be prevented or those in which the frequency of occurrence at least can be reduced.

**cooperative advertising** Situation where a vendor shares advertising cost with a retailer.

**counterfeit** Exact copies of items that are registered with the U.S. Patent and Trademark Office.

**couture** Original, one-of-a-kind garments made with the highest standards of the highest quality fabrics.

**couturier** The main creator and designer for a haute couture firm.

**cover letter** A one-page formal letter telling the employer of the applicant's interest in the specific position for which the applicant is applying, briefly describing why the applicant is qualified, and referring the employer to the enclosed resume.

## D

**demand** The quantity of a product that customers are willing and able to buy.

**demographic information** Age, gender, ethnic group, nationality, education, and income.

**designer** High-quality, high-fashion items that are sold under one of the well-known designer labels.

**discount** The low-end fashion price line.

**disposable income** The money that is left after needs are met and bills are paid.

**distribution** Moving a product each step from the design idea to the consumer.

**door** Fashion jargon for a retail store.

## E

**economy of scale** Occurs when the price per garment is low due to large-volume production.

**elements of design** Include lines, shapes, texture, and color.

**entrepreneurs** People who start their own businesses.

**environmental risks** Risks that relate to safe conditions within the business; they are usually pure risks that are preventable, predictable, and generally insurable.

**estimated financial statements** Expected costs and cash flows used to project the potential for a new business.

**ethics** A system of deciding what is right or wrong in a reasoned and impartial manner.

**exclusive rights** An agreement that a vendor will sell a particular style or color to only one store.

## F

**fads** Those items that quickly move through the three phases of the fashion life cycle and disappear from the fashion scene.

**fashion advertising** Paid communication between the product maker or seller and the audience or customer about a fashion item.

**fashion cycle** The time from when a style is introduced until it is no longer purchased.

**fibers** Thin threads that are spun into yarn.

**filament** A long, continuous fiber.

**financial plan** A major part of a complete business plan consisting of summary statements of financial data that make up a complete budget.

**financing** Planning ways to cover the costs of successfully operating a business.

**findings** All of the notions that are needed to complete garments; include zippers, buttons, thread, lining materials, and trims.

**fit model** A person who is representative of the target customer.

**floor-ready merchandise** Garments that are ready for immediate sale when received by the retailer.

**forecaster** Person who predicts trends and decides on colors and details that make next season's fashions exciting.

## G

**global sourcing** Working with manufacturers throughout the world.

## H

**haute couture** High-fashion, individually designed, original, handmade garments.

## I

**income statement** Financial record that reports a business's revenues and expenses.

**infomercials** Commercials that are the length of a regular hour or half-hour TV show and feature information about the sponsor's products in a show format.

**initial public offering (IPO)** The point at which a business moves from private ownership to public ownership by selling shares of the company on the stock market.

**insurable risks** Pure risks that possibly could happen to a large number of businesses, where the chances and amount of the loss can be predicted.

**inventory control** The process used to track the quantities, wholesale value, and retail value of garments received and sold.

**inventory optimization** Maintaining a level of inventory that can be minimized while keeping sales constant or growing.

**inventory turnover** The rate at which merchandise is sold and new merchandise brought in during a time period.

## J

**just-in-time inventory** Items that are received at the time they are needed.

## K

**knockoffs** Copies of haute couture garments available for purchase at reasonable prices.

## L

**leadership** The ability to influence the behavior of others.

**limited-liability company (LLC)** A business that is similar to a corporation but has the management and tax advantages of a partnership and doesn't issue stock.

**liquidators** Businesses that purchase closeouts of excess inventory.

**luminaire** A complete lamp, including parts to focus the lamp.

## M

**man-made fibers** Fibers that include both cellulose and synthetic fibers.

**margin** The difference between the selling price and the cost of the fashion items.

**markdown** Taken when the original retail price is reduced to speed up sales.

**markdown optimization** Careful analysis of what is being marked down by vendor, style, size, and color in order to limit the need for future markdowns.

**marker** The plan that shows how the pattern pieces will be placed on the fabric for its most efficient use.

**market price** The price at which consumers are willing to buy enough for the producer to make a profit.

**market share** Percent of the total market represented by customers in a target group.

**marketing** Planning and executing the conception, pricing, promotion, and distribution of ideas, goods, and services to create exchanges that satisfy individual and organizational objectives.

**marketing mix** How the basic marketing elements—product, price, promotion, and distribution—are combined to meet customer needs and wants.

**marketing research** The process of gathering information about current and potential customers.

**marketing segments** Subgroups based on demographics or psychographics that the group members have in common.

**marketing-information management** Gathering and using information about what customers want.

**marketing-information system (MktiS)** A system that collects, stores, reports, analyzes, and uses information on products and customers.

**markup** Amount added to the cost to cover operating expenses and desired profit.

**mass market** A large number of potential customers with no specific similarities.

**mature markets** Markets that have reached their full potential, with steady demand but little room for continued growth.

**merchandise plan** A list of current inventory, projected sales, quantity already on order, and quantity of inventory still needed to cover projected sales.

**merchandiser** Person who plans the styles, prices, and number of garments to be produced based on what the marketing information indicates will sell.

**merchandising** Obtaining and presenting apparel and accessories for sale to customers.

**moda pronta** Italian ready-to-wear apparel.

**moderate** Middle-priced garment.

## N

**net profit** The balance left after the operating expenses are paid.

**networking** Attending functions that allow you to meet and connect with other people interested in doing business.

## O

**open-to-buy** Amount of money the buyer has available to commit to the purchase of new apparel for a given period of time.

**order forecast** An estimate of the number and size of orders that need to be placed to cover the sales that have been forecast.

**overruns** The garments left when a manufacturer has produced too many of an item.

## P

**Pareto Principle** A theory that a small number of causes is responsible for most of the results.

**partnership** An agreement between two or more people to share in the ownership of a business.

**patent** A legal agreement that protects a design from being copied.

**personal financial statement** Financial record that includes a list of an owner's assets and liabilities, personal net worth, bank references, and past credit history.

**persuasive language** Messages relevant to potential customers.

**piracy** The creation of illegal copies of apparel that are sold at a lower price.

**press kit** Promotional tool used to attract the media to an event.

**price** The amount that customers pay for products.

**price elasticity** Range between the lowest price a retailer can afford to charge and the top price a customer is willing to pay.

**price point** A specific price within a specific price range.

**pricing** The process of setting the value or cost of a product at the right level.

**principles of design** Fundamental rules that guide good design; include balance, contrast, rhythm, unity, and proportion.

**private label** A line of garments produced for only one retailer.

**product** What a business offers customers to satisfy needs.

**product features** Benefits to the customer.

**product mix** All the products an organization sells.

**product/service management** Designing, producing, maintaining, improving, and/or acquiring products or services to meet customer needs.

**production pattern** The pattern shape of each piece of a garment.

**productivity** Measured by the dollar amount of apparel and accessories sold per square foot of store space per year.

**professional organizations** Groups of career-minded individuals with common interests organized around a purpose.

**promotion** Communicating with customers about the product to achieve customer demand for and purchase of the product.

**promotional mix** The four components of promotion—advertising, public relations, publicity, and personal selling.

**prototype** A model of a garment.

**psychographics** Characteristics such as ideology, values, attitudes, and interests used to group people.

**pure risk** A risk where there is no chance to gain from the event.

**R**

**reference** Information provided by a former employer about a person's job qualifications and personal qualities.

**resume** A summary of information about a job applicant.

**retail** What the final consumer pays for a garment.

**return on investment (ROI)** The increased money received above an initial investment.

**risks** Exposures to loss or injury.

**runway shows** Fashion shows that feature designs worn by live models.

**S**

**sales forecast** A plan that estimates the dollar volume of sales ahead of time.

**same-store sales reports** Reports that compare what is happening today to what happened on the same date a year ago.

**seam** The joint at which two pieces of fabric meet.

**selling** Assisting the customer in identifying and satisfying a want or a need.

**Service Corps of Retired Executives (SCORE)** A nonprofit association made up of retired executives and former business owners who are dedicated to helping small businesses start up and succeed.

**softlines** Those items generally made of fabrics or leather.

**sole proprietorship** A business owned and operated by one person.

**special events** Promotional activities that are out of the ordinary.

**speculative risk** A risk where gains or losses are possible.

**spreading** Layering fabric on a table so that the marker can be placed on top.

**stitching** The interlocking or interlooping of thread used to join two pieces of fabric.

**style** A particular look in fashion that sets it apart.

**subchapter S corporation** A business that combines advantages of a "C" corporation and a partnership but retains the filing and stockholder complexity of a corporation.

**suggestion selling** An offer of additional related items.

**supply** Product quantity that the producer is willing and able to make available.

**supply chain** Everyone involved in the fashion process, from supplier to manufacturer to wholesaler to retailer to consumer.

**synergy** An increase in productivity when stores locate near other highly productive stores in order to sell more merchandise.
**synthetics** Fibers produced with only chemicals.

# T

**target market** A specific audience of people—for example, all of the people in the United States ages 13 to 18 years.
**tariff** A tax on goods being brought into or exported out of the United States.
**terms of payment** Guidelines that include how many days after receipt of merchandise the retailer has before payment is due, any discount for early payment, and who will pay for the shipping costs.
**trading bloc** Organization whose members agree to remove trade barriers between the member nations while imposing barriers on countries that are not members.
**trend** When fashion takes a particular direction and the style is acknowledged as being right for the time.
**trendy** Forward-looking fashion or an updated version of a classic.
**trunk show** Informal fashion show that is held in a retail store as a way of promoting one individual designer's collection.

# U

**uncontrollable risk** A risk where any action cannot prevent the event from occurring.
**uninsurable risk** A risk where the chances occurring cannot be predicted or the amount of loss cannot be estimated.

**union** A legal organization of workers that obtains a majority consent to represent them to the management of a business.
**upstream risk** The chance that manufacturers may not perform as needed.

# V

**value-priced** Good quality, but not high fashion, garments that have an excellent value-to-price ratio.
**vendor-managed inventory** A system where the manufacturer decides how much of a product the retailer needs based on point-of-sale data.
**venture capitalists** Business partners who provide funds to start or expand a company in exchange for part-ownership.
**versatile fixtures** Store fixtures that are easily changed to meet a new need.
**vertical integration** When companies perform more than two business activities, such as financing and marketing.
**visual merchandising** The promotional presentation of fashion apparel and accessories.

# W

**wholesale** The manufacturer's price to the retailer.
**World Trade Organization (WTO)** A global organization that fosters trade and provides a forum for the 144 member countries to negotiate and handle trade-related disputes.

# Y

**young designer** Garments that are usually very creative, created by designers who are just starting out.

# INDEX

## A

A. & L. Tirocchi Gowns, 42
abercrombie, 17
Abercrombie & Fitch, 17, 64
Accent lighting, 181
Active Collection, 117
Activewear, 15
Adidas, 155
Advertising
  and effectiveness, 128
  budgeting for, 130
  creating, 131
  defined, 67
  media selection for, 130
  targeting, 129
Advertising allowance, 130
Al-Sabah, Majed, 115
Alife Rivington Club, 155
All American Tees, 239
Alloy, 196
Amalgamated Clothing and Textile
  Workers Union, 248
Amazon Conservation Team, 68
American Apparel, 239
American Express, 130
*American Fabrics,* 46
American Fashion Awards, 137
American fashion centers
  Canada, 106
  Central America, 106
  Los Angeles, 106
  New York, 104–105
  South America, 106
American fashion designers
  Combs, Sean, 108
  Gutierrez, Daphne, 108
  Hilfiger, Tommy, 107
  Karan, Donna, 107
  Klein, Calvin, 107
  Som, Peter, 108
American Society of Interior
  Designers, 46
Americanization, 31
AmericasMart, 106
Andersen, Kurt, 264
Ann Taylor, 58

Ann Taylor Loft, 58
Arden, Elizabeth, 231
Armani, Giorgio, 77
Arpeja, 224
Arthur Andersen, 89
ASDA Supermarkets, 55
Asia Pacific Leather Fair, 116
Asian fashion centers
  China, 116
  Guangdong, 117
  Hong Kong, 116
  Japan, 117
Asian fashion designers
  Cheong-Leen, Flora, 119
  Kawakubo, Rei, 119
  Mukherjee, Sabyasachi, 119
Assembly, 152
Assets, 89
Association of Southeast Asian
  Nations, 118
Assortment plan, 185
Atelier, 28

## B

Back-end, 156
Balenciaga, Cristobal, 112
Banana Republic, 218
Banc of America Securities LLC,
  96
Bank of America Corporation,
  96
Bar codes, 156
Barney's, 63, 103, 120
Barraza Associates Ltd., 130
Barraza, Maria, 130
Bartlett, John, 38
Bass Pro Shops Outdoor World,
  171
Baum, Deborah, 271
Beckford, Tyson, 268–269
Benetton USA, 129
*Bibi,* 31
Bill of materials, 151
*Black Enterprise Magazine,*
  228

Bloomingdale's, 108, 217
Blue Nile, Inc., 160
Board of Trade in England, 60
Bonwit Teller, 179
Boutiques, 14
Brand building, 129
Brand names, 60
British Fashion Council, 111,
  252
*British Vogue,* 56
Broadcast media, 131
Brooks Brothers, 153
Brown, Joyce F., 270
Bruce fashion label, 108
Burka, 31
Burlington Coat Factory, 79
Bush, George W., 36
Bush, Laura, 34
Business activities, 54
Business description, 222
Business management risks,
  225
Business plan
  defined, 221
  parts of, 222
Business plans, developing,
  218–221
  opening shop, 221
  setting selection, 220–221
  structure selection, 219–220
Business structures
  "C" corporation, 219–220
  limited-liability company, 220
  partnership, 219
  sole proprietorship, 219
  subchapter S corporation, 220
Buyers
  and differentiation, 186
  and planning, 184–185
  and product development,
    186
  defined, 184
  relationships with, 186
  working with vendors,
    185–186
Buying office, 263

## C

"C" corporation, 219
CaliforniaMart, 106
Calvin Klein, Inc., 78
Camera Nationale della Moda
   Italiana, 111
Campbell, Naomi, 110
Campbell, Paul, 270
Camper, 15
Capital
   defined, 89
   raising, 95–96
Capital expense, 95
Careerwear, 15
Catwalks, 58, 134
CAUS News, 46
Céline, 112
Cellulose fibers, 43–44
Central Intelligence Agency, 27
Chain stores, 14
Chamber of Commerce,
   67–68
Chambre Syndicale de la Couture
   Parisienne, 28, 29
Chanel, Coco, 83, 112, 128
Channels of distribution
   defined, 59
   direct, 59
   indirect, 59
Chapan, 10
Chardonnet, Hillaire de, 44
Charney, Dov, 239
Chase, Edna Woolman, 231
Cheong-Leen, Flora, 119
Chicago Apparel Mart, 221
Chico's FAS, 6
Child labor, 247
Children's Advertising Review Unit
   (CARU), 105
Chloé, 110
Cholis, 31
Christian Dior SA, 112
Classic styles, 10, 14
Clinique, 69
Clorox Company, 243
Closed shop, 248
Coach, 54
Coldwater Creek™, 89
Collaborative Planning,
   Forecasting, and
   Replenishment®, 161, 207
Collection opening, 111
Collective bargaining, 248
College Television Network (CTN),
   67

Color
   defined, 39
   forecasts, 40
   traditions, 40
Color Association of the United
   States (CAUS), 40, 46
Color Marketing Group, 40
Color Source Book, 46
Combs, Sean, 108
Comme Des Garcons, 119
Commission, 140
Competition
   and benefits, 82–83
   and productivity, 83
   defined, 64
Computer-aided design (CAD)
   systems, 152
Computer-aided manufacturing
   (CAM) systems, 153
Concession, 198
Condé Nast Publications,
   264
Contractors, 59
Contrast, 38
Controllable risks, 225
Converse, Inc., 242
Coon, Jeanette, 265
Cooperative advertising, 130
Copy, 129
Cortina, Betty, 199
Cost units, 88
Cotton, 43
Cotton Incorporated, 43
Cotton Incorporated's Lifestyle
   Monitor™, 141, 195, 199
Coty Inc.'s Lancaster Group
   Worldwide, 209
Council of Better Business
   Bureaus, Inc., 105
Council of Fashion Designers of
   America (CFDA), 105, 111, 120,
   137, 241
Counterfeit, 250
Couture, 14
Couturiers, 29
Credit
   beneficial, 93
   consumer, 94
   obtaining, 93
Credit checks, 94
Credit policy, 94
Cross Colour, 228
Cruz, Penélope, 136
Culture
   elements of, 31

   multicultural consumer, 31
   restrictions, 31
Customer
   expectations, 56
   information, 56
Cyber Marketing feature
   apparelsearch.com, 39
   care label rules, 243
   DS Retail Technologies, Inc.,
      219
   eLuxury.com, 19
   GlobalShop, 173
   Hermès, 69
   Hoover's Online, 200
   JCPenney®, 7
   Lands' End Custom™, 140
   Lightolier, 178
   Loro Milan, 45
   Moja Design, 266
   Nielsen//Netratings, 208
   online shopping, 131
   Robinsons, 119
   Shop.org, 229
   Shoshkele™, 162
   Smart Bargains, Inc., 83
   TeleCheck, 94
   The Triangle Fire, 246
   Tommy.com, 151
   Vogue, 56
   Who's Next, 113
   Worth Global Style Network
      (WGSN), 274
Cyber media, 131

## D

DailyShopper Network, Inc.,
   219
Dali, Salvador, 179
Dallas Apparel Mart, 184
Dallas Times Herald, 11
Davies, George, 55
Davis, Evan, 222
De Beers, 112
DECA Prep
   business services marketing
      role play, 51
   creative marketing project,
      125
   customer service role play,
      101
   entrepreneurship participating
      event, 237
   fashion merchandising
      promotion plan, 137

marketing management role
play, 193
marketing management series
role play, 259
retail marketing research event,
75, 215
retail merchandise
management, 283
retail merchandising
associate level role play, 169
specialty store promotion
planning, 25
Decline phase, 10
Delta Epsilon Chi, 230–231
Demand
defined, 33, 78
factors of, 33–34
Demographic information, 54
Department stores, 13
Designer, 14
*Details,* 264
Dickens, Charles, 29
Dillard's®, 13, 173
Direct mail media, 131
Direct-payment subsidies, 80
Discount stores, 13
Disposable income, 79
Distribution, 5, 6
Distributive Education Clubs of
America (DECA), 230–231
Division, 187
Divisional merchandise manager
(DMM), 187
DJM Asset Management, 262
Dominguez, Liliana, 133
Doneger Creative Services, 263
Donna Karan, 112
Downstream, 151
Drexler, Millard, 70
DS Retail Technologies, Inc.,
219
DuPont Co., 162
DuPont LYCRA®, 137
Dupre, Seeju, 198

**E**

East Coast Fashion Group of
Advanstar Communications,
271
eBay, 163
E-commerce, 162
Economy of scale, 59
Egoist, 18
Electronic Check Acceptance®, 94

Electronic data interchange (EDI),
161
Electronic Retailing Association,
157
Elements of design, 39
*Elle,* 136
Emerging fashion centers
Korea, 118–119
Madagascar, 118
Vietnam, 118
Emerging technology
e-commerce, 162–163
smart garments, 162
Employment Training Panel
(ETP), 150
Entrepreneurs, 92
Environmental risks, 225
Envirosell, Inc., 210
Enyce, 222
Esprit de Corps, 184
*Essence Magazine,* 141
Estée Lauder, 69, 87
Ethics, 252
European fashion centers
France, 111–112
Italy, 111
United Kingdom, 111
European fashion designers
Ford, Tom, 113
Prada, Miuccia, 113
Versace, Donatella, 113
European Union (EU), 84–85, 242
Eveningwear, 15
Everard, Louis, 217, 222
Everard's Clothing, 217, 220
Exclusive rights, 186
Exported, 60
Express, 96

**F**

Fads, 10
Fair Labor Association (FLA),
247
Fairchild, John, 11
Fashion
and technology, 18–19
history of, 28–30
predicting, 58
Fashion advertising, 128
Fashion Business Incubator, 230
Fashion businesses
producers, 263
publishers, 263–265
trend forecasters, 262–263

Fashion careers
apparel and accessories
designing, 268–269
fashion educator, 270
modeling, 269
trade show organizer, 271
Fashion careers, finding and
keeping, 276–278
applications, 276–277
cover letters, 276
interviews, 277
job openings, 276
resume, 276
thank-you letters, 277
Fashion careers, preparing for,
273–275
education, 274–275
experience, 275
researching, 273
Fashion channels, 59–60
Fashion cycle
defined, 9
phases of, 9–10
Fashion Do's & Don'ts feature
Abercrombie & Fitch, 64
Arthur Andersen, 89
bowling shoes, 15
code of ethics, 157
*Details,* 264
fashion cooperation and
competition, 186
London Fashion Week, 252
Saks Fifth Avenue, 203
school dress codes, 34
shock ads, 129
Skechers USA, Inc., 105
Wal-Mart®, 220
Fashion ethics
developing morals, 252–253
making choices, 253
Fashion Flashback feature
Balenciaga, Cristobal, 112
Board of Trade in England,
60
Bonwit Teller, 179
Fashion Group International
(FGI), 231
fashion promotion, 135
inventory control, 197
Lowe, Ann, 269
Marshall Field's, 11
Polo Ralph Lauren, 79
price fixing, 241
price tags, 156
skeleton suit, 29

Fashion Group International, 120, 230–231, 232
Fashion Institute of Technology, 107, 270
Fashion marketing, 45
Fashion show, organizing, 133–136
Federal Trade Commission (FTC), 241, 243
Federated Department Stores, 13, 156
Felix, Lando, 222
*femme*, 271
Fendi, 115
Ferragamo, 115
Ferrari, 10
Fibers, 42
Fields, C. Virginia, 127
Fila Sportswear, 222
Filament, 43
Financial plan, 87, 222
Financial reports, 205
Financial statements
　balance sheet, 89
　budget, 88
　cash flow statements, 88
　estimated financial statements, 88
　income statement, 89
　personal financial statement, 89
　startup cost statement, 88
Financing, 6
Findings, 45
Fit model, 151
Fixtures, 171, 180
Floor-ready merchandise, 161
Florio, Steven T., 264–265
Florio, Tom, 265
Foley's, 232
*Footwear News,* 96
Ford Motor Company, 38
Ford, Tom, 113
Forecasters, 59
Forever 21, 245
Formal balance, 38
Formula One, 10
French, R. Scott, 6, 11
Frequent revision, 178

**G**

Gap, Inc., 70, 218
Garment production
　cost of, 151
　designing, 151
　preparing, 151
　producing, 151
　researching, 150
　sourcing, 151
Gen Art, 273
General merchandise manager, 187
Givenchy, 112
*Glamour,* 67, 264
Global markets, 56
Global sourcing, 118
*GlobalShop,* 173–174
Glow perfume, 209
Goody's Family Clothing, 181
Gorman, Evelyn, 88
*GQ,* 264
Graham-Pepper, Joanie, 224
Griffin, Laura, 17
Griffin, Tim, 171
Groupe Socota Industries, 118
Gucci Group, 110, 113, 115
Gutierrez, Daphne, 108

**H**

Haute couture, 29, 112
Head, Edith, 231
Hempel Corporation, 116
Hermès, 69
Herrera, Carolina, 106
Hilfiger, Tommy, 107
Hisada, Shoko, 117
Hobby, Janet, 184
Hollister Co., 17
Home Marketing Association (HMA), Inc., 265–266
Hong Kong Trade Development Council, 116
House and Garden, 265

**I**

I.B. Diffusion, 221
Inditex, 53
Infomercials, 137
Informal balance, 38
Information, managing, 55–56
Information technology, 156
Initial public offering (IPO), 95
Insurable risks, 225
International AntiCounterfeiting Coalition (IACC), 250, 254
International Apparel Mart, 106
International Council of Shopping Centers, 266
International Fashion Fair, 117
International Labour Organization (ILO), 247
International Ladies Garment Workers Union, 248
International Textile and Garment Industry Exhibition, 118
Interpersonal skills, 229
Introductory phase, 9
Inventory control
　and accuracy, 202
　defined, 202
Inventory optimization, 204
Inventory turnover
　defined, 157, 203
　excess inventory, 203
　fast turns, 203–204
I-TexStyle, 271
Iverson, Annemarie, 131

**J**

Jarrett, Jaclynn, 265
Jarrett, Marvin, 265
JCPenney®, 7, 13, 34, 139, 199
Jones Apparel Group, 95
Jordan, Michael, 129
Judson, Lisa, 163
Juliana Collezione, 265–266
Just-in-time inventory, 157

**K**

Karakul, 10
Karan, Donna, 70, 107
Karin Models, 133
Karl Kani-Infinity, 228
Karzai, Hamid, 10–11
Kawakubo, Rei, 119
Kbond, 155
Kellwood, 263
Kennedy, Jacqueline, 34, 112, 269
Kennedy, John, 36, 269
Kenneth Cole, 15
Key marketing functions, using, 5–7
KhiMetrics, Inc., 202
Kiehl's Since 1851, 68, 137
Kim, Grace, 184
Klein, Calvin, 11, 107
Kmart, 13, 262
Knight, Phil, 247
Knockoffs, 30

Kohl's®, 173–174, 180–181, 199
Kos, Julijana, 266

# L

Labels, requirements, 242–243
  business name, 243
  care instructions, 243
  country of origin, 243
  fiber content, 243
Laczay, Thomas, 262
Laird + Partners, 70
Lambertson, Richard, 38
Lands' End, 140, 156
Lands' End Custom™, 140
*Latina Magazine,* 199
Lauren, Ralph, 3, 79, 95, 107, 269
Lavis, Maro, 221
Lawrence, Mary Wells, 40
Lead time, 205
Leadership, 228
Leadership, characteristics of,
  228–230
  communications, 228
  ethical behavior, 230
  knowledge acquisition, 229–230
  problem solving, 229
  resource management, 229
  team membership, 229
Lectra, 149
Legislation, 240–241
Leight, Larry, 38
Lerner New York, 18
Levi Strauss, 162
Lewin, Harley, 251
Liabilities, 89
Liable, 226
Licensing agreement, 60
Lighting, 180
Lightolier, 178
Limited Brands, 96
Limited, Inc., 96
Limited-liability company (LLC),
  220
Lines, 39
Liquidators, 163
LivePerson, 164
*Living Colors: The Definitive
  Guide to Color Palettes through
  the Ages*, 46
Liz Claiborne, 89
LoCascio, Robert, 164
London Fashion Week, 252
Lopez, Jennifer, 209
Lopez, Marilyn, 268–269

Loro Milan, 45
Louis Vuitton Moët Hennessy
  (LVMH), 107, 112–113
Lowe, Ann, 269
Luminaire, 182

# M

MAC, 87
Macklin, Pamela, 141
Macy's, 13, 108, 119
Mahecha, Theissy, 106
Mall layout, 172
Malone, Maurice, 261
Man-made fibers, 44
Management plan, 222
Mannequins, 178
Manufacturing retailers, 59
Margin, 63
Markdown, 62, 158
Markdown optimization, 158
Marker, 151
Market price, 80
Market segments, 54–55
Market share, 64
Marketing, 4
Marketing concepts, 55
  fashion marketing, 4–5
Marketing functions, key, 5
Marketing mix, 5
Marketing research
  and projections, 155–156
  defined, 199
Marketing segments, 199
Marketing-information
  management, 5
Marketing-information system
  (MktIS)
  analyzing data, 197
  collecting data, 197
  defined, 196
  reporting data, 197
  storing data, 197
  using data, 197
Markets, global, 56
Markup, 63
Marshall Field's, 11
Marshalls, 14, 79
Marvel Comics, 133
Mass market, 199
Mass production, 30
Mature markets, 116
May Department Stores, 13, 46,
  89
McCartney, Linda, 110

McCartney, Sir Paul, 110
McCartney, Stella, 110, 253
MCM, 119
Merchandise plan, 185
Merchandiser, 58
Merchandising
  and marketing, 187–188
  defined, 187
Merchant processing account, 94
Meyer, Gene, 38
Miller, Nicole, 127
Miu Miu line, 113
"Mix: Modern Clothes," 88
Miyake, Issey, 174
Moda pronta, 111
Moja Design, 261, 266
Motorola, Inc., 162
Mukherjee, Sabyasachi, 119
Myrie, Jamil, 261

# N

Nano-Tex, 162
Nast, Condé, 265
National Association of Store
  Fixture Manufacturers, 171, 180
National Football League, 127
National Merit Scholarship
  Corporation, 15
National Public Radio, 264
National Retail Federation, 158,
  229, 230
Needs, 78
Negative cash flow, 88
Neiman-Marcus, 60, 140, 224
Net cash flow, 88
Net profit, 63
Networking, 271
New Balance, 254
*New York Daily News,* 130
New York Stock Exchange, 95,
  142
Niche, 18
Nike, 46, 129, 155, 247
Nima New York's Jewelry, 268
Nordstrom, 4, 13, 14
Nygård, Peter, 106
*Nylon,* 265

# O

Occupational Safety and Health
  Administration (OSHA), 225
*Ocean Drive*, 261
Off-price stores, 14

Oklahoma Fixture Company (OFC), 171
Oldham, Todd, 68
Oliver Peoples Eyewear, 38
Olsen, Kathy, 221
Open-to-buy, 106
Operating expenses, 62
Order forecast, 209
Overruns, 79

**P**

Pareto Principle, 205
Partnership, 219
Patent, 242
Peak phase, 9
Pegasus Apparel Group, Inc., 263
Pegus, Claudia, 106
Peres, Daniel, 264
Personal selling, 68
Persuasive language, 129
Phillips NV, 162
Piracy
    consumer attitudes toward, 251
    counterfeit apparel, 250
    defined, 250
    international enforcement against, 251–252
Polo Ralph Lauren, 3, 79, 95, 269, 270
Portella, Niria, 268–269
Positive cash flow, 88
Prada, 15, 92, 113, 115, 158, 172, 174
Prada, Mario, 113
Prada, Miuccia, 113
Press kit, 135
Prêt-à-porter, 28
Prêt À Porter Paris®, 111
Price, 5
Price elasticity, 200
Price ranges
    better, 65
    bridge, 65
    budget, 65
    couture, 65
    defined, 65
    designer, 65
    discount, 65
    moderate, 65
    value-priced, 65
Pricing
    categorizing, 65
    defined, 6

policies, 64
    setting, 62–63
Principles of design, 38
Print media, 130
Private labels, 60
Product, 5
Product availability, 205
Product features, 129
Product mix, 13
Product/service management, 6
Production pattern, 151
Productivity, 83
Professional organizations
    DECA, 231
    defined, 230
    Delta Epsilon Chi, 231
    Fashion Group International, Inc., 231
    National Retail Federation, 231
Projects
    business risk, managing (Ch. 10), 237
    buying trip, planning (Ch. 5), 125
    codes of ethics (Ch. 11), 259
    credit policy, developing (Ch. 4), 101
    displays, designing (Ch. 8), 193
    fashion career, planning (Ch. 12), 283
    fashion show, planning (Ch. 6), 147
    marketing proposal (Ch. 7), 169
    marketing research (Ch. 3), 75
    marketing research survey (Ch. 9), 215
    product mix, selecting (Ch. 1), 25
    trend predictions (Ch. 2), 51
Promotion
    components of, 67
    defined, 5–6
Promotional mix, 67
Promotional plan, 222
Promotional planning, 68–70
Proportion, 39
Prototype, 151
Psychographics, 54
Public relations (PR), 67
Publicity, 68
Pucci, Emilio, 112, 142
Puma, 155
Pure risk, 224

**R**

Ralph Lauren, 136
Ramos, Estevan, 104
Ratcheting, 45
Reebok, 247
Reid, William, 38
Reiko, Nakane, 82
Retail
    and distribution, 265–266
    defined, 62
Return on investment (ROI), 203
Rhode Island School of Design, 42
Rhythm, 39
Risk management, 205
Risks
    business management, 225
    controllable, 225
    defined, 224
    environmental, 225
    insurable, 225
    pure, 224
    speculative, 225
    uncontrollable, 225
    uninsurable, 225
Risks, categorizing, 224
    risk control, 225
    risk insurance, 225
    risk results, 224–225
Risks, controlling, 226
    business management, 226
    environmental, 226
Risks, marketing, 225
    business management, 225
    environmental, 225
Riva Jewelry, 248
Robinsons, 119
Roosevelt, Eleanor, 231
Royalty, 60
Ruzow, Stephen, 263

**S**

Saks Fifth Avenue, 103, 108, 140, 171, 203
Sales forecast, 88, 207–208
Sales knowledge, 69
Salinas, Jorge Luis, 273
Same-store sales reports, 197
Sanders, Jil, 155
Sara Lee Branded Apparel, 207
Scales, Melissa, 15
Scarcity, 78
Scott, H. Lee, 266
Seam, 45

Sears, 13, 94, 129, 139, 156
Selling
    defined, 7, 139
    keys to successful, 139–140
    steps, 141–142
Sensatec, Inc., 162
Seo, Danny, 80
Serge de Nimes, 43
Service Corps of Retired
    Executives (SCORE), 222
Seventeen, 131
Seventh on Sixth, Inc., 105, 241
Shapes, 39
Share of stock, 219
Shellman, Tony, 222
Shields, Brooke, 107
Shop worn, 203
Shoshkele™, 162
Signage, 180–181
Silhouette, 9
Silk, 42
Simplicity, 178
Size and measurement table, 151
Skechers USA, Inc., 105
Smart Bargains, Inc., 83
Smart garments, 162
Softlines
    children's wear, 36
    defined, 35
    men's wear, 35–36
    women's wear, 35
Sole proprietorship, 219
Som, Peter, 108
Sourcing, 151
Space lighting, 181
Special events
    defined, 133
    fashion awards, 137
    fundraisers, 137
    infomercials, 137
    trunk shows, 136
Speculative risk, 225
Spitalnick, Irwin, 266
Sportswear, 14–15
Spreading, 152
Standards
    classification, 160–161
    voluntary, 161
Stella McCartney, 115
Stitching, 45
Store design strategies
    and the customer, 174–175
    convenience, 173–174
    designing, 174
    entertainment, 174

Strauss, Levi, 43
Style, 33
Styles
    characterizing, 14
    classifying, 14–15
    pricing, 15
Subchapter S corporation, 220
Suggestion selling, 141
Supply, 79
Supply and demand, 78–80
Supply chain, 161
Susan G. Komen Foundation,
    127
Sweatshop Watch, 245
Sweatshops, 245
Synergy, 83
Synthetics, 44

T
T. J. Maxx®, 14
TAG Heuer, 112
Talbots, 14, 56
Talent Ensemble International,
    106
Target®, 13, 139, 173, 199
Target customer, 55
Target market, 9, 199–200
Tariffs
    cooperation with, 242
    defined, 60, 160
    retaliation against, 242
Task lighting, 181
Technology, impacts of
    customization, 153
    mass production, 152–153
Teen People, 199, 264
TeleCheck, 94
Terms of payment, 186
Textile Act, 242
Textile Industry Affairs, 243
Textiles
    fabrics, 42–44
    fibers, 42–44
Texture, 39
Thai Silk Company, 27
The Armani Group, 77
The Bon Marché, 219
The Carlyle Hotel, 103
The Co-op, 63
The Doneger Group, 263
The Latest Style feature
    A. & L. Tirocchi Gowns, 42
    Abercrombie & Fitch, 17
    Alloy, 196

Ann Taylor and Ann Taylor Loft,
    58
Blue Nile, Inc., 160
Chambre Syndicale de la
    Couture Parisienne, 28
Chanel No. 5 perfume, 128
Coach, 54
Collaborative Planning,
    Forecasting, and
    Replenishment (CPFR), 207
comic books and fashion, 133
cross-promotion, 67
discount stores, 78
DJM Asset Management, 262
Employment Training Panel
    (ETP), 150
Fifth Avenue window displays,
    177
Ford Thunderbird, 38
Gen Art, 273
International AntiCounterfeiting
    Coalition (IACC), 250
KhiMetrics, Inc., 202
lipstick sales, 87
mass retailers and teens, 139
McCartney, Stella, 110
Nordstrom, 4
Prada, 92, 172
Ramos, Estevan, 104
Reiko, Nakane, 82
silhouettes, 9
sneakers, 155
Sweatshop Watch, 245
teen trends, 33
transshipment, 240
turtlenecks, 13
Villa Moda, 115
Virtual Runway, 184
Wal-Mart®, 62
Williams, Carl, 228
Wong, Sue, 224
Yurman, David and Sybil, 268
ZoZa, 218
The Limited, 14, 18
The New Mart, 106
The New York Times, 134
The Triangle Fire, 245–246
The Wall Street Journal, 15, 70,
    96, 130, 247, 262
Thompson, Jim, 27
Tian Art, 119
Tiffany & Co., 248
Time Out feature
    African-American female
        spending habits, 35

Barneys, 63
Barraza, Maria, 130
*Bibi,* 31
Campbell, Paul, 270
Chico's FAS, 6
China, 84
Chinese fashion, 116
Converse, Inc., 242
Cotton Incorporated, 43
counterfeiting, 251
Davies, George, 55
Egoist, 18
employee theft, 205
environmentally conscious
   fashion, 80
Enyce, 222
Fashion Business Incubator,
   230
Ferrari activewear, 10
*GlobalShop,* 174
Glow perfume, 209
Kiehl's Since 1851, 68
Korean-Americans, 59
Lawrence, Mary Wells, 40
Limited, Inc., 96
London Fashion Week, 111
"Made in the USA" apparel, 152
minority shoppers, 141
Nast, Condé, 265
New York Experience
   Conference, 275
Nordstrom, 14
Pegus, Claudia, 106
Prêt-à-Porter, 185
Ralph Lauren trunk show, 136
size standardization, 158
small businesses, 225
startup costs, 88
store fixture design competition,
   180
teen trendspotters, 199
Union of Needletrades,
   Industrial and Textile
   Employees (UNITE), 248
Wal-Mart®, 163
Tirocchi, Anna, 42
Tirocchi, Laura, 42
Tokyo Fashion Designers'
   Association, 117
Tootsie's, 14, 20
*Town & Country,* 136
Trade and Development Act of
   2000, 247
Trading bloc, 84
Traffic, 67

Transshipment, 240
Trend Setters feature
   Agins, Teri, 278
   French, Scott, 120
   Greenberg, Mindy, 188
   Jarmon, Selven O'Keef, 20
   Kuykendall, Linda, 232
   Laird, Trey, 70
   Lawrence, Mary Wells, 142
   Lewin, Harley I., 254
   online personal shoppers, 164
   Silverstein, Susan, 96
   Underhill, Paco, 210
   Walch, Margaret, 46
Trends
   defined, 17
   researching, 18
   targeting, 18
Trendspotters, 199
Trendy, 14
Triangle Shirtwaist Company,
   245
Truex, John, 38
Trunk show, 136
TSC Apparel, 239
*Twist,* 269


**U**

U.S. Congress, 240
U.S. Congressional Trade and
   Developmental Act of 2000,
   118
U.S. Customs Service, 160, 240
U.S. Department of Commerce,
   240, 242
U.S. Department of Labor,
   247–248
U.S. Office of Strategic Services,
   27
U.S. Patent and Trademark
   Office, 250
U.S. Small Business
   Administration, 222
Uncontrollable risk, 225
Uniform Code Council (UCC),
   161
Uninsurable risk, 225
Union, 248
Union of Needletrades, Industrial
   and Textile Employees (UNITE),
   248
Unity, 39
Upstream risk, 205
*USA Today,* 129, 218

**V**

Value-to-price ratio, 62
*Vanity Fair,* 264–265
Vendor, 62
Vendor-managed inventory,
   157
Venture capitalists, 95
Versace, Donatella, 113
Versace, Gianni, 113
Versatile fixtures, 180
Vertical integration, 59
Victoria's Secret, 96
Villa Moda, 115
Virtual Runway, 184
Visual merchandising, 177
*VM+SD,* 180
*Vogue Magazine,* 56, 103,
   264–265
Voluntary Interindustry Commerce
   Standards (VICS) Association,
   161, 207


**W**

Wal-Mart®, 54–55, 62, 65, 95,
   139, 163, 203, 207, 220,
   266
Wang, Vera, 103
Wants, 78
Warnaco Group, Inc., 78, 95
Waterford Wedgwood USA,
   103
Wedding apparel, 15
Wells Rich Greene, 142
Wet processing, 152
*Who's Next,* 113
Wholesale, 62
Window displays, creating,
   178
   steps in, 178–179
Winning Strategies feature
   American Apparel, 239
   Cotton Incorporated's Lifestyle
      Monitor™, 195
   Everard's Clothing, 217
   Lectra, 149
   Miller, Nicole, 127
   Moja Design, 261
   Oklahoma Fixture Company
      (OFC), 171
   Polo Ralph Lauren, 3
   Thai Silk Company, 27
   The Armani Group, 77
   Wang, Vera, 103
   Zara, 53

Wolfe, David, 263
Wolman, Adam, 261
*Women's Wear Daily,* 35, 96, 131,
134, 136, 142, 163, 195, 203,
210, 248, 264
Wong, Sue, 224
Wool, 43
Wool Act, 242
Worker Rights Consortium (WRC),
246–247
Workers' rights, 245–247

World trade, developing nations,
85
World Trade Organization (WTO),
84, 116, 242, 251
Worth Global Style Network, 19

**Y**

Yamamoto, Yohji, 155
Young designer, 14
YouthAIDS, 137

Yurman, David, 268
Yurman, Sybil, 268
Yves Saint Laurent (YSL), 113

**Z**

Zara, 53, 59
Zehren, Anne, 199
Ziegler, Mel, 218
Ziegler, Patricia, 218
ZoZa, 218, 220

# PHOTO CREDITS

**Chapter 1**    pages 2, 4, 10, 14, 19 © Photodisc, Inc.; page 17 Photography by Natasha Andjelic

**Chapter 2**    pages 26, 28, 30, 35, 36, 38, 40, 43, 44, 45 © Photodisc, Inc.; page 33 Photography by Natasha Andjelic

**Chapter 3**    pages 52, 55, 64, 69 © Photodisc, Inc.; pages 58, 65 Courtesy of R. Scott French

**Chapter 4**    pages 76, 78, 80, 82, 84, 85, 87, 92, 93, 95 © Photodisc, Inc.

**Chapter 5**    pages 102, 104, 108, 112, 115, 116, 117, 118 © Photodisc, Inc.; page 110 Photography by Natasha Andjelic

**Chapter 6**    page 126 Courtesy of PRÊT À PORTER PARIS® Show, photographer standem favart photo; pages 128, 139, 141Courtesy of Everard's Clothing, Washington, D.C., photography by Jason Miccolo Johnson; page 134 © Photodisc, Inc.; page 137 Courtesy of R. Scott French

**Chapter 7**    pages 148, 153, 156, 158, 161, 163 © Photodisc, Inc.

**Chapter 8**    pages 170, 179, 181 Courtesy of Everard's Clothing, Washington, D.C., photography by Jason Miccolo Johnson; pages 174, 177, 180, 182, 187 © Photodisc, Inc.; page 175 © Digital Vision

**Chapter 9**    pages 194, 196 © Photodisc, Inc.

**Chapter 10**   page 216 Courtesy of Everard's Clothing, Washington, D.C., photography by Jason Miccolo Johnson; pages 221, 224, 228 © Photodisc, Inc.

**Chapter 11**   pages 238, 240, 242, 251, 253 © Photodisc, Inc.; page 245 © Corbis, Inc.

**Chapter 12**   pages 260, 262, 263, 265, 270, 274, 277 © Photodisc, Inc.; page 271 Courtesy of PRÊT À PORTER PARIS® Show, photographer standem favart photo; page 264 © Digital Vision